Islam and the Limits of the State

Leiden Studies in Islam and Society

VOLUME 3

The titles published in this series are listed at *brill.com/lsis*

Islam and the Limits of the State

Reconfigurations of Practice, Community and Authority in Contemporary Aceh

Edited by

R. Michael Feener
David Kloos
Annemarie Samuels

TUTA SUB AEGIDE PALLAS · 1683 ·

BRILL

LEIDEN | BOSTON

Cover illustration: Girls snacking on Aceh's west coast. Photo by Michael Feener.

Library of Congress Cataloging-in-Publication Data

Islam and the limits of the state : reconfigurations of practice, community and authority in contemporary Aceh / edited by R. Michael Feener, David Kloos, Annemarie Samuels.
pages cm. – (Leiden studies in islam and society ; v. 3)
Includes bibliographical references and index.
ISBN 978-90-04-30485-7 (pbk. : alk. paper) – ISBN 978-90-04-30486-4 (e-book)
1. Islam and state–Indonesia–Aceh. 2. Islamic law–Indonesia–Aceh. I. Feener, R. Michael, editor. II. Kloos, David, editor. III. Samuels, Annemarie, editor.

BP63.I52A165 2016
322'.10959811–dc23

2015034533

This publication has been typeset in the multilingual "Brill" typeface. With over 5,100 characters covering Latin, IPA, Greek, and Cyrillic, this typeface is especially suitable for use in the humanities. For more information, please see www.brill.com/brill-typeface.

ISSN 2210-8920
ISBN 978-90-04-30485-7 (paperback)
ISBN 978-90-04-30486-4 (e-book)

This book is printed on acid-free paper.

Contents

Preface

During the past decade, the Indonesian province of Aceh has experienced dramatic political, socio-economic, and cultural transformations. Tightly interwoven with this atmosphere of change is an ongoing debate about the role and meaning of Islam in Acehnese society. The state, both as an actor and as an arena for contestation, has taken an increasingly central stage in this debate. This volume deals with relationships between the state and lived realities in Acehnese society. Its central premise, informing the ways in which individual contributions have been assembled and edited, is that the state is both a formative and a limited force with regard to religious and social transformation. It is formative, in the sense that it has actively engaged in the formulation and enforcement of Islamic rules and regulations. The state is limited, in the sense that a large part of religious life and experience in Aceh takes place outside the limits of the state, and because the boundaries between 'state' and 'society' are contingent and subject to continuous re-negotiation. As a result, diverse local actors have affected state Shariʿa as much as state Shariʿa has affected them.

Central in this regard has been the gradual implementation of an Islamic legal system. A new 'special autonomy' law passed in 1999 made provisions for Aceh's provincial government to exercise control over aspects of religious life that were previously beyond the domain of state law. This allowed for the creation of a state Shariʿa system in which new government institutions and legislation were created to regulate such issues as Islamic creed, religious symbolism, and public behaviour. However, the impact of Shariʿa on contemporary society in Aceh cannot be reduced to laws and policies. In addition to developing concrete measures (which vary greatly in terms of range and effectiveness), state agents have engaged in an advanced discourse of 'state Islam' directed at improving local governance, public behaviour, 'bad' or socially disruptive practices, and social deviance. At the same time, the implementation of Shariʿa, or aspects of it, has been the subject of passionate resistance. Efforts to advance an official standard of Islamic morality across the province have led to diverse outcomes dependent on local contexts. Absolutely crucial in this respect is that Shariʿa implementation in Aceh, both as an idea and as a functioning legal system, has been part of a complex political environment, marked by a fragile peace and the consequences of a cataclysmic natural disaster.

The complex political situation in which state Shariʿa was introduced was the result of decades of armed conflict. In 1976, Hasan di Tiro, an Acehnese diplomat, businessman, and grandson of a famous religious teacher from Pidie district (on the Acehnese North coast) founded the Free Aceh Movement (Gerakan Aceh Merdeka/ GAM), an organization of armed insurgents fighting for a separate Acehnese state. Driven by a combination of ethno-nationalist ideology and control over natural resources (including large quantities of oil and gas), the Aceh conflict caused more than 28,000 deaths. Besides these casualties (most of which were innocent civilians), people in Aceh, especially those living in rural areas, were subjected to widespread acts of intimidation, displacement and torture, committed both by the Indonesian military and by GAM. On 26 December 2004, shortly after a period of martial law had seemed to dash all hopes to end the conflict, a 9.1 magnitude earthquake and resulting tidal wave—commonly known as the 'Indian Ocean tsunami'—destroyed much of the provincial capital Banda Aceh and Aceh's West coast, claiming an estimated 170,000 lives across the province (and ten thousands more in other parts of Asia). The disaster accelerated developments in what had been a halting peace process as both sides agreed to a ceasefire. At the same time, domestic as well as foreign relief workers in one of the largest humanitarian interventions in human history acted as informal observers of the truce. In August 2005, a peace treaty was signed in Helsinki, following on negotiations between the Indonesian government and the GAM leadership in exile. As a consequence, GAM was formally disbanded, disarmed—transforming into a political party, Partai Aceh (PA), which took control of Aceh's provincial government by winning local elections in April 2009. At present, the political situation is stable but fragile, with tensions rising especially around election times.

Aceh's Islamic legal system was thus established in contexts of dramatic political and social upheaval. At the same time, Shari'a implementation has to be understood in relation to the deeper and complex history of Islam in Aceh. Aceh has long been regarded as a place where Islam has a pronounced role in society. Its long traditions of Islamic religious scholarship and the prominence of religious leadership have made Aceh an important field for the study of Muslim societies for over a century. In contrast to Java and many other parts of the Indonesian archipelago where, until recently, works of international scholarship have tended to downplay the role of Islam in society, scholars working on Aceh have tended to place considerable emphasis on the social and political roles of Islam. This tradition of scholarship has produced important work covering areas ranging from epigraphy to ethnography, providing a rich background for understanding the historical contexts for contemporary developments. At the same time, the dominant historical and political narrative of Islam in Aceh, and the associated focus on politics and normative Islam, continues to be a source of stereotypes. Images of 'fanatical' Acehnese are fed by a history of violent conflicts, going back to the Acehnese resistance against

Dutch colonial domination in the nineteenth and early twentieth century. Such stereotypes have worked to disguise regional differences, local variations, and significant cultural change.

The role of Shari'a and its representation in scholarly and non-scholarly reports is a case in point. Often, the 'rebellious nature' of Aceh is stated as a causal factor in a seemingly self-evident, unidirectional, or unambiguous process of state-directed 'Islamization.' This volume challenges such simplistic views of Acehnese exceptionalism as it focuses on the question of how the implementation of Islamic law and its pronounced agenda of state-directed social change has both influenced, and been shaped by, the complex cultural contexts of a society undergoing dramatic social transformations in the post-disaster, post-conflict period. Together, the chapters in this volume show that, rather than the 'simple' result of a pre-ordained cultural identity, Shari'a law both draws upon, and opens up, a number of complex questions and debates around issues of Acehnese ethnic and political identity, including local contestations about the rights, duties, and moral responsibilities of everyone—ethnically Acehnese or not—who claims to be part of this place and its history.

One side effect of post-tsunami reconstruction and the peace building process was a revival of multi-disciplinary academic research about Aceh. Over the past decade, Indonesian and international researchers flocked to the province in unprecedented numbers to study social and political developments there. At the same time, foreign donors worked together with local universities in projects of academic capacity building. While many of the authors—and all of the editors—have been a part of this development in one way or another, one aspect should be particularly emphasized here. During the conflict, and especially since the 1990s, conducting fieldwork in Aceh was difficult. Thus, while the recent history and politics of Aceh have been relatively well analyzed, grounded ethnographic studies have been extremely rare up until the ending of the conflict. This also explains, at least partly, why the dominant narrative of Acehnese history and society has long been characterized by a focus on formal politics (including the relations between Aceh and Jakarta), the views and experiences of political and religious leaders, and conflict. In contrast, little attention has been given to the ways in which different segments of Acehnese society have dealt with, and tried to influence, the religious norms and regulations established by formal institutions. This volume is part of a much larger effort to address this imbalance.

Many recent publications about Aceh have focused on political institutions, the humanitarian effort, and state-civil society relations. Together they have produced a more complex picture of Aceh than the one that is usually presented in (international and domestic) media. The unprecedented openness of Aceh has also facilitated the work of a new generation of scholars working on diverse aspects of Islam and society. Exciting new lines of investigation have been directed at the complex ways in which Islamic belief and practice are configured within the everyday experiences of Muslims as they navigate the diverse transformations of society. This volume brings together an international group of researchers who have recently conducted extensive fieldwork on various aspects of Muslim religious life in Aceh, and among different social groups. This work presents insight into diverse expressions and interpretations of Islam all across the province that can help us to better understand the range and extent of ways in which Islam both informs and reflects dynamics of political and cultural change in contemporary Aceh.

Most of the chapters are adaptations of papers presented at the international conference "Islam in Contemporary Aceh: Reconfigurations of Ritual, Doctrine, Community and Authority" which was held in Leiden in September 2011. They help us to understand how diverse expressions and interpretations of Islam in relation to the current state Shariʿa project have come to inform and reflect broader dynamics of political and cultural change across the province. Given Aceh's iconic position in the history of Islam in Indonesia, and taking into account the broader field of the anthropology of Muslim societies, this volume aims to contribute to discussions about patterns of continuity and change in the fields of lived experience, the officialization of religious thought and practice, and the role of Shariʿa and the state in contemporary Muslim societies. It starts out with an overview of the process of Shariʿa implementation, and a further elaboration of the central theme of the volume. Subsequent chapters focus on such issues as gender relations, the role of civil society, the drafting of religious laws, leadership dynamics, public morality, punishment, public space, the remaking of everyday life in post-conflict, post-tsunami contexts, and changing ideas about community and individuality. As such, we hope that this book will invite further debate, and help propel and sustain the flowering of Aceh scholarship into a wider field of academic and non-academic discussion.

The editors are grateful to all those whose work and generous support made the 2011 conference possible. In particular, we would like to thank LUCIS (Leiden University Centre for the Study of Islam and Society), who funded the event and the Leiden University faculty who participated, including Léon Buskens, Kees van Dijk and Nico Kaptein. Our discussions there were also significantly enriched by the contributions of Arskal Salim and Daniel Birchok. We are grateful to Jaap Fokkema of VU University Amsterdam, who produced the Aceh administrative map printed here. We would also like to acknowledge all of the encouragement and assistance of Nienke Brienen-Moolenaar, Teddi Dols and Kathy van Vliet at Brill in helping us bring this book to publication, as well as the editorial assistance of Hongyan Li and Wajihah Hamid at the National University of Singapore's Asia Research Institute, and an anonymous reviewer for his/her helpful comments.

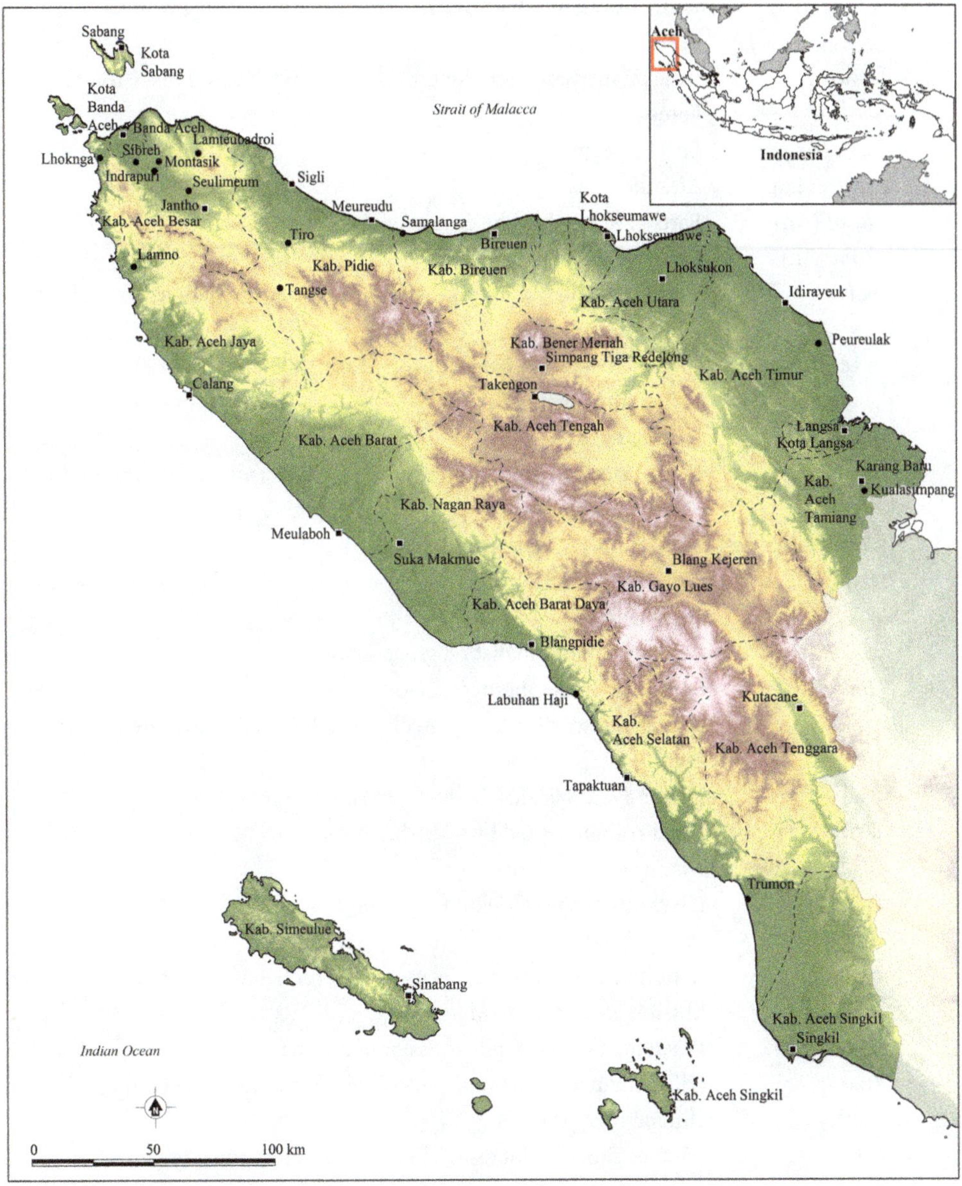

MAP 1 *Administrative map of Aceh*

Glossary and Abbreviations

The terms appearing below in *italics* are from Indonesian/Malay, except where otherwise specifically noted as Arabic (Ar.), Acehnese (Ac.), or Javanese (Jv.).

ABRI	(Angkatan Bersenjata Republik Indonesia) The Indonesian Armed Forces
adat (Ar.)	Local custom
akhirat (Ar.)	Afterlife
aurat (Ar.)	Parts of the body to be covered as required by Islam
azan (Ar.)	Call to prayer
balai	Simple wooden structure used for community gatherings and for religious study
BRR	(Badan Rehabilitasi dan Rekonstruksi) Rehabilitation and Reconstruction Agency
bupati	District head
CEDAW	Convention on the Elimination of All Forms of Discrimination against Women
dakwah (Ar. *daʿwa*)	Islamic religious propagation
Darul Islam (DI)	Armed insurrection against the Indonesian Republic to establish an Islamic state
dayah (Ac.)	Acehnese traditionalist religious school
dhikr (Ar.)	Sufi ritual 'remembrance' of God
DPRA	(Dewan Perwakilan Rakyat Aceh) Aceh Provincial Legislative Assembly
DSI	(Dinas Syariat Islam) Aceh's State Shariʿa Agency
fatwa (Ar.)	Legal opinion issued by a Muslim jurist
fikih (Ar. *fiqh*)	Islamic jurisprudence
GAM	(Gerakan Aceh Merdeka) Free Aceh Movement
geuchik (Ac.)	Village head
hadith (Ar.)	Report of the words and deeds of the Prophet Muhammad
hajj (Ar.)	Muslim pilgrimage to Mecca
hikmah (Ar.)	Wisdom, often with religious connotations
HMI	(Himpunan Mahasiswa Islam) Islamic Students' Association
HRW	Human Rights Watch
HTI	(Hizbut Tahrir Indonesia) The Indonesian national organization of the trans-national movement Hizb ut-Tahrir
HUDA	(Himpunan Ulama Dayah Aceh) An association of traditionalist ulama in Aceh

hudud (Ar.)	Stipulated Quranic punishments for particular offenses against Islamic law
IAIN	(Institut Agama Islam Negeri) State Islamic Studies Institute
ibadat (Ar.)	Ritual practice; worship
ICAIOS	International Center for Aceh and Indian Ocean Studies (Banda Aceh)
ICG	International Crisis Group
ICMI	(Ikatan Cendekiawan Muslim Indonesia) Indonesian Association of Muslim Intellectuals
ijtihad (Ar.)	Independent jurisprudential reasoning in Islamic law
ilmu (Ar.)	Literally 'knowledge,' referring in different contexts to religious learning, modern science, or esoteric/magical knowledge
iman (Ar.)	Faith
imeum meunasah (Ac.)	Village-level religious leader
jihad (Ar.)	Literally 'struggle,' used popularly in the sense of 'holy war'
jilbab	Muslim women's headscarf
JMSPS	(Jaringan Masyarakat Sipil Peduli Syariah) An Islamic NGO in Aceh
JPUK	(Jaringan Perempuan Untuk Kebijakan) A women's NGO in Aceh
kabupaten	District
kafir (Ar.)	Unbeliever; infidel
kecamatan	Sub-district
KAMMI	(Kesatuan Aksi Mahasiswa Muslim Indonesia) Indonesian Union for Muslim Student Action
kampung (Ac. *gampong*)	Village, or neighbourhood
kenduri	Religious meal, or celebration
khalwat (Ar.)	Inappropriate association between marriageable men and women
khamar (Ar.)	Wine, or intoxicating drink
Kiai (Jv.)	Title for the leader of a *pesantren*
(*Hari*) *Kiamat* (Ar.)	Judgment Day
kitab kuning	Literally 'yellow books,' referring to the religious texts used in traditional institutions of Islamic learning in Southeast Asia (*pesantren, dayah*, etc.)
KOHATI	(Korps HMI-Wati) Women's wing of the Islamic Students' Association (HMI)
KPU	(Komisi Pemilihan Umum) Election Commission
KTP	(Kartu Tanda Penduduk) Indonesian state-issued identity card
LOGA	Law on the Governing of Aceh
madrasah (Ar.)	A 'modern-style' Islamic religious school in Indonesia
Mahkamah Syariah	Shari'a Court
maisir (Ar.)	Gambling

majelis taklim	An assembly for purposes of Islamic learning, often used today for public preaching events
Majelis Ulama	Council of Ulama
merantau	Long-term sojourn away from home for purposes of work or education
meunasah (Ac.)	Traditional village institution, used for basic Islamic education, prayer and other communal functions
MISPI	(Mitra Sejati Perempuan Indonesia) A prominent women's NGO in Aceh
MPU	(Majelis Permusyawaratan Ulama) Aceh's provincial-level Ulama Council
MUDA	(Majelis Ulama Daerah Aceh) A provincial-level assocation of ulama
Muhammadiyah	Indonesian modernist Islamic mass organization
MUNA	(Majelis Ulama Nanggroe Aceh) A provincial-level assocation of ulama
MUI	(Majelis Ulama Indonesia) Indonesian National Ulama Council
New Order	The authoritarian developmentalist state under Suharto (1965–1998)
NGO	Non-Governmental Organization
NU (Nadhlatul Ulama)	Indonesian traditionalist Islamic mass organization
Nyai (Jv.)	Wife or daughter of *pesantren* leader (Java)
PA	(Partai Aceh) Aceh Party
pemuda	'Youth'
Perda	(Peraturan Daerah) Regional level regulations
Perti	(Persatuan Tarbijah Islamijah) Islamic Educational Movement
pesantren (Jv.)	Islamic boarding school
PKS	(Partai Keadilan Sejahtera) Prosperity and Justice Party
PII	Pelajar Islam Indonesia, a national association of Muslim students
PNS	(Pegawai Negeri Sipil) Civil servant
PPP	(Partai Persatuan Pembangunan) United Development Party
PUSA	(Persatuan Ulama Seluruh Aceh) All Aceh Union of Ulama
qanun (Ar.)	Term used for regional regulations, including Islamic legislation in contemporary Aceh
Qanun Jinayat	Aceh's Islamic criminal law code
rajam (Ar.)	Punishment of death by stoning
razia	'Raid' by the police or WH
Reformasi	The post-New Order period of 'Reform' in Indonesia
RPUK	(Relawan Perempuan untuk Kemanusiaan) Women's Volunteers for Humanity
RTA	Rabitah Taliban Aceh, an organization of students and alumni of traditional Islamic boarding schools (*dayah*) in Aceh

santri dayah (Ac.)	Students from Aceh's traditional Islamic schools
Satpol PP	(Satuan Polisi Pamong Praja) Civilian police force
SIRA	(Sentral Informasi Referendum Aceh) Aceh Referendum Information Center
sosialisasi	Term commonly used in connection with projects for the public promotion of state Shari'a
Shari'a	Literally 'path' or 'way,' commonly translated as 'Islamic law'
syiar (Ar. *shi'ār*)	'Symbolism' of Islam
tarekat (Ar.)	Sufi order
Teuku (Ac.)	Title used by the traditional Acehnese landed nobility (*uleebalang*)
Teungku (Ac.)	Title used for Acehnese ulama
ulama (Ar.)	Islamic religious scholar; in Indonesia, this plural form is also used for an individual scholar (Ar. *alim*)
uleebalang (Ac.)	The traditional Acehnese landed nobility
umat (Ar. *umma*)	Islamic community
UNIFEM	United Nations Development Fund for Women
wali nanggroe	Symbolic 'head of state'
WH	(Wilayatul Hisbah) Aceh's 'Shari'a police'
YICM	Yayasan Insan Cita Madani, an Acehnese NGO
zina (Ar.)	Fornication, or adultery

List of Maps

List of Contributors

R. Michael Feener
is Research Leader of the Religion and Globalization Research Cluster at the Asia Research Institute and Associate Professor in the Department of History at the National University of Singapore. Previously he taught at Reed College and the University of California, Riverside. He has also held visiting professor positions and research fellowships at Harvard, Kyoto University, École des Hautes Études en Sciences Sociales (Paris), the University of Copenhagen, The Doris Duke Foundation for Islamic Art (Honolulu), and the International Institute for Asian Studies (IIAS) in Leiden, the Netherlands. His research focuses on the cultural and intellectual history of Islam in Southeast Asia. His previous books on Aceh include *Sharīʿa and Social Engineering: The Implementation of Islamic Law in Contemporary Aceh, Indonesia* (Oxford University Press, 2013); and two volumes co-edited with Patrick Daly & Anthony Reid: *From the Ground Up: Perspectives on Post-Tsunami and Post-Conflict Aceh* (ISEAS Press, 2012); and *Mapping the Acehnese Past* (KITLV Press, 2011).

Annemarie Samuels
is a postdoctoral researcher at the University of Amsterdam. She received her PhD in Cultural Anthropology from Leiden University in 2012 for a dissertation about the remaking of everyday life after the tsunami in Aceh. She is currently revising her dissertation for publication and working on a new ethnographic research project that focuses on HIV/AIDS, morality and care in Aceh. Her publications on Aceh include: "Narratives of Uncertainty: The Affective Force of Child-Trafficking Rumors in Postdisaster Aceh," *American Anthropologist* (2015), "'Aceh Thanks the World': The Possibilities of the Gift in a Post-disaster Society," *Anthropology Today* (2013), and "Moving from Great Love: Gendered Mobilities in a Post-Tsunami Relocation Neighborhood in Aceh, Indonesia," *International Journal of Urban and Regional Research* (2012).

David Kloos
is a researcher at KITLV/Royal Netherlands Institute of Southeast Asian and Caribbean Studies in Leiden, The Netherlands. He obtained his PhD at VU University Amsterdam (2013) on the basis of an historical and anthropological study of religious practice and authority in Aceh, which is currently being revised for publication. His current research project, "Female Islamic Leadership and Visual Rhetoric in Southeast Asia," explores the ways in which female religious authorities in Malaysia and Indonesia make use of visual

images to communicate with their audience. Publications on Aceh include: "A Crazy State? Violence, Psychiatry, and Colonialism in Aceh, Indonesia, ca. 1910–1942," *Bijdragen tot de taal-, land- en volkenkunde* (2014) and "In the Name of *Syariah*? Vigilante Violence, Territoriality, and Moral Authority in Aceh, Indonesia," *Indonesia* (2014).

Kristina Großmann
is Assistant Professor at the Chair of Comparative Development and Cultural Studies—Southeast Asia at the University of Passau, Germany. Her main research interests are: theories of action, gender studies, processes of modernization, Islam, peace and conflict studies as well as social and political ecology in Southeast Asia, especially Indonesia. Her recent publications include the book *Gender, Islam, Aktivismus: Handlungsräume muslimischer Aktivistinnen nach dem Tsunami in Aceh* [Gender, Islam, Activism: Scopes of Acting of Muslim Activists in Aceh after the Tsunami] (Berlin: Regiospectra, 2013); *Handbuch Indonesien* [Handbook Indonesia], co-edited with Gunnar Stange and Rolf Jordan (Angermünde: Horlemann, 2015); and the chapter: "Contested Unity in Diversity: Indonesia"—Muslim Women and Violent Political Protest, in the *Encyclopedia of Women and Islamic Cultures*. (Brill online, 2014; general editor: Suad Joseph).

Dina Afrianty
is a lecturer and researcher at the State Islamic University in Jakarta, Indonesia. She is currently working for The Asia Foundation in the Civil Society Strengthening Program and for the Legal Reform Component of Australia-Indonesia Partnership for Justice. Dina Afrianty is a research fellow at the Center for Social Difference at Columbia University and an associate of the Centre for Indonesian Law, Islam and Society, University of Melbourne. She is an Endeavor Post-Doctoral Research Fellow at the University of Melbourne.

Eka Srimulyani
is Professor at the State Islamic University (UIN) Ar-Raniry, and was trained in Islamic Studies at Leiden University and Asia-Pacific Studies at the University of Technology, Sydney, Australia. Between 2010 and 2012 she was a research fellow at IIAS within the framework of a KNAW postdoctoral fellowship. She is also a senior researcher at The International Centre for Aceh and Indian Ocean Studies (ICAIOS). Her research focuses on (Muslim) women and education. She published a book titled *Women from Traditional Islamic Educational Institutions in Indonesia: Negotiating Public Spaces* (Amsterdam University Press, 2012) and several articles and book chapters including: "Muslim Women and Education

in Indonesia: The Pondok Pesantren Experience," *Asia Pacific Journal of Education* (2007); "Pesantren Seblak of Jombang East Java: Women's Educational Leadership," *Review of Indonesian and Malaysian Affairs* (2008); "Negotiating Public Space: Three Nyai Generations in a Jombang Pesantren," in: *Indonesian Islam in a New Era: How Women Negotiate their Muslim Identities*, edited by Susan Blackburn, Bianca Smith and Siti Syamsiyatun, Monash Asia Institute (2008); and "Gender in Contemporary Acehnese Dayah: Moving Beyond Docile Agency?" in: *Gender and Power in Indonesian Islam: Leaders, Feminists, Sufis and Pesantren Selves*, edited by Bianca J. Smith and Mark Woodward, Routledge (2014).

Reza Idria
is a lecturer at the State Islamic University (UIN) Ar-Raniry, Banda Aceh. He obtained his MA in Islamic Studies from Leiden University, the Netherlands (2010). Currently, he is a PhD student in Social Anthropology at the Department of Anthropology, Graduate School of Arts and Sciences (GSAS), Harvard University, USA. He is co-founder of Komunitas Tikar Pandan and research fellow at the International Centre for Aceh and Indian Ocean Studies (ICAIOS) in Banda Aceh.

Benjamin Otto
studied Criminology at VU University Amsterdam. In 2009 he lived in Banda Aceh for a period of six months to conduct research for his MA thesis. Previously he lived in Bandung and Yogyakarta where he learned Indonesian and worked as an intern for Lembaga Bantuan Hukum. Currently he works as a detective at the Amsterdam Police Department.

Jan Michiel Otto
is Professor of law and governance in developing countries at Leiden University, where he heads the Van Vollenhoven Institute for Law, Governance, and Development. He is lead author and editor of *Sharia incorporated: A Comparative Overview of the Legal Systems of Twelve Muslim Countries in Past and Present* (2010). Prof. Otto has been trained in law and development administration and spent long periods of fieldwork in Egypt and Indonesia. Recently he co-authored and co-edited *Searching for Justice in Post-Gaddafi Libya: A Socio-Legal Exploration of People's Concerns and Institutional Responses at Home and From Abroad* (2013).

Antje Missbach
studied Southeast Asian Studies and Anthropology at the Humboldt University in Berlin. In 2010 she obtained her PhD from the Australian National University in Canberra for a thesis about the long-distance politics of the Acehnese diaspora. She has taught at universities in Berlin and Heidelberg before becoming a McKenzie Postdoctoral Fellow at the University of Melbourne. Currently she is a lecturer at the Department of Anthropology at Monash University in Melbourne. Her research has been supported by the Australian Research Council, Fritz-Thyssen-Stiftung, and the German-Academic Exchange Service (DAAD). Her main research areas center on transit migration, diaspora politics as well as border and mobility studies.

CHAPTER 1

State Shariʿa and Its Limits

R. Michael Feener

Aceh has experienced dramatic social change over the past decade, with devastating natural disaster followed by unprecedentedly ambitious projects of reconstruction and development.[1] The shock of this unforeseen tragedy redefined priorities, transformed conversations about the future of Acehnese society, and accelerated ongoing negotiations to bring an end to armed conflict in the region. The peace agreement was formally concluded in July 2005 at Helsinki, bringing to an end decades of violent struggle between the Indonesian central government and the Free Aceh Movement (Gerakan Aceh Merdeka/GAM). These developments contributed to the establishment of a level of stability that allowed for attention to be refocused on issues of social order under a civilian administration—which in turn set the stage for a reworking of the earlier special autonomy measures that provided for the state implementation of Islamic law. It also greatly facilitated the work of international development agencies and NGOs to carry out massive projects of reconstruction in Aceh. Consequently, enormous amounts of money flowed in, allowing a range of international NGOs to field-test their latest theories of linking disaster relief and recovery with longer-term, future-oriented development projects.

Under the popular motto of "Building Back Better," reconstruction in Aceh looked beyond purely physical rebuilding to include also a broad range of programs aimed at the improvement of economic and social conditions. This ambitious constellation of projects aimed not only to manage the reconstruction of homes and physical infrastructure in disaster-affected areas, but also to construct and implement new models of quality assurance, transparency, good governance, and gender equity in post-tsunami Aceh. Well beyond the

1 Research for this chapter was undertaken partially with the support of the Singapore Ministry of Education's Academic Research Fund (MoE AcRF # R-110-000-029-750). I would like to thank Mahdi Abdullah Syihab for his invaluable assistance in collecting some of the primary materials consulted for this study, as well as Prasenjit Duara, Ben Arps, Julius Bautista, Philip Fountain, Arif Jamal, Jeremy Kingsley, Deepa Nair, Liang Yongjia, Yijiang Zhong, Annemarie Samuels, David Kloos, and all the participants at the Leiden workshop for their critical comments on earlier drafts of this chapter.

 | DOI: 10.1163/9789004304864_002

specific projects of the state, international development organizations, and NGOs, Acehnese public discourse became saturated with ideals and idioms of 'improvement' during the post-tsunami/post-conflict period. In fields ranging from physical infrastructure to Islamic law, there developed an expansive vision of 'total reconstruction' that would remake Aceh literally 'from the ground up.'[2] Combined with the euphoric discourses surrounding the dawn of a new peace, in a region long plagued by violent conflict, reconstruction projects fostered the emergence of possibilities for creating a 'new Aceh' that would transform the lives of a people who had suffered so much war and devastation.

As Annemarie Samuels (2012) has demonstrated, the higher-level policy discussions of reconstruction and economic development were elaborated within more diffuse projects of the 'remaking of everyday life.' In her contribution to this volume, she turns attention to the diverse narratives of 'improvement' that have been developed and deployed by individuals in Aceh to help them explain and understand the tragedy. These processes involved some significant reconfigurations of local understandings of Islam, including its place within the personal experience of individuals in relation to broader aspects of social life. These diverse experiences and interpretations of Islam in contemporary Aceh continue to draw on a rich and complex constellation of traditions, growing out of the region's historical religious and cultural legacies. This volume aims to open a set of windows on to these developments through studies highlighting the diversity of ways in which Muslims in Aceh have worked to negotiate these dramatic social transformations. The importance here lies not only in a richer empirical picture of recent developments there, but also in helping to develop a more nuanced critical perspective on relations between Islamic doctrine and practice, official government institutions, civil society organizations, and the experiences of individual Muslims in local communities. This move to provide a more diverse and complex matrix of understandings and experiences within which to contextualize the provincial government's project of Shariʿa social engineering is what we intend here by the idea of looking at Islam 'beyond the limits of the state.'[3]

The contributors to this volume pursue this idea through a series of ethnographic explorations of cases ranging from NGOs and diaspora politics to female ulama and punk rockers. In order to provide some broader contexts for these discussions, this introductory essay will begin with an historical overview

2 For more on the processes of reconstruction, see Daly, Feener, and Reid (2012).

3 The overview of Aceh's state Shariʿa system presented on the pages that follow uses material drawn from my recent monograph on the subject (Feener 2013). More extensive discussions of particular points and full citations to primary source material can be found there.

of Islam in Aceh, with a focus on those aspects that have significantly informed the contemporary cases presented in the chapters that follow.[4]

Aceh's Historical Legacies as an 'Abode of Islam'

The northern tip of Sumatra has been home to some of the earliest Muslim port polities in the Indonesian Archipelago. From the late thirteenth century, their courts patronized Islamic scholars and Sufis from across the Islamic world; and they brought with them diverse models of belief and practice that have left a continuing imprint on the subsequent development of Islam in Aceh. In the seventeenth century, the court of Aceh's sultans was the site of pronounced competition between different forms of Sufism, as their proponents competed for royal favour. With the waning of the sultanate's power and control over its once extensive domains in the eighteenth century, new forms of Islam made inroads, resulting in further reconfigurations—particularly with regard to the development of Sufi orders beyond the circles of the court. During the nineteenth century, local Muslim leaders drawing on aspects of these traditions of Sufism emerged to mobilize resistance to the incursion of the Dutch. The Dutch launched their first invasion of Aceh in 1873, in response to which the Acehnese waged a long war of anti-colonial resistance cast in terms of a *jihad* in the defence of Islam against invading infidels. Calls for these campaigns of resistance drew on the traditions of activist Sufism that had taken root in the region over the course of the eighteenth and early nineteenth centuries—including the Sumatran scholar ʿAbd al-Samad al-Palimbani (al-Jawi)'s treatise on *jihad*.[5] Over the late nineteenth century, these ideas of Islamic mysticism and militant mobilization came to be expressed through a new genre of 'holy war' texts in Acehnese verse, generally referred to as *Hikayat Prang Sabi*.[6]

---

4 For a more extensive introduction to major developments in, and sources for, the history of Islam in Aceh, see Feener (2011).

5 One early exemplar of the Acehnese genre of 'Holy War' texts—Nya' Ahmat's 1894 exhortation to *jihad* against the incursion of the Dutch entitled *Nasihat ureueng muprang*–draws on the work of Palimbani's *Nasihat al-muslimin wa tadhkirat al-mu'minun fi fada'il al-jihad fi sabil Allah* (Snouck Hurgronje 1906: II, 119). For more on 'Palimbani,' see: Feener (2015).

6 There is a considerable body of modern writing on Acehnese *Prang Sabi* texts—and in fact this particular genre of texts has received attention disproportionate to its place within the broader tradition of Acehnese literature. See, for example: Alfian (2006, 109–120); Amirul Hadi (2011, 183–198); and Damsté (1928, 545–609).

By the early decades of the twentieth century, however, the Dutch colonial state had consolidated its control over Aceh, while local ulama also came to solidify their own autonomous institutional foundations in the form of educational institutions known in Acehnese as *dayah*. These Islamic religious boarding schools came to serve as the primary organizational structures of Islam in Aceh in the early twentieth century and provided the ulama with avenues of considerable social influence in particular local communities. The forms of Islam promoted within Acehnese *dayah* were diverse, but there did emerge a broad general tendency for most to share traditions of Shafiʿi jurisprudence (*fiqh*) and Khalidi-Naqshbandi Sufism.[7] These traditional modes of Islamic belief and practice were, however, at the same time becoming the object of sharp critiques by a new generation of modernist reformers associated with a new style of *madrasa* schools spreading through the region. These modern reformers drew on discourses that articulated new visions of Islam that were then developing in the Middle East and South Asia, in which the Shariʿa was envisioned as serving as the foundation for a thorough reconstitution of society (Siegel 1969, 98–133).

In Aceh, these modernist reformers came to be organized in a new 'union' of ulama known locally as PUSA (Persatuan Ulama Seluruh Aceh, the All-Acehnese Organization of Ulama), which was largely concentrated in the area surrounding Banda Aceh and in the towns along Aceh's north coast. PUSA's leadership was often antagonistic toward aspects of Acehnese tradition, and its members aggressively critiqued a range of customary practices that had come to be associated with Islam as blameworthy 'innovations' that had to be suppressed. Many of them were also stridently opposed to the forms of Sufism that had become so widely established in Aceh at that time. These stark positions on prominent expressions of Islam contributed to tensions between 'modernist' and 'traditionalist' Muslims in Aceh, which took the form of political struggles and even violent conflict during the early years of Indonesian independence. In ways not unlike that of the PUSA Modernists, Aceh's traditionalist ulama also mobilized themselves into organizations including a militia named the Barisan Hizbullah and a political party called PERTI (Persatuan Tarbiyah Islamijah), which was led by Teungku Muda Waly in South Aceh.[8]

---

7 This sub-tradition of the Naqshbandiyya traces its origins to Iraq and the teachings of Shaykh Khalid al-Kurdi (d. 1827). For more on its introduction to and development in Indonesia, see Kraus (1990); van Bruinessen (2007).

8 An introduction to PERTI and an overview of the development of its politics can be found in Koto (1997). For more on the PERTI political activism of Muda Waly in particular, see van Bruinessen (1992, 143–146).

It was PUSA, however, that was most successful in establishing itself as the dominant Islamic organization in Aceh at mid-century. This ascendency was aided, in part, by the role of some of PUSA's leadership in collaborating with the Japanese during their wartime occupation of Sumatra (1942–1945). Under the Japanese occupation, PUSA was able to claim important positions within the new structures of state authority. The relationship of PUSA with the Japanese occupational forces was, however, a complex one and the ulama were not the only beneficiaries of new policies under the Japanese military administration. Like the Dutch before them, the Japanese pursued strategies that played off the divisions between the ulama and the local landed aristocracy (*uleebalang*) in ways that served to strengthen their control over Aceh. In this way, the policies of the Japanese occupation maintained and deepened local divisions and rivalries among the Acehnese over issues of religious and political authority (Shiraishi 1975, 33–35).

Aceh, Islam, and Independent Indonesia

At the end of the war, PUSA moved swiftly against their primary political rivals, the *uleebalang*, who were now branded as the last remaining allies of the fallen Dutch colonial order. From December 1945 to January 1946, violent clashes erupted across Aceh, in what came to be known as the 'Social Revolution' (*Revolusi Sosial*). By the end of it, most of the *uleebalang* in the crucial districts of Pidie and North Aceh were killed, and many of those who survived fled from Aceh—thereby leaving the former power of the *uleebalang* much diminished (Reid 1979). This left the field open for a reconstitution of a professional administrative class in Aceh, the ranks of whom soon swelled with young Muslim professionals with allegiance to PUSA. At the forefront of this new ascendency of Aceh's Modernist Muslims was PUSA's charismatic leader, Daud Beureueh, who emerged from the war not only as Aceh's foremost Islamic reformist leader, but also as its military governor and chief administrator. PUSA affiliates thus came to dominate many sectors of the civil administration in post-war Aceh. With Daud Beureueh at its head, PUSA capitalized on their newly privileged position in society to energetically promote its vision of Islam in the making of a new, modern Aceh.[9] This included the expansion of the jurisdiction of the Shariʿa

9 This included a stepping up of its earlier campaigns against customary practices. See for example, the 1948 PUSA proclamation on Traditionalist funerary practices, recently reprinted in Analiansyah and Jamhuri (2008, 4–5).

courts and attempts at promoting new legislation governing aspects of public morality including gambling, alcohol consumption, and relations between the sexes.[10]

PUSA's position of dominance was, however, significantly compromised when the Indonesian central government moved to consolidate control over the country by dissolving the province of Aceh and annexing its territory to the neighbouring province of North Sumatra, with its capital in Medan. PUSA's reactions to this loss of control over local administration, together with a complex of other social and economic factors, ultimately culminated in the declaration of armed opposition to the central Indonesian state in 1953 (Feith 1962, 345–346). This rebellion against the Republic of Indonesia was referred to as the 'Darul Islam' ('Abode of Islam') movement, and it came to be linked together with other armed campaigns under that name for the establishment of an 'Islamic state' of Indonesia (Formichi 2012, 109–243; van Dijk 1981, 309–336). The Darul Islam movement in Aceh waged a long struggle to establish a modern Islamic state, but it was ultimately unsuccessful. Agreements to end hostilities were reached with most of the rebel leaders in 1959, when Aceh was granted the status of a 'special' province with concessions of autonomy in the fields of religion, customary law (*adat*) and education.

After the formal end of the Darul Islam revolt, the next major political and social transformations for Aceh came in the wake of the collapse of Soekarno's founding regime of the Indonesian Republic and the establishment of Suharto's New Order in 1965. At that time, the dynamics of interaction between Aceh and the Indonesian central government underwent a new evolution, including a reframing of visions of the role of Islam in defining Acehnese identity in official discourse. The most prolific and high-profile figure in producing the New Order narrative of Acehnese Islam was Ali Hasjmy. Hasjmy had been affiliated with PUSA during his youth, but after being 'rehabilitated' in Jakarta, he came to play key roles in the integration of Aceh into the Indonesian New Order state.

Over the course of his career in Aceh, Hasjmy helped form a number of modern Islamic institutions, all designed to garner broader Muslim support for the assertion of Indonesian national control over the province by actively promoting the New Order's emerging developmentalist ideals as being in line with 'proper' understandings of Islam. Working with Islamic religious leaders, he

10 These same core concerns have also been at the center of twenty-first-century Shari'a legislation in Aceh. The historical relations between contemporary *qanun* and mid-twentieth-century projects of Islamic religious and social reform are discussed extensively in Feener (2013).

developed new structures through which they could contribute their authority in support of various government policies and programs, and in which they also saw opportunities to utilize the resources of the state to further their own agendas for the definition and management of Islam in Aceh. During the latter decades of the twentieth century, the administration of Aceh's provincial bureaucracy was largely headed by a class of technocrats who were entrusted not only with the implementation of economic development projects, but also with counteracting rival ideologies that could inspire opposition to the central Indonesian state (Schlegel 1979). Many of these technocrats were themselves descendants of PUSA-affiliated ulama, with strong personal commitments to Islam, but who had also come to feel that they had a significant stake in the consolidation and perpetuation of Aceh's position within the broader Indonesian nation.

These technocrats tended to be viewed by most outside observers as proponents of a developmentalist modernity with agendas of secularization (McDougall 1979). At least some of the technocrats, however, had formed visions of development that incorporated particular understandings of Islam. I have discussed these visions elsewhere in terms of a '*daʿwa* paradigm' that combined ideas of Islamic reform, Indonesian nationalism, and economic development together in powerful new ways (Feener 2013). The connections between *daʿwa* and developmentalism were, however, particularly pronounced in Aceh. In many ways, Aceh can be seen as a kind of social laboratory for New Order experiments with the state management of Islam. These experiments included the establishment of Indonesia's first state Ulama Council in 1965 and the nation's pioneering Faculty of Dakwah, which was established first in 1968 at the Banda Aceh campus of the State Institute for Islamic Studies (I. Institut Agama Islam Negeri/IAIN, presently UIN) and paved the way for similar faculties to develop at other campuses across the country in the 1970s and 1980s.

Institutions of this type have served to emphasize and impress the centrality of Islam to the reform and control of Acehnese society upon civil servants and the Muslim middle class more broadly over the latter years of the New Order period. They were simultaneously Acehnese Muslims with a strong sense of local identity, and participants in broader trends of Islamic revival that had been gaining ground across Indonesia since the 1970s. These sectors of Acehnese society tended to see their interests as congruent with those of the central Indonesian state (Hefner 1993; Platzdasch 2009). In Aceh, their position was at times considerably more complicated during the years of violent conflict between the Indonesian armed forces and the 'Free Aceh Movement' (I. Gerakan Aceh Merdeka/GAM) that started in the 1970s and ultimately survived the collapse of the New Order to intensify further in the early years of the twenty-first century.

By that time, both Aceh's Islamic religious leaders and the high command of the Indonesian armed forces in the province had come to explicitly link the issue of Shariʿa to that of ending the conflict with GAM. It was in these contexts that the basic parameters of Aceh's current state Shariʿa system began to take shape. In February 2004, the top Indonesian military officer in the province proclaimed that "whoever supports the Shariʿa also supports the extermination of GAM ... because GAM's actions deviate greatly from the Islamic faith." GAM leaders, for their part, retorted that the state implementation of Shariʿa was "a plot by the central government to depict the Acehnese as fanatics in the eyes of the outside world" (Aspinall 2009, 207–214).[11] Critiques of Aceh's state Shariʿa system as a cynical political ploy have been common among former supporters of GAM and particularly among Acehnese living in the diaspora, as discussed by Antje Missbach in her chapter below. These views have thence become widely echoed in circles of NGO activists and academics, both within Aceh and beyond—thus contributing further dimensions to local debates over the place of the state in the management of Islamic affairs.

At the same time, within Aceh itself many Islamic leaders, and particularly a number of prominent academics associated with the IAIN, actively supported the state implementation of Islamic law as a means of restoring public order and undermining the separatist claims of GAM over the final years of the twentieth century. The motivations of these actors reflect not only the extent to which they may have been beholden to structures of established political power, but also the aspirational appeal of Shariʿa as a model of divinely ordained justice and a means of addressing worldly needs for security and stability. At the turn of the twenty-first century, Aceh's state Shariʿa project prioritized conceptions of personal morality and the modernizing rationalization of individual religious practice that had been characteristic of earlier models of New Order developmentalist *daʿwa* all across Indonesia. These particular formulations of Islam enjoyed a considerable resonance beyond Aceh, and were seen by some supporters of the state Shariʿa project, both locally and in Jakarta, as facilitating the re-integration of Aceh into the wider Indonesian nation.

The formal implementation of Islamic law in Aceh progressed particularly slowly during the first years of the project. It was only in the wake of the 2004 tsunami that the state Shariʿa project made significant advances, building upon aspects of a broader religious revival and rapidly developing dis-

11 The first quotation in this paragraph is quoted by Aspinall from *Serambi*, 23 February 2004.

courses of remaking society in the post-disaster/post-conflict period. Within these contexts the proponents of Aceh's recently-established, but until then little-enforced, Islamic legal system quickly seized the opportunity to promote their languishing Shariʿa project as an important part of rebuilding Aceh in the post-conflict/post-tsunami period. The traumatic experiences of natural disaster and the chaos of war gave increased occasion for many Muslims in Aceh to look into their own diverse understandings of Islam as frameworks for negotiating everyday life in a trying world. Combined with a rhetoric of 'total reconstruction,' promoted by the Indonesian state and international development agencies—as well as the euphoric discourses surrounding the dawn of a new peace in a region long-plagued by violent conflict—religious sensibilities contributed to the emergence of a pervasive sense of the possibility of creating a 'new Aceh' that would transform lives in this long-troubled and recently devastated region. At the same time, engagement with diverse aspects of the broader reconstruction project had the effect of bringing Islamic institutions and leadership further into the orbit of the Indonesian state in complex ways. This involved the redefinition of existing governmental institutions, as well as the creation of new ones.

Aceh's contemporary Islamic legal system can thus be seen as a 'high modern' project of promoting ideals of rationalizing religious reform through the educational and coercive apparatus of the state (Scott 1999). At the same time, however, these understandings of Islam and its role in actively promoting particular agendas of social change were far from universal among Muslims in Aceh itself. This is evident, for example, in the considerable dissent expressed in private complaints, public forums, and the popular media. These aspects of contemporary Acehnese discourse on state Shariʿa are explored in the chapters that follow by Dina Afrianty, Antje Missbach, Reza Idria, and Benjamin and Jan Michiel Otto.

Aceh's Contemporary State Shariʿa System

Aceh's Islamic legal system is one of the most complex experiments with the state implementation of Islamic law in the contemporary world, as it deals simultaneously with a complex of dramatic social transformations, while attempting to establish a new legal system within the broader constitutional framework of the Indonesian nation-state.[12] Aceh has, of course, a long and

12 For comparative perspectives on the contemporary Islamic legal systems of Saudi Arabia, Pakistan, Afghanistan, Nigeria, and Sudan, see Vogel (2000); Lau (2006, 2008); Ostien,

rich history of incorporating aspects of Shariʿa within evolving frameworks of pre-colonial Muslim state structures.[13] The current Islamic legal system is, however, configured in ways that differ significantly from the forms of legal and political structures of earlier periods—particularly with reference to the ways in which Aceh's 'special autonomy' status frames the application of Shariʿa there, within the national legal system.[14]

At the turn of the twenty-first century, new 'Special Autonomy' measures were introduced by the Indonesian central government in an attempt to undercut local support for GAM. This made it possible to reform existing institutions for the administration of Islamic law in the province, and also to establish new ones. Law No. 44/1999 formally recognized the 'Special Status of the Province of Aceh Special Region' in the fields of religion, education and *adat*, and Law No. 18/2001 conferred in principle, broader powers of provincial self-governance. These laws established the framework for the development of new substantive Shariʿa legislation to address issues of religious observance and public morality, as well as other laws defining the new institutions by which Islamic law would be implemented.[15]

Provisions for the state implementation of Islamic law are contained in regional regulations referred to locally as '*qanun*.'[16] Aside from two *qanun* dealing with the formation of specific Shariʿa institutions, the first of these new laws passed was Qanun No. 11/2002, which marked a new level of symbolic state engagement with the particulars of Islamic belief and practice by bringing these aspects of religious observance under the rubric of a regional regulation (*qanun*).[17] In terms of formal law enforcement, however, the most significant of Aceh's current Shariʿa regulations have been three laws passed in 2003: No. 12

Nasir, and Kogelmann (2005); and Layish and Warburg (2002); and Otto (2010), respectively.

13 On Islamic law and legal institutions in pre-modern Aceh, see Ito (1984); Lombard (1967).

14 For more extensive discussions of the institutions of state Shariʿa in Aceh, see Feener (2013).

15 On the political contexts surrounding the initial implementation of Islamic law in contemporary Aceh, see Aspinall (2009); Lindsey et al. (2007); Miller and Feener (2010); Moch. Nur Ichwan (2007).

16 The standard published source for legislation on the implementation of Islamic law in contemporary Aceh is Himpunan Undang-undang, Keputusan Presiden, Peraturan Daerah/ Qanun, Instruksi Gubernur dan Edaran Gubernur berkaitan Pelaksanaan Syariʿat Islam, Edisi Ketujuh (Banda Aceh: Dinas Syariʿat Islam Aceh, 2009).

17 Peraturan Dearah Provinsi Nanggroe Aceh Darussalam No. 33/2001 tentang Susunan Organisasi dan Tata Kerja Dinas Syariat Islam; and Qanun Provinsi Nanggroe Darussalam No. 10/2002 tentang Peradilan Syariat Islam.

on the consumption of alcohol, No. 13 on gambling, and No. 14 on inappropriate mixing of the sexes (*khalwat*). As the only new statements on the content of Shariʿa to be applied in Aceh to date, these have been the focus of much of the formal legal work of the new, or newly reformulated, institutions of Islamic law there.[18]

Aceh's current Shariʿa bureaucracy comprises a number of distinct but interrelated bodies. In this system, the State Shariʿa Agency (Dinas Syariat Islam/DSI) performs coordinating functions in working with the other major institutions involved with the implementation of Islamic law in contemporary Aceh: the Shariʿa Courts (Mahkamah Syariah/MS), the 'Ulama' Council (Majelis Permusyawaratan Ulama/MPU), and the 'Shariʿa Police' (Wilayatul Hisbah/WH).

The oldest institution of state Shariʿa in Aceh is the system of Islamic courts. While there were mechanisms established for the application of Islamic law under the sultanates, the Islamic courts operative in Aceh today trace their history back only to the mid-twentieth century, when they were established by the Japanese during their wartime occupation of Sumatra (1942–1945). Although under the Darul Islam movement in Aceh, these courts laid claim to a broader jurisdiction, over the second half of the twentieth century, Aceh's Islamic Courts generally operated much like those in other parts of Indonesia. Today, the vast majority of the cases before the court continue to be related to divorce, followed in number by inheritance—and these cases are generally decided according to rules and norms commonly found in the decisions of religious courts elsewhere in Indonesia. The number of cases involving gambling, alcohol consumption and *khalwat* in 2006–2007 have never amounted to a significant portion of the Shariʿa Courts' caseload. Since 2008, there has moreover been an overall decrease in the number of such cases appearing before Aceh's Islamic Courts.

Another previously existing institution for the state regulation of Islamic affairs that took on new roles and responsibilities in the twenty-first century is the Council of Ulama. Aceh's Ulama Council is the oldest state-affiliated body of its kind in Indonesia, dating to 1965. Since its inception it has served to actively promote the New Order's emerging developmentalist ideals, proclaiming that these were in accordance with proper understandings of Islam. In its current form, the Acehnese Council of Ulama (Majelis Permusyawaratan Ulama/MPU)

18 These particular concerns and goals of the current Shariʿa system are in fact not unprecedented impositions by the Indonesian central government, but actually reflect earlier attempts of certain segments of Aceh's Islamic leadership to advance an agenda of prescriptive social reform through the modern legislative apparatus of the state dating back to draft legislation of the 1960s.

was established through Regional Regulation (PerDa) 3/2000, and strengthened by the 2006 Law on Governing Aceh (LOGA). The Ulama Council is given, at least on paper, a very powerful position in the new legal order of Acehnese society. It is designated by law to be an equal partner with the provincial government and supposed to be deeply involved in the processes of conceptualizing and drafting legislation. The MPU is likewise invested with the right to issue *fatwas* (legal opinions)—whether solicited or not—on matters of government, development, economy and social development. To date, however, the MPU has been unable to exercise many of these powers and in fact, has faced some considerable obstacles in terms of internal tensions, competition with other institutions, and public ambivalence to some of its pronouncements.

Of the new institutions established under Aceh's state Shari'a system, the most often discussed (and highly contested) has been the 'Shari'a Police' (Wilayatul Hisbah/WH). The WH was first created through the enactment of Regional Regulation No. 5/2000, and further defined in sections of Qanun No. 11/2002, where its officers are invested with the authority to 'reprimand' (I. *tegur*) and 'advise' (I. *nasehat*) those caught violating the Shari'a as defined by Acehnese *qanun*. The WH does not, however, have the authority to formally charge or detain alleged offenders and thus must work together with the civil police and the public prosecutor's office in order to bring a case to the Islamic Courts. In principle the WH can be constituted and deployed at all levels of provincial administration down to that of the village (Ac. *gampong*) level. This kind of reach has, however, proven impossible to achieve due to the chronic and acute shortage of resources allocated to them. To cope with their manifest inability to handle the enforcement of Aceh's Shari'a laws on their own, the WH have developed modes of cooperation with village level officials (Ac. *geuchik; imeum meunasah*) and with *adat* institutions within the model of 'community policing.'

This solution has, however, presented another set of problems along a slippery slope, running from village justice toward vengeful vigilantism—particularly in cases perceived as offenses against the 'honour' of the local community. Over the past decade, the excessively zealous application of humiliating and at times violent punishments by both spontaneous mobs of village men and more organized bands of vigilantes—some comprised of students from Islamic schools (Ac. *santri dayah*)—have made news headlines and filled the air of coffee shops in many parts of Aceh.[19] Such incidents often attract unfavourable attention to the official state apparatus of the WH as well, not all of which

19 On vigilantism in contemporary Aceh, see Kloos (2014); Mahdi Syihab (2010).

is un-deserved.[20] The vocal public criticism directed most visibly toward the WH—both for its own actions and through their popular association with both other state institutions and unofficial agents for the enforcement of public morality—is discussed in detail in the chapters by Benjamin and Jan Michiel Otto, and by Reza Idria in this volume.

Before the supervision of the WH was transferred to the authority of the civilian police force (I. *Satpol*) in 2008, the WH was under the administration of another new institution of Aceh's Islamic legal system, the State Shariʿa Agency (Dinas Syariat Islam/DSI). The DSI is structured into four main sections, of which only one is primarily involved with activity in the formal legal sphere. Most of the Agency's work is directed toward the promotion of religious and social agendas that extend well beyond the drafting and enforcement of black-letter law. This is particularly evident in the Agency's more active unit for 'Propagation and Religious Practice' (I. *dakwah dan peribadatan*). This unit is tasked with administering *daʿwa* programs, providing facilities for ritual observance, providing and maintaining houses of worship, facilitating the work of other religious institutions, and generally promoting the public observance and symbolism of Islam (I. *Syiar*).

The express intention of the Agency's work in these areas is to use the instruments of the new Islamic legal system to bring about sweeping changes in both the regulation of society and the character of individual Muslims. The concern with *daʿwa* is, in fact, seen as central to the work of the Agency, as repeatedly stressed in the formal statements and voluminous publications of the DSI's founding director, Alyasa Abubakar. As he put it, the primary goal of the state Shariʿa project in Aceh is one of improving and perfecting the Islam of individual Muslims. He argues that if this is accomplished, the Acehnese as a whole will become more "honest, frugal, studious, diligent, loyal, intelligent, and emotionally mature" (Alyasa 2005, 1–5). As one of the primary architects of Aceh's contemporary Shariʿa system, Alyasa elaborates the aspirations for this project of social engineering, through Islamic law in terms of an all-encompassing system regulating every aspect of both individual and social life (Alyasa 2005, 21–26). This ideal is popularly expressed in Aceh, and elsewhere across Indonesia as '*Islam yang kaffah*.'[21] This phrase also appears prominently in the official

20 One of the most horrific cases of this involved the gang rape of a woman by three WH officers after being taken into custody in Langsa in January 2010. "Oknum WH Mesum Harus Dihukum," *Rakyat Aceh* (21 April 2007): 11.

21 This Indonesian-language phrase draws on the Qur'anic verse (*al-baqara*/2: 208) that calls for believers to 'fully' or 'completely' (*kaffah*) embrace Islam (Ar. *udkhulu fi'l-Islam kaffatan*).

'Clarification' (*Penjelasan*) of Qanun 11, and has become a central referent in the public discourse associated with programs promoting the further Islamization of law in contemporary Aceh. In Alyasa's own writing, the term is used frequently to refer to a comprehensive system regulating all aspects of individual and social life, including the necessary role of official state structures in remaking Acehnese society through the implementation of Shari'a.[22]

Shari'a and the Limits of the State

This 'top-down' perspective may appear to at least have the advantage of moving along what is viewed by many as the primary trajectory of modernizing religious reform, which since the late nineteenth century has been seen as increasingly one of rationalized systematization and social activism. Christopher Bayly, in his monumental study *The Birth of the Modern World*, has synthesized a vast body of work on the history of religions, arguing that all across the globe during the modern period processes of modernization have not undermined or eliminated religion, but rather facilitated the rise of a 'new style' for its expression in the public sphere. He thus claims that since the nineteenth century, religious reformers in many parts of the world have increasingly drawn "on rationalistic traditions and philosophies which had long been present in their respective religious traditions," to sharpen and clarify their identities while "expanding 'down' into particular societies by imposing uniformity" (Bayly 2004, 328–333). Such vectors of modernization have come to be identified as important dynamics within diverse religious traditions, thereby expanding the Weberian paradigm well beyond his famous Christian example into what has been a fruitful line of research in Islamic Studies. Ideas about 'Protestant Islam' have been discussed as significant factors in the modern transformations of Islamic practice in many parts of the world.[23] Such developments are, however, still only part of the story of the complex realities of lived experience in diverse Muslim societies.

22 It pervades much of the text of the 400+ page 'official' treatise on the subject authored by him (Alyasa 2005).

23 In discussing modern trends in this direction in Subsaharan Africa, for example, Roman Loimeier writes, "Even if we do not accept the idea that there is something like an 'Islamic Reformation,' it is quite obvious that we are witness to a 'second Islamization' of Subsaharan Muslim societies which is expressed, in particular, in social terms." (Loimeier 2005, 249).

Indeed, the view that processes of modernization have inevitably lead to the dominance of rationalizing religious reform and systematization, has more recently begun to be called into question by historians. In his ground-breaking study of the diversity of religious movements in a 'modernizing' colonial port city of India, Nile Green calls for a reframing of such perspectives on modernizing religious reform, arguing that, "While an English-educated comprador class demanded a 'Protestant' Islam of scripture and sobriety, the workers in their warehouses sought a religion of carnival holidays and practical little miracles" (Green 2011, 23). He thus highlights the importance of simultaneously keeping in view the diverse range of developments in religious practice that may contradict "familiar trajectories of socio-historical development" (Green 2011, 11). In fact, he argues that during the late nineteenth and early twentieth centuries, processes of modernization actually "encouraged the creation of an ever-increasing diversity of religious producers and consumers, with the latter made more demanding through their exposure to a growing marketplace of religious products and services" (Green 2011, 10).[24] Green's call for careful consideration of the "multiplicity of religious competitors" that emerge even in the face of powerful movements for totalizing systematization, is as important for students of contemporary Muslim societies as it is for historians of the nineteenth and twentieth centuries (Green 2011, 241).

Taking into account such countervailing tendencies within the complex processes of religious and social change can help us refine our understanding of developments in Aceh and elsewhere in the Muslim world that have attracted attention because of large-scale programs of religious redefinition over recent years. For example, processes of technocratic religious reform have been gaining ground in neighbouring Malaysia for decades, and over that time they have progressed a considerable way toward transforming dominant understandings of Islam there. Michael Peletz has characterized these developments as "extremely dislocating and otherwise deeply painful for rural Malays and all ordinary Muslims," and he has sought to explain, "why ordinary Malays are not inclined to resist [...] even though many proponents of rationalization, particularly *dakwah* people, have targeted beliefs, practices, and values long central to their (ordinary Malays') cultural identities" (Peletz 2002, 274, 196–197). Peletz sees any potential resistance constrained by a range of factors including the grave political risk of challenging the hegemony of the *dakwah* movement as

24 Well beyond Bombay, nineteenth-century print technology facilitated developments along diverse trajectories of Muslim religious traditions, including "a proliferation of images of saints" (Elias 2012, 38).

the state exercises the right "to define all alternative discourses as [...] an affront to the dignity of Malays and/or Islam," as well as a pervasive sense of surveillance and social forms of what he calls "invisible censorship" (Peletz 2002, 232–235). Similar factors have also been at work to some degree in Aceh. However there are other, less deterministic and state-focused ways to read the development of projects for 'Islamization' in contemporary Muslim societies that can help us to better appreciate the contexts of, and limitations upon, programs of state-directed religious reform.

In his ethnography of the Chitral community in Northwest Pakistan, Magnus Marsden has argued "against simplistic formulations treating local Islam as inherently vulnerable to global trends and forces in contemporary Islam" (Marsden 2005, 9). He does this by emphasizing the ways in which Chitral Muslims critically engage with processes of Islamization to provide a clearer picture of how Muslims in that particular context, "think, consider, reflect and exercise independent judgment in matters of faith, and how far they are uncritically deferential to men of religious authority on these issues" (Marsden 2005, 11–12). The energized public sphere of post-conflict, post-tsunami Aceh provides a very different, but nonetheless equally clear case of the complexity of internal Muslim discourse that demonstrates the limits of "sweeping accounts of the wave of global Islamic revival" (Marsden 2005, 251).

In Aceh, despite state support of Islamist institutions and their role in the transformation of Acehnese Muslim belief and practice, broad reformist trends are often tempered with concessions to select forms of established local practice. This is the case, for example, with the litany of prayers for the deceased known locally as the *Samadiyya*. Despite being suspect in the eyes of many modernist reformers, this particular form of traditionalist ritual recitation is explicitly endorsed in the official State Shari'a Agency's handbook for village-level religious leaders (*imeum meunasah*), who are expected to lead the funerary observances of which it is a part (Suhaidy 2007, 135). *Samadiyya* recitations draw on (and indeed take their name from) Qur'anic verse and thus have, in some sense, a foundation in scripture.[25] At the same time, however, the *Samadiyya* also involve contested conceptions of the transfer of merit to the deceased and interactions with disembodied spirits.[26] In his work on such traditions in the Gayo highlands of Central Aceh, John Bowen showed that these

25 The name of the practice itself clearly indexes a rare Arabic term (*al-Samad*) that appears prominently in one of the most oft-recited sections of the Qur'an (*al-Ikhlas*/112.2).

26 *Samadiyya* recitations are often performed in connection with Muslim funerary rites (I. *kenduri kematian*) in which some practitioners see the ritual reading of this text as a means to 'open a bridge' for the spirits of the dead.

rituals have been sharply criticised by 'Modernist' reformers for much of the twentieth century (Bowen 1993, 259–272). In a more recent study of analogous Muslim rituals for the dead in Kluet (South Aceh), however, Sehat Ihsan has also reported that local Muhammadiyah activists have come to admit 'defeat' in their attempts to put an end to such practices, in the greater interests of peace and mutual welfare (Sehat Ihsan Shadiqin 2010, 271).

While opposition to rationalizing reform agendas has served to constrain the ambitions of some modernizing reformers, not all proponents of projects for transforming Islamic belief and practice in the region have become thus resigned—particularly those with a stronger involvement with the role of state institutions in Aceh's Islamic legal system. The continuing back and forth between advocates of State Shariʿa (as an instrument of reform) and others in Aceh (with different views on the role of religion in society) takes place within a context in which the very categories of 'religion' and 'politics' have been configured within processes of secularizing modernization, that have shaped developments in many post-colonial Muslim societies.[27] Here it is important to note that speaking of secularization in this sense does not entail a diminishing of the importance of religion in the lives of individuals.[28] Rather the idea of secularization here can be seen in a more limited way—referring, as Martin Riesebrodt has expressed it, "to the process of institutional differentiation through which secular spheres—that is social spheres free of religious premises and norms—emerge." It refers, in other words, to "a transformation of social orders, namely to the process of freeing social institutions from religious control" (Riesebrodt 2010, 175–177).

In her recent study of Islamism in Pakistan, Humeira Iqtidar has followed the work of Talal Asad (2003) in re-conceptualizing the secular not in terms of "a one time separation of religion and the state but as the continuous management of religious thought and practice by the state" (Iqtidar 2011, 21). Such top-down dynamics of official interventions into the definition of religious thought and practice are also clearly seen in Aceh, where the management of religion is likewise framed by the institutions of a modern nation-state. Iqtidar also draws upon the idea of Islamism as 'an agent of secularization' developed by

---

27 Academic definitions of what secularization is, have been myriad, but much current debate engages with the seminal work of Talal Asad (2003) and Charles Taylor (2007). See also Scott and Hirschkind (2006).

28 In fact, Riesebrodt has emphasized, 'religion' can (and in many modern contexts does) come to take on increasing importance with relation to a now more clearly delineated and autonomous 'religious sphere' within a broader 'secularized' system. See Riesebrodt (2010, 177).

Olivier Roy (1994) to demonstrate that the rationalization and objectification of religion characteristic of secularization processes facilitate the increasing importance of individual choice, and consequently of competition between advocates of different models of proper Islamic religious thought and practice (Iqtidar 2011, 22–23). As such a situation develops, she argues, "Religious practice can no longer be a matter of the communal following of norms; it has been changed into a largely individualized decision that must be justified internally, that is, within a subject and, externally, to others around the subject" (Iqtidar 2011, 157). All this has the effect of significantly raising the stakes on efforts to "get Islam right" on the levels of both the individual and society—thus potentially also exacerbating tensions between projects for standardizing systematization and individuating processes involved in the construction of modern subjects. The ways in which such complex negotiations of the relationships between individuals, religious leaders, and the state are managed in contemporary Aceh are insightfully explored here in the chapters by Annemarie Samuels and David Kloos.

In such contexts, I would argue, we might use case studies from Aceh to interrogate issues of importance to discussions well beyond the borders of that Indonesian province. In the dramatic contexts of the post-disaster/post-conflict period, Aceh's state Shariʿa system was energized by totalizing rhetorics of 'reconstruction' that were aggressively promoted by internal relief and development agencies and served to ratchet up the rhetoric of literally building a "new Aceh." With these heightened aspirations in mind, however, the results of their efforts at social transformation through the implementation of Islamic law have come to be seen by many proponents of state Shariʿa in Aceh as disappointing.[29] In voicing their frustration over this, mention is often made of such contingencies as fluctuations of political support, funding issues, and the training and management of personnel. These problems, while considerable, remain conceptualized as basically issues that could potentially be resolved by increased resources and better technical administration. If, however, we were to accept Iqtidar's argument that the modern state plays a central role in animating the very social processes that configure religion as a matter of individual decision, then it would appear that the realization of establishing hegemonic command over defining and regulating religion by the coercive apparatus of the modern state would be not just difficult, but ultimately impossible. Indeed, in this sense the very 'secularizing' framework of the modern state, may fun-

29 On the disappointment with the government's performance in implementing Shariʿa, and on the need to further develop *siyasa* see, for example Adan (2008, 30–34).

damentally compromise the ability for it to be used as an instrument for the promotion of a totalizing program for the uniform transformation of the religious belief and practice of its citizens. It thus becomes clear that even in a context in which the intent of using Shariʿa as a tool of social engineering is explicitly announced and energetically promoted, it remains crucial for us to contextualize the aspirations and accomplishments of such a project in relation to diverse aspects of Islamic belief and practice that persist and evolve well beyond the limits of the state's power to define them.

This, however, is not to say that the efforts of Aceh's proponents of state Shariʿa have not accomplished anything over the past decade. For even if the goal of establishing a totalizing vision of Islam for the province may be by definition unattainable, they have made measurable progress toward pushing the parameters for defining acceptable Islamic thought and practice in the directions that they deemed desirable. These developments are often commented upon anecdotally with reference to, for example, the changing public profile of Sufi devotionalism and changing patterns of everyday dress. The papers written for this volume, however, go beyond this to provide a rich array of ethnographic material through which to explore the complexities of Islam in contemporary Acehnese society in more nuanced ways, including co-optation, confrontation, avoidance, and ambivalence.

The chapters that follow present windows onto the ways in which the rapid changes that have marked the post-disaster/post-conflict period in Aceh have not only served to facilitate the engagement of local Muslims with modern projects of democratization, gender equality, economic development, and state Shariʿa, but also alternative forms of Islamic ideas and institutions with deeper roots historical in Aceh. In his chapter, David Kloos emphasizes the crucial point that even in the context of contemporary Aceh's dramatic social transformations, there are "strong currents of continuity at work in the ways in which Acehnese lead their daily lives." The volume as a whole thus aims to highlight the complex interactions between elements of continuity and change to provide a richer sense of the lived realities of Muslims in contemporary Aceh and their individual imaginations and experiences of Islam beyond the limits of the state.

References

Adan, Hasanuddin Yusuf. 2008. *Syariʿat Islam di Aceh: Antara Implementasi dan Diskriminasi*. Banda Aceh: Adnin Foundation.

Alfian, Teuku Ibrahim. 2006. "Aceh and the Holy War (Prang Sabil)." In *Verandah of*

Violence: The Background to the Aceh Problem, edited by Anthony Reid, 109–120. Singapore: National University of Singapore Press.

Alyasa Abubakar. 2005. *Sekilas Syariat Islam di Aceh*. Banda Aceh: Dinas Syariat Islam.

Analiansyah and Jamhuri. 2008. *Syariat Islam Di Nanggroe Aceh Darussalam: Inventarisasi Dokumen*. Banda Aceh: Dinas Syariat Islam Provinsi Nanggroe Aceh Darussalam.

Asad, Talal. 2003. *Formations of the Secular: Christianity, Islam, Modernity*. Stanford: Stanford University Press.

Aspinall, Edward. 2009. *Islam and Nation: Separatist Rebellion in Aceh, Indonesia*. Stanford: Stanford University Press.

Bayly, Christopher A. 2004. *The Birth of the Modern World, 1780–1914*. Malden, Mass: Blackwell Publishing.

Bowen, John. 1993. *Muslims through Discourse: Religion and Ritual in Gayo Society*. Princeton: Princeton University Press.

Bruinessen, Martin van. 1992. *Tarekat Naqsyabandiyah di Indonesia*. Bandung: Mizan.

———. 2007. "After the Days of Abû Qubays: Indonesian Transformations of the Naqshbandiyya-Khâlidiyya," *Journal of the History of Sufism* 5:225–251.

Daly, Patrick, R. Michael Feener, and Anthony Reid, eds. 2012. *From the Ground Up: Perspectives on Post-tsunami, and Post-conflict Aceh*. Singapore: ISEAS Press.

Damsté, H.T. 1928. "Hikajat Prang Sabi." *Bijdragen tot de Taal-, Land- en Volkenkunde* 84:545–609.

Dijk, C. van. 1981. *Rebellion under the Banner of Islam: The Darul Islam in Indonesia*. Leiden: KITLV Press.

Elias, Jamal J. 2012. *Aisha's Cushion: Religious Art, Perception, and Practice in Islam*. Cambridge, Mass.: Harvard University Press.

Feener, R. Michael. 2011. "The Acehnese Past and its Present State of Study." In *Mapping the Acehnese Past*, edited by R. Michael Feener, Patrick Daly, and Anthony Reid, 1–24. Leiden: KITLV Press.

———. 2013. *Shari'a and Social Engineering: The Implementation of Islamic Law in Contemporary Aceh, Indonesia*. Oxford: Oxford University Press.

———. 2015. "Abd al-Samad in Arabia: The Yemeni Years of a Shaykh from Sumatra," *Southeast Asian Studies* 4(2):259–277.

Feener, R. Michael and Mark Cammack, eds. 2007. *Islamic Law in Contemporary Indonesia: Ideas and Institutions*. Cambridge, Mass.: Harvard University Press.

Feener, R. Michael, Patrick Daly, and Anthony Reid, eds. 2011. *Mapping the Acehnese Past*. Leiden: KITLV Press.

Feith, Herbert. 1962. *The Decline of Constitutional Democracy in Indonesia*. Ithaca: Cornell University Press.

Formichi, Chiara. 2012. *Islam and the Making of the Nation: Kartosuwiryo and Political Islam in Twentieth-Century Indonesia*. Leiden: KITLV Press.

Green, Nile. 2011. *Bombay Islam: The Religious Economy of the West Indian Ocean, 1840–1915*. Cambridge: Cambridge University Press.

Hadi, Amirul. 2011. "Exploring Acehnese Understandings of Jihad: A Study of the *Hikayat Prang Sabi*." In *Mapping the Acehnese Past*, edited by R. Michael Feener, Patrick Daly, & Anthony Reid, 183–198. Leiden: KITLV press.

Hefner, Robert W. 1993. "Islam, State, and Civil Society: ICMI and the Struggle for the Indonesian Middle Class." *Indonesia* 56:1–36.

Iqtidar, Humeira. 2011. *Secularizing Islamists? Jamaʿat-e-Islami and Jamaʿat-ud-Daʿwa in Urban Pakistan*. Chicago: University of Chicago Press.

Ito, Takeshi. 1984. "The World of the Adat Aceh: A Historical Study of the Sultanate of Aceh." PhD diss., Australian National University.

Kloos, David. 2014. "In the Name of *Syariah*? Vigilante Violence, Territoriality, and Moral Authority in Aceh, Indonesia," *Indonesia* 98:59–90.

Koto, Alaiddin. 1997. *Pemikiran Politik Perti (Persatuan Tarbiyah Islamiyah), 1945–1970*. Jakarta: Nimas Multima.

Kraus, Werner. 1990. "Some Notes on the Introduction of the Naqshbandiyya-Khalidiyya into Indonesia." In *Naqshbandis: Cheminements et Situation Actuelle d'un Order Mystique Musulman*, edited by M. Gaborieau, A. Popovic and T. Zarcone, 691–706. Istanbul and Paris: Éd. Isis.

Lau, Martin. 2006. *The Role of Islam in the Legal System of Pakistan*. Leiden: Martinus Nijhoff Publisher.

———. 2008. "Legal Reconstruction and Islamic Law in Afghanistan." In *The Law Applied: Contextualizing the Islamic Sharia, A Volume in Honor of Frank E. Vogel*, edited by Peri Bearman, Wolfhart Heinrichs, and Bernard Weiss, 216–234. New York: I.B. Tauris.

Layish, A. and G.R. Warburg. 2002. *The Reinstatement of Islamic Law in Sudan Under Numayri: An Evaluation of a Legal Experiment in the Light of Its Historical Context, Methodology, and Repercussions*. Leiden: E.J. Brill.

Lindsey, Tim and M.B. Hooker, with Ross Clarke and Jeremy Kingsley. 2007. "Shariʿa Revival in Aceh." In *Islamic Law in Contemporary Indonesia: Ideas and Institutions*, edited by R. Michael Feener and Mark E. Cammack, 216–254. Cambridge, Mass: Harvard University Press.

Loimeier, Roman. 2005. "Is there Something like a 'Protestant Islam'?" *Die Welt des Islams* 45(2):216–264.

Lombard, Denys. 1967. *Le Sultanat D'Atjeh au Temps D'Iskandar Muda 1607–1636*. Paris: Ecole Francaise D'Extreme-Orient.

Marsden, Magnus. 2005. *Living Islam: Muslim Religious Experience in Pakistan's North-West Frontier*. Cambridge: Cambridge University Press.

McDougall, John James. 1979. "The Technocrat's Ideology of Modernity." In *What is Modern Indonesian Culture?* Edited by Gloria Davis, 232–248. Athens, Ohio: Ohio University Center for International Studies.

Miller, Michelle Ann and R. Michael Feener. 2010. "Emergency and Islamic Law in Aceh." In *Emergency Powers in Asia: Exploring the Limits of Legality*, edited by Victor Ramraj and Arun Thiruvengadam, 213–236. Cambridge: Cambridge University Press.

Nur Ichwan, Moch. 2007. "The Politics of Shariʿatization: Central Governmental and Regional Discourses of Sharīʿa implementation in Aceh." In *Islamic Law in Contemporary Indonesia: Ideas and Institutions*, edited by R. Michael Feener and Mark E. Cammack, 193–215. Cambridge, Mass.: Harvard University Press.

Ostien, Philip, Jamila Nasir, and Franz Kogelmann eds. 2005. *Comparative Perspectives on Shariʿah in Nigeria*. Ibadan: Spectrum Books Limited.

Otto, Jan Michiel, ed. 2010. *Sharia Incorporated: A Comparative Overview of the Legal Systems of Twelve Muslim Countries in Past and Present*. Leiden: Leiden University Press.

Peletz, Michael G. 2002. *Islamic Modern: Religious Courts and Cultural Politics in Malaysia*. Princeton: Princeton University Press.

Platzdasch, Bernhard. 2009. *Islamism in Indonesia: Politics in the Emerging Democracy*. Singapore: ISEAS Press.

Reid, Anthony. 1979. *The blood of the People: Revolution and the End of Traditional Rule in Northern Sumatra*. Oxford: Oxford University Press.

Riesebrodt, Martin. 2010. *The Promise of Salvation: A Theory of Religion*. Chicago: University of Chicago Press.

Roy, Olivier. 1994. *The Failure of Political Islam*. Cambridge, Mass.: Harvard University Press.

Samuels, Annemarie. 2012. "After the Tsunami: The Remaking of Everyday Life in Banda Aceh, Indonesia." PhD diss., Leiden University.

Schlegel, Stuart A. 1979. "Technocrats in a Muslim Society: Symbolic Community in Aceh." In *What is Modern Indonesian Culture?* Edited by Gloria Davis, 232–248. Athens, Ohio: Ohio University Center for International Studies.

Scott, David and Charles Hirschkind, eds. 2006. *Powers of the Secular Modern: Talal Asad and his Interlocutors*. Stanford: Stanford University Press.

Scott, James. 1999. *Seeing Like a State: How Certain Schemes to Improve the Human Condition Have Failed*. New Haven and London: Yale University Press.

Sehat Ihsan Shadiqin. 2010. "Kenduri Kematian di Kluet Aceh Selatan: Pemaknaan yang Beraneka Ragam." In *Serambi Mekkah yang Berubah: Views from Within*, edited by Arskal Salim and Adlin Sila, 253–284. Jakarta: Pustaka Alvabet and Aceh Research Training Institute.

Shiraishi, Saya. 1975. *Aceh under the Japanese Occupation: Rival Leaders in Aceh Besar and Pidie*. Tokyo: Tokyo International Christian University.

Siegel, James. 1969. *The Rope of God*. Berkeley: University of California Press.

Snouck Hurgronje, Christiaan. 1906. *The Achehnese* (2 vols.). Leiden: E.J. Brill.

Suhaidy, Saleh. 2007. *Buku Pegangan Teungku Imeum Meunasah*. Banda Aceh: Dinas Syariat Islam Provinsi Nanggroe Aceh Darussalam.

Syihab, Mahdi. 2010. "Penegakan Syariat: Etnografi Aksi Razia Santri Dayah di Aceh Utara." In *Serambi Mekkah yang Berubah: Views from Within*, edited by Arskal Salim and Adnin Sila, 57–91. Jakarta: Pustaka Alvabet and Aceh Research Training Institute.

Taylor, Charles. 2007. *A Secular Age*. Cambridge, Mass.: The Belknap Press of Harvard University Press.

Vogel, Frank. 2000. *Islamic Law and Legal System: Studies of Saudi Arabia*. Leiden: E.J. Brill.

CHAPTER 2

Hikmah and Narratives of Change: How Different Temporalities Shape the Present and the Future in Post-Tsunami Aceh

Annemarie Samuels

> Why in Aceh? God has not yet given [the tsunami] to other people, He gave [it] to Aceh first, right? Perhaps it is also a test. Now people live according to Shariʿa rules again, perhaps it was a test. A warning, so that the Acehnese will become better people in the future.
>
> PAK JAMALUDDIN, owner of a coffeehouse, December 2007

The tsunami that struck Aceh on 26 December 2004 left a trail of death and destruction.[1] It also brought about social changes and hopes for better futures. The post-tsunami years in Banda Aceh were full of different ideas about improvement, as many people felt that the tsunami had created opportunities for building a better society. The two major normative frameworks for improvement, which I call 'improvement narratives,' were that of moral and religious 'improvement' on the one hand and socio-economic 'development' on the other.[2] In this chapter, I will show that aspirations for and expectations of these

1 The fieldwork on which this chapter is based was made possible by the generous financial support of Leiden University, the Catharine van Tussenbroek Fonds, the Leiden University Fund, and the Aceh Research Training Institute (ARTI). I am very grateful to Patricia Spyer for her inspiring comments on earlier drafts of this chapter. I thank Michael Feener and David Kloos, who have read several versions of this chapter and provided me with most valuable suggestions for improvement. Finally, I wish to thank all the participants of the Leiden workshop for their thoughtful comments and the stimulating discussions.

2 In this chapter, I use the concept of 'improvement narratives' to refer to these two specific normative frameworks for change. I use the concept of 'imaginaries' to discuss ideas about the future more broadly. Finally, the concept of 'discourse' will be reserved for all other publicly articulated ideas about society.

 | DOI: 10.1163/9789004304864_003

kinds of improvement were closely intertwined in people's everyday lives in the years after the tsunami.

These improvement narratives were shaped by different concepts of time: whereas the narrative on moral improvement builds on an apocalyptic concept of time in which the expectation of the future end of the world influences present actions, the narrative on socio-economic development builds on a temporality of never-ending growth. However, although based on different concepts of time, through both narratives the tsunami came to figure as a starting point, or even an opportunity, for change. These improvement narratives emerged within contexts of rapidly changing institutions and the promotion of state discourses on development and on the strengthening of Islamic law (Feener 2013; Phelps et al. 2011). In this chapter, I will focus on the improvement narratives of ordinary Muslims in Banda Aceh, showing how they were informed, but never completely determined by state discourses, while simultaneously building on different temporalities and aspirations for the future. I argue that the tsunami heightened the importance of certain temporal relations, connecting the past, present, near and distant futures in new ways that both made a sense of the 'end of days' imminent, and opened up new possibilities for 'improvements' of various kinds in the near future.

To understand the improvement narratives of Islam and socio-economic development in contemporary Aceh, it is crucial to explore the diverse ways in which people there have come to understand and explain the tsunami. Many people in Banda Aceh discuss the past experiences of the disaster in relation to the future-oriented imaginaries of both actual and aspirational social and personal change. Among these future imaginaries, the two improvement narratives discussed in this chapter stand out, because of their importance to both public debates and personal ways of understanding the disaster. These improvement narratives were fundamentally influenced by different conceptions of time, two of which will be discussed in detail in this chapter.

The first is what might be considered an 'Islamic' conception of time. Although space doesn't allow me to engage with the encompassing topic of time and Islam comprehensively here, in light of the discussions in this chapter it is important to briefly discuss the centrality of the notions of fate, eternity and the Day of Judgment in Islamic conceptions of time. Gerhard Böwering has shown how the Qur'an breaks with pre-Islamic notions of time as it puts destiny into the hands of God. This means that God determines everything that happens, including the beginnings and ends of the lives of individuals (Böwering 1997, 57). Early Muslim philosophers and theologians developed Greek ideas on atomism to show that God created the world anew in every moment within eternity (op. cit. 59). Most important, perhaps, in the context of this chapter are the notions of the Day of Covenant (the moment of creation) and the Day of Judgment (when the world will end and individuals will be judged), which are both "anchored in eternity" (op. cit. 60). In Aceh, this conception of time in which the world has a beginning and an end, informed the idea that the tsunami signalled that the end of the world was approaching. Interpreted as a God-given warning, test, or punishment, many Muslims explained the tsunami as a sign that they should improve their religiosity in the present to ensure a better position in the afterlife.[3]

A second influential conception of time is a linear and progressive one. It is this idea of time that underlies the improvement narrative of socio-economic development, which promises never-ending progress. In Indonesia, this view of development has been promoted by the state since the colonial period (Li 1999, 2007). It became the state philosophy during the New Order, and gained new momentum in Aceh after the tsunami (see Feener 2013). However, for many people in Aceh, progress is not just a linear temporal process, but also a return to a mythic past of a glorious, prosperous and cosmopolitan Aceh. Arguably, this nostalgic notion of the return to a glorious past as a way of progress toward the future might be considered a third conception of time influencing the two above-mentioned improvement narratives. Importantly, these different conceptions of time as well as the different improvement narratives do not only coexist, but are also entangled in everyday life and in the explanations for the occurrence of the tsunami. References to the different improvement narratives are selectively deployed by people in Aceh in relation to shifting contexts (for example in discussions on morality and society and in discussions on the economy or foreign relations).

In this chapter, I will suggest that the way in which, after the tsunami, people used the Islamic concept of *hikmah* (divine wisdom) signals the intersection of the two improvement narratives. By pointing out that *hikmah* could be seen in the tsunami's intended effects on both morality and socio-economic development, the post-tsunami use of the concept of *hikmah* exemplifies the long-term connections between religious ideals and modern ideologies of development (Feener 2013).

My focus on future imaginaries contributes to a growing body of literature on Islam and everyday life in Aceh (Birchok 2013; Ihsan 2010; Kloos this volume,

3 Below, I will discuss some of the most common Islamic explanations for the tsunami. For detailed accounts of the repertoire of (religious) tsunami explanations, see Feener (2013), Feener and Daly (Forthcoming), Idria (2010), and Wieringa (2011).

2013; Samuels 2012; Smith 2012). It is through this particular focus that I aim to emphasize how ideas about time and improvement not only developed in a specific historical context and gained momentum in the post-tsunami and post-conflict period, but also how, as temporal narratives making sense of the disaster, they became an important part of the remaking of the everyday after the tsunami.

This chapter results from my research project on the remaking of everyday life in post-tsunami Banda Aceh. For this project, I conducted ethnographic fieldwork in and around Banda Aceh for more than twelve months in total.[4] During this time, I lived with two host families in tsunami affected neighbourhoods, one near Banda Aceh's city centre and the other seven kilometres outside the municipal boundaries in the district of Aceh Besar. I conducted in-depth interviews and participant observation in the places where I lived, as well as in several other locations, including Banda Aceh's city centre, a severely affected fishermen's neighbourhood, and a relocation site 15 kilometres out of town. In the process of these interviews, I talked with men and women of different ages, class backgrounds and ethnicities. By focusing on their stories I aim to contribute to the understanding of the role of religion in post-disaster societies, thereby exploring the influences and limits of the state. After a brief introduction on the concepts of time and improvement, I will discuss Islamic tsunami explanations, the Islamic notion of *hikmah* that brings together different narratives of improvement, and the role of the developmental discourse in the post-tsunami society.

Time and Improvement

The tsunami brought to prominence two different conceptions of time, which are both intimately related to narratives of improvement. The first is a religious temporality, through which the tsunami was explained as making people aware of the imminent end of the world. The second is a developmental temporality, through which the tsunami was seen as providing an opportunity to embark upon a linear process of progress. In this section I will elaborate on the relation between these temporalities and post-tsunami narratives of improvement.

4 I conducted fieldwork for this project in Banda Aceh from October 2007 to March 2008, from February to August 2009, in May/June 2010 and in January 2012.

Most people in Aceh give religiously informed explanations for the tsunami—including those along the lines mentioned by Pak Jamaluddin, in the epigraph that opened this chapter.[5] In this repertoire of explanations (which will be discussed in detail below), the tsunami is not only seen as a divine intervention, but also as an opportunity for Muslims to become more pious and for the society as a whole to improve morally. The need to become more pious is strongly anchored in the future end of the world. The way in which the future end inspires present actions is what Frank Kermode (1967) has called 'the sense of an ending.' In this religious temporality, there is a beginning and an end. People now are 'in the middest' but the end will certainly come and the living can still change their fate. This 'sense of an ending' bestows meaning on the present in relation to the expected future and influences present behaviour (Kermode 1967, 17; see also Spyer 2000). As Spyer (2000, 177) argues, "[i]n this way, social action becomes charged with a meaning and efficacy that ultimately derives from its relation to this end."

Interestingly, this 'messianic time' of the end is more about an understanding of the present than about the future. As Giorgio Agamben, drawing on the work of Walter Benjamin, has pointed out, messianic time is not about waiting for the Messiah to come, but about the potentialities of the present, for "the sole possibility to truly grasp the present is to conceive of it as the end." (Leland de la Durantaye 2009, 376, quoted from Agamben 2001). These reflections on the importance of the present in relation to the end of the world in a religious conception of time are not unrelated to Böwering's discussion of the Islamic philosophy of time—in which God creates the world anew in each moment and in which the Day of Judgment will be the end of the world anchored in eternity (Böwering 1997). It is this religious conception of time (akin to what Benjamin called "messianic time") that was strengthened by the tsunami.

Yet it is important to note that the appeals of the distant future of the 'end' and the afterlife, as well as the call for near future reform in this world, are not new to Aceh. James Siegel has analysed the focus on paradise and the afterlife in his discussion of the *Hikayat Prang Sabi* ('Story of the Holy War'), the popular epic narrating the war against the Dutch (Siegel 1979) and the change toward a focus on this-worldly Islamic reform from the 1930s onwards (Siegel 2000 [1969]).[6] Like the war against the Dutch (which started in 1873), the tsunami

5 All the personal names that I use in this paper to refer to my interlocutors in Aceh are pseudonyms.

6 According to Siegel's account, the appeal of worldly Islamic reform movements was highly gendered. It was the men who superseded village level social structures to connect to 'the

foregrounded the idea of the end of the world and therefore instilled the need for religious improvement with a particular sense of urgency.[7]

Becoming more pious, however, is not the only form of moral improvement that people in Aceh are concerned with. As anthropologists of Islam have recently argued, in everyday life different "moral registers" coexist or sometimes painfully contradict each other (Schielke 2009a; see also Kloos this volume; Marsden 2005, 2009; Schielke 2009b; Soares 2006), for example when Islamic ideals of chastity are confronted with expectations of romantic love, or when aspirations of consumption and well-being are confronted with religious disregard for attachment to worldly possessions (Schielke 2009b). "Morality in this sense," Schielke argues, "is not only unsystematic and ambiguous, it is also accompanied by declaredly amoral aims and strategies that people deem necessary to fill the 'emptiness' of the everyday and to reach material well-being" (2009a, s31). Others have analysed this ambiguity in the context of *islam mondain*, emphasizing that religious values and ethical working on the self do not exclude worldly aspirations (Otayek and Soares 2007; Soares and Osella 2009, s11–s12. For discussions on this topic in the Southeast Asian context, see Fealy and White 2008; Njoto-Feillard 2012; Rudnyckyj 2010).

Although these different kinds of aspirations are not necessarily without tensions, in this chapter I emphasize how they coexist in Aceh's post-tsunami everyday.[8] The moral and religious improvement deemed necessary in light of the coming end of the world by no means excluded people's aspirations

---

rope of God.' Siapno (2002) shows that, at least during her research in the 1990s, this was not the case (anymore). Many of the ideas about the tsunami and the future described in this chapter were voiced by men as well as women. My point is not to downplay gender differences in imaginings of the future, but to underscore that women as well as men create and recreate these broadly shared ideas about improvement and temporality.

7 As Edwin Wieringa has shown, the Acehnese war literature warns that sinfulness is causing disaster (in this case the Aceh war) and that the Acehnese can only reach paradise by committing to their faith through fighting the Holy War against the Dutch (Wieringa 1998; see also Feener 2013). Interestingly, the *Hikayat Prang Sabi* became popular again in the context of another recent moment of significant social transformation in Aceh, namely the 1999 peaceful social movement that demanded a referendum about Acehnese independence from Indonesia (Kloos forthcoming).

8 In public debate, different moral registers indeed may stand in a hierarchical relation. As Schielke (2009a, s32) remarks about Egypt: "While values can be debated, declaring them religious often ends the debate. All other moral registers have either to accept or ignore the supremacy of religion, but they cannot openly contest it." However, in everyday life, people draw on different moral registers without reflecting on them all, or by painfully admitting that they cannot live up to the standards of perfect piety (Schielke 2009a; 2009b).

and expectations of more 'worldly' future improvement. People in Aceh frequently voiced aspirations for, especially, improvement of personal and collective material well-being and improvement of Aceh's international position, its place-in-the-world (Ferguson 2006). Different from the religious 'sense of an ending,' these aspirations echo the development discourse that builds on a temporality of linear and never-ending progress; a process in which the tsunami formed a new and dramatic intervention.

After the tsunami, many people expressed their hopes for improvement of the educational system and for more economic investments that would lead to more jobs and prosperity. They hoped that the international attention for Aceh, which came about because of the tsunami, would secure lasting international recognition, attract tourists and economic investment, and increase the possibilities for studying abroad and traveling for business. Young men and women in particular aspired for economic improvement that would enable them to pursue their studies, start businesses and enjoy a middle-class lifestyle that would include hanging out in Banda Aceh's new hip road side cafés or the relatively expensive Pizza Hut, using internet on a smart phone and driving a car or a brand new motorcycle. As much as these aspirations may be inspired by images of middle-class lifestyles circulating on television and in magazines, they were certainly also fuelled by the post-tsunami reconstruction industry that brought cafés, cars, and an air-conditioned shopping mall.

In this sense, the tsunami had the effect of increasing rather than diminishing the 'capacity to aspire' (Appadurai 2004), an increased sense that improvement toward the 'good life' was a real possibility. These aspirations, accompanied by expectations of modernity (Ferguson 1999), provide a strong and important imaginary of the future in post-tsunami Aceh. However, when 'modernity' does not come as expected, or not for all, the unfulfilled promise of money and status may cause great frustration and disappointment (Ferguson 1999; Schielke 2009b).

The appeal of the development discourse of improvement toward modernity was not only part of a long tradition of 'development' in Indonesia (Anderson 1983; Heryanto 1988; Li 1999), but also informed by many changes in post-tsunami and post-conflict Aceh. The peace agreement, political change, the presence of hundreds of national and international NGOs and governmental agencies with huge budgets and ambitious 'improvement schemes' (Li 2007), as well as the opening up of the province for travel, contributed to the improvement momentum. Crucially, improvement—in the form of development—was promised by the national government and international organizations that frequently used the phrase 'building back better' as the slogan for the work of post-tsunami reconstruction in Aceh. 'Building back better' is an ongoing effort in the present without necessarily having a clear end point in the future and lacking a view of the past. Connected to the popular disaster reconstruction approach of 'linking relief reconstruction and development' (LRRD),[9] through 'building back better,' governments and aid agencies aim to go beyond immediate disaster relief and physical reconstruction to generate social and economic changes (Feener 2013).[10] In Aceh, 'building back better' did not just include socio-economic development. As Feener (2013) points out, the Indonesian government promoted discourses of both development and of religious reform in Aceh after the tsunami.

Importantly, different ideas about the future evolve in a field of differential power relations. The voices of religious leaders, the Indonesian government, international organizations and other powerful actors influence, but do not totally determine the everyday expectations and aspirations I analyse in this chapter. Rather, people position themselves in relation to different narratives and imaginaries in the context of their daily lives. 'The will to improve' (Li 2007) was indeed the major drive for change in post-tsunami Aceh. However, this will was not only formulated by experts in 'improvement schemes,' but also voiced and acted upon by Islamic leaders and many ordinary Acehnese in diverse ways. It is through this continuous process of positioning, adjustment and interaction that we can look beyond the state and its official discourse on Islam and development, to discern their limits in the lived experiences of individuals and local communities.

It should be emphasized here that the post-tsunami idea of development was not only grounded in a state-developmental discourse, but also in a historically grown sense of Acehnese identity. The interpretation of the Acehnese past is very important in contemporary Aceh (Feener 2011, 19). Present expectations of Acehnese modernity both inform, and are informed by, the imaginary of Aceh's glorious past; evoking a nostalgia for the Acehnese Golden Age in the

9 For an early overview of the LRRD approach, see Buchanan-Smith and Maxwell (1994). For a critical account of the influence of this approach in the post-disaster reconstruction process in Aceh, see Christoplos and Wu (2012).

10 Based on a comparative study of 'Building back better' practices in post-tsunami Aceh and Sri-Lanka, Kennedy et al. (2008) conclude that because of the multiple interpretations one could give to 'better,' the slogan should be changed to 'building back safer.' 'Safer,' according to Kennedy et. al., applies both to highly technical aspects of reconstruction (such as physical structures) and to less technical aspects such as education and disaster risk reduction. Arguably, however, it is exactly the broad scope and versatility of the concept 'better' that allows governments and aid agencies to see the disaster as an opportunity for societal change and thereby put it to political use.

pervasive aspiration to 're-connect' to globalization (see Ferguson 1999, 2008).[11] An Acehnese identity as opposed to an Indonesian identity emerged in the second half of the twentieth century (Aspinall 2009, 46–47). The idea of the past and future glorious nation of Aceh developed first in relation to modernity and colonialism and as a part of Indonesian 'roots' and only later as opposed to Indonesia (ibid.).

Today, an Acehnese identity strongly influences how people in Aceh talk about the future. People often discuss the future (development) of 'Aceh' as a nation. After the tsunami, many people had the feeling that suddenly it had become possible not only to be part of the Islamic *umma* and the globalized world, but also to be part of modernity as Acehnese. Through this idea of the development of Aceh, the state's development discourse gets a particular local meaning. Before exploring this development discourse and temporality further, I will first look into Islamic interpretations of the tsunami and their relation to the development of Acehnese discourses on the imperative of moral improvement.

God's Will

Many Acehnese Muslims considered the tsunami to be *takdir*; fate or destiny. This meant that for the people who lost their lives in the tsunami the predestined time of death (*ajal*) had already come, while for the survivors apparently it had not come yet (*belum ajal*). A related, frequently used expression was that the survivors had been given more time to live (*masih dikasih umur*). Thus, according to many of my interlocutors, both those who died and those who survived were confronted through the tsunami with their predetermined fate (*takdir*).

The idea of a predestined future that is known by God but not by humans has a prominent presence in everyday life in Aceh. Fate is called upon to explain bad things that happen (*musibah*, disasters) and good things that happen (*rezeki*, fortune), although both *musibah* and especially *rezeki*, which also has other, related, meanings, may also be the consequence of past actions. In everyday speech, both *insya' Allah* (God willing) and *kalau umur panjang* (if

11 The Acehnese "Golden Age" (*Zaman Mas*) refers to the late sixteenth to early seventeenth century, when the Aceh sultanate was at the height of its power, and Islamic law was—or so it is assumed—forcefully upheld. Edward Aspinall describes this as Aceh's "first great historical myth" that would be "a recurrent motif for later sultans, rebels, Islamic scholars, Indonesian nationalists, and secessionists alike." (Aspinall, 2009, 22).

[we] live long enough) are frequently used when people talk about things that may happen in the future, indicating that people can never be sure that God wants it to happen that way. In short, as the notion of fate is deeply embedded in everyday life in Aceh, it is not surprising that it became important in the context of explaining the tsunami as well.[12] For some people, referring to *takdir* meant that they did not question the meaning of the tsunami any further, as further explanations of why God had sent the disaster were mere possibilities; no one would ever know for sure. However, this did not prevent a majority of the people I spoke with from raising one or more of these possible explanations and pointing at signs that provided extra 'proof' (*bukti*) that the tsunami had been God's will.

Such 'proof' included foretelling signs that, in retrospect, predicted the tsunami, such as the particular behaviour of relatives who would die in the tsunami, dreams and visions, and stories about divine revelations or foretelling feelings. For example, some people told me how a pre-tsunami dream had been a sign of what was about to happen. Such was the experience of Ibu Rina, a young mother, who had lost many family members in the tsunami. She lived in one of Banda Aceh's neighbourhoods that had been seriously damaged, but after the tsunami she had quickly renovated her damaged house, together with her husband. In front of the house, they had made a small store in which she sold credit for mobile phones and worked as a tailor. While sitting in her store and talking about her experience of the tsunami on an afternoon in early 2008, she told me about the dream she had on the night before the disaster:[13]

> In this dream my mother and my younger sister came to me. My sister said: "Sister, please forgive me." That was in my dream. "Why do you ask for forgiveness? What have you done wrong?" [I asked.] I felt that my mother

---

12 For the Acehnese I spoke with, the emphasis on fate did not mean that in case of a calamity one could just sit and wait for death to come. Rather, as many people said, one should work to take care of oneself and others (*berusaha*).

13 Siegel (2000, 326–329) mentions three categories of dreams in Aceh, of which only one, *loempòë*, is 'true': "It is true, however, because it contains a message. It is a sign of what will happen. Moreover, it is sent not by djinns but by God." (op. cit. 328). Grayman et al. (2009) also encounter this category of dreams and add that people rarely discuss these dreams. In his famous nineteenth century ethnography, Snouck Hurgronje already wrote about premonitions and dream interpretations (mostly of foretelling dreams) (Snouck Hurgronje 1894, 43–46). These dream interpretations are part of the long-established Malayo-Muslim genre of *Ta'bir Mimpi* (Snouck Hurgronje 1894, 45; see also Overbeck 1929). On the history of visionary dreams in Islam, see Green (2003).

> was there. And then my mother said: "Just forgive." Alright, I forgive. But the following morning the tsunami came. They disappeared.

Only after the tsunami, Rina realized that this dream had announced their parting. Other people told me how strange behaviour of their relatives had been a sign of their coming deaths or how in retrospect their relatives had sensed that they would die. One of the people who told me such a story was Pak Nazaruddin. Before the tsunami, he had been a businessman in Jakarta, where he lived with his wife and children. His parents, who both died in the tsunami, had lived in their village of origin, a fishermen's neighbourhood in Banda Aceh, where his father had been a local imam. Soon after the tsunami, Pak Nazaruddin moved back to Aceh permanently to start his own shop in his old neighbourhood. In one of our conversations in his shop, he told me how perhaps his father had sensed his own death: "One month before the tsunami he called me [in Jakarta]. He asked all of us to come home; as if he already knew he would die." Pak Nazaruddin explained how his family in Aceh started to send all kinds of special Acehnese food to Jakarta and went on to say: "So I called him; and he asked to take the children home to Aceh. He meant that I should take them home to Aceh because, how did he say it, he said: perhaps I will die and then I won't see them again."[14]

Perhaps the most visible sign that was often referred to as an indication that the tsunami was given by God, was the image of mosques still standing in a landscape in which everything had been washed away. For most Acehnese, the pictures of the lonely mosques show God's power: while destroying everything, He left the mosques standing. Apart from such lasting images, many circulating miracle stories were interpreted as symbolizing the religious meaning, or *hikmah* (divine wisdom), of the event. Some were very personal. A teenager I knew well related how he became stuck in a net of barbed wire deep down in the water. He prayed and prayed that if the time of his death had come (*ajal*), God would make death come quickly, but that if he still had time to live, the wire would come loose. Immediately after his prayer, he could free himself. Others told me how they felt that they were picked up by a snake under water and lifted up to the surface or how they had seen that a sudden ray of light lifted people to the top of a mosque. Other stories tell of holy places that were spared by the water or how people were saved after they promised to fast for a certain number of days. These tropes of snakes, of people being lifted up to the top of

14 As others in Aceh told me, it is common that people sense their death forty days in advance. They sense it without being fully aware of it, so they may give signs or say goodbye without being aware that they are doing this.

the mosque and of survival after a promise or prayer, came up in the stories of various people I spoke with and appeared in different magazines and books about the tsunami.[15]

The stories of pre-tsunami signs that predicted the disaster build on the notion of predestination. Some people sensed that their own death was coming and although people with *ilmu* (special knowledge) warned for the disaster, most ordinary people only recognized the signs afterwards, when they became objects of interpretation and commentary or when they realized that a personal dream had actually announced the disaster. As some people explained to me, God does give signs and warnings, but they are implicit; in dreams, in children's behaviour. Apart from confirming that the disaster and death were fated, these signs and the miracles that happened during the tsunami emphasized that the tsunami as well as the fate of individuals were part of a divine plan. In many respects, they connect to a broader repertoire of tsunami explanations and their consequences for present and future behaviour.

It is important to note that many people in Aceh discuss dealing with fate or destiny in terms of *qadha* and *qadhar* (Smith 2012, 202–206). As Catherine Smith shows in her excellent ethnography of the concept of *trauma* in Aceh, *qadha* is the fixed destiny of each individual, determined by God (op. cit. 202). The individual has the obligation to accept *qadha*. Death is always *qadha* and thus needs to be accepted. *Qadhar*, however, is "a form of potential destiny that an individual ought to strive toward." (ibid.). As Smith points out, individuals have to recognize what is *qadha* and what is *qadhar*, then accept *qadha* and strive toward achieving *qadhar* (ibid.). This distinction is important to keep in mind in the discussion of the tsunami explanations below. While many people in Aceh see the tsunami itself as predetermined fate that has to be accepted, the various explanations they give for the occurrence of the disaster inform their narratives on improvement in the present and the future.

Tsunami Explanations

Most people told me that the heavy earthquake in the Indian Ocean had caused the tsunami, but the deeper explanation of why this had happened to Aceh (or

15 See, for example, "Tabib Diselamatkan Ular" (*Tabib* saved by a snake), *Aceh Magazine* (April 2006, 40–42) and various stories in *Tsunami dan Kisah Mereka* (The tsunami and their stories) (Damanhuri bin Abbas et al. 2006, Banda Aceh: Badan Arsip Provinsi NAD), such as "Dua Kali Menyelam" (Two times gone under) (70–71) and "Ular Kiri Kanan" (Snakes to the left and to the right) (200–201).

to a person in particular) was almost always framed in religious terms.[16] The tsunami was then alternately explained as a test, a warning, a punishment, or a way to stop the conflict.[17] These explanations often overlapped and many people mentioned several explanations at once. Therefore, rather than describing them as mutually exclusive options, they can be seen as part of a dynamic religious repertoire. In this section, I explore some of the explanations within this repertoire that have important consequences for ideas about the present and the future. As we will see, these different explanations come up in different contexts. For example, while the tsunami was often explained as a test or a warning when people talked about the individual lessons they learned from the disaster, interpretations of the tsunami as a way to stop the conflict or as a punishment for sins that had been committed were often invoked when reflecting on (hoped for) societal changes. To clarify this, in the rest of this section I will discuss some of these explanations in detail.

People often explained the occurrence of the tsunami as a test or trial (*cobaan*). God had given the people of Aceh (as a group or as individuals) a difficult trial through which they could show the strength of their faith (*iman*). In addition, by overcoming the disaster, they would strengthen their faith even more. Some people emphasized that the tsunami was thus given to the Acehnese people because God loved them and therefore had given them the opportunity to pass this test. For Ibu Wira, a woman in her late thirties, this was the most important explanation in her process of coming to terms with the disaster. In a long conversation in December 2007, exactly three years after the disaster, she told me how she lost her only daughter in the tsunami and how this still made her extremely sad. However, after the tsunami she had started to increase her religious understanding through reading and praying and because of that she felt a little better every day. She referred to this process as one of individual *introspeksi*, saying that the tsunami had been a test that offered her the opportunity to move up a grade (*naik kelas*). Her learning and praying were

---

16 This line of reasoning is also used by Islamic scholars and religious teachers. For example, in a book titled *Tsunami, Tanda Kekuasaan Allah* ("Tsunami, a sign of God's power"), Abdurrahman al Baghdady explains that the statement that earthquakes and tsunamis are just natural phenomena is wrong. He argues that they are indeed natural phenomena, but that God decides when they occur (Abdurrahman al Baghdady 2005, 64–72). For a more elaborate discussion of theological perspectives on the tsunami in books, articles, and online publications, see Idria (2010).

17 For other overviews of different explanations, see Fanany (2010), Idria (2010) and Feener (2013). Wieringa (2011) analyses how religious interpretations of the tsunami are reflected in tsunami poetry.

therefore not only a crucial way to deal with her grief, but also a conscious effort of personal ethical improvement (Kloos, this volume), resulting from the interpretation of the tsunami as a test. While for Ibu Wira this was an individual process, others perceived of the tsunami as an opportunity for the Acehnese to become more pious collectively.

Frequently, people explained the tsunami as a direct consequence of the conflict in Aceh. They would say, for example, that the disaster was God's way to 'wipe Aceh clean' (sometimes the English word *cleaning* was used), because of the chaos (*kekacauan*). Chaos in this context referred to the conflict that had troubled the province for decades and that had heavily impacted daily life in Banda Aceh in the last years before the tsunami.[18] More than eight months after the disaster (in August 2005), the conflicting parties signed a peace agreement. Although other factors were arguably much more fundamental for this agreement to come about (Aspinall 2009), many of Banda Aceh's residents saw peace as a direct consequence of the disaster—and the tsunami thus as God's way to enforce peace.[19] Such was the view of Pak Ilham, a man in his early thirties, who lived in a village that was hit hard by the tsunami. On an afternoon in 2008, I spoke with Pak Ilham and his wife about the tsunami and the reconstruction process. We were sitting in a tsunami aid house that they temporarily rented from a family member, while waiting for their own house to be finished. After they both told me about what happened to them during the tsunami, Pak Ilham explained why, according to him, the tsunami had happened. His words reveal not only the perceived relation between the conflict and the tsunami, but also the sense of the tsunami as a radical break with the past providing a new beginning:

> According to us [the tsunami] is a warning. Perhaps here everything had gone too far already. First, if we look at it from this perspective, there was the conflict. There were murders; houses were burned down, that kind of things. Chaos (*kekacauan*); let it be over at once. Like that. God gave [it]: everything was over. *Cleaning*. *Clear* [English], clean, cleaned up. To begin a new life. That is it, according to my personal opinion.

One explanation is then that God was angry because of the violence in Aceh. However, according to many, God was also angry because of the profusion of

---

18 For a long time the conflict was heavily felt only in rural Aceh. It was only after the end of Suharto's rule in 1998 that the conflict started to encompass also the urban areas of the province, including Banda Aceh (Miller and Bunnell 2010).

19 See Waizenegger and Hyndman (2010) for a discussion of the relation between the tsunami and the peace process.

sinful behaviour and moral degradation. 'Sin' in this context was sometimes referred to as *dosa*, the general Indonesian term for sin, but more often as *maksiat*, which is generally used in the meaning of sexual immorality. As women are often bestowed with the burden of guarding sexual morality, *maksiat* is a gendered concept.[20] This attention to moral degradation and sexual immorality can be seen as part of a broader trend of growing moral vigilantism and public attention to women's dress and moral behaviour.[21] Michelle Miller (2010) points out how some religious leaders argued that the tsunami was caused by women's immoral conduct. However, though often referring to *maksiat* as a plausible cause, the Acehnese people I spoke with rarely explicitly blamed women as a group for causing the tsunami. Nevertheless, this narrative of the tsunami as a punishment for sins feeds best into the rhetoric of moral lectures given by religious leaders that focus on the future in order to change the present; and the present in order to change the future (see below).[22]

In this respect, one particular tsunami explanation kept re-appearing. According to this explanation, on the evening before the tsunami (Christmas, 25 December 2004) people were having a party near the grave of *Syeikh Abdurrauf Singkil*, a famous Islamic scholar from the seventeenth century. He is also widely known as *Teungku Syiah Kuala* and the grave is usually referred to as the *Syiah Kuala* grave. According to many, the people partying near the grave that night were Indonesian military, i.e. non-Acehnese. They drank lots of alcohol and 'played with women' (*main perempuan*), sins according to Islam. The guard of the grave warned them that they should stop the party, but they did not, which aroused the wrath of God. The next day the tsunami struck Aceh as a direct punishment for what happened.

Several things stand out in this story that has a very broad circulation. First of all, even though people often mention that the partygoers were 'playing with women,' the emphasis is clearly on men as the wrongdoers, who would not

20 I thank David Kloos for bringing this to my attention.

21 On the rise of vigilantism with regards to supposed moral transgressions in Aceh, see Kloos (2014) and Newman (2009).

22 Miller's broader argument is that because people saw the disaster as divine punishment for their sins, feelings of guilt made them accept the strict Shari'a rules rather easily. Although divine punishment is one important explanation, I think we should be cautious in depicting guilt as the pervasive feeling. Arguably, while divine punishment is the explanation most often adopted by religious leaders, interpreting the tsunami as a warning or a test given because God loves the Acehnese is of similar importance in society at large. Concomitantly, guilt may have been only one among a range of sentiments of which in the long term, for example, that of acceptance seemed to be much more important.

listen to the guard and aroused God's anger. Secondly, many people describe the men on the beach as military men. Thus, the story of what happened near *Syiah Kuala*'s grave connects the narratives of immorality and of conflict chaos as explanations for God's decision to send the tsunami.

Finally, in this story, apparently a very small group of wrongdoers caused the deaths of 170,000 people. Interestingly, across the whole repertoire of tsunami explanations, individual and collective responsibilities are alternately invoked. While Ibu Wira saw the tsunami as something she could personally learn from, in other narratives the disaster was a collective test given to the Acehnese, or a sign for the whole Islamic *umma* that the end of the world was near (see below). Further, individual deaths were explained both on collective and individual levels. One explanation that was often offered, was that for each sinful person ten others had to be taken as well. An explanation for the death of loved ones, especially children, was also that God had chosen those whom he loved most. In this context, one woman emphasized that not the people who survived, but those who were in heaven with God now were saved (*selamat*).[23]

One recurrent tsunami explanation with profound implications for present behaviour was that the tsunami was a warning (*peringatan*). God sent the tsunami to remind the Acehnese that the Day of Judgment (*kiamat*),[24] on which they will be confronted with their sins, was near. However, the survivors still had some time to change; to improve their conduct and become good Muslims. In informal conversations about the tsunami, the people I have quoted in this chapter as well as many others frequently brought up religious explanations as well as the hope for a better future. These topics were also often discussed in more public settings, such as the neighbourhood women's meeting to which I will turn now.

Religious Improvement

On a Saturday afternoon in May 2009 I join the monthly neighbourhood *arisan* (women's gathering rotating savings club). The hostess has invited a religious teacher (*ustadz*) to give a lecture. After a long prayer *ustadz* Ibrahim begins to talk about the tsunami, stating that in spite of the tsunami there are still many people who are committing sins. We should

23 She deliberately played with the word *selamat* here, as it can both mean that someone survived (the disaster) and that someone was 'saved' (and in heaven now).

24 *Kiamat* (Ar. *qiyama*) in Islam is the Resurrection that follows the annihilation of the world and precedes the Judgment (Gardet 2011).

> be aware that our soul (*rohani*) and our heart are important, not our material possessions (*harta*). He goes on to explain that the tsunami is already announced in the Qur'an. What is also announced is that there will be signs that the end of the world is drawing near. Nowadays there are more and more disasters, the *ustadz* explains; even today there has been a disaster in Nigeria. The world is old, seven thousand years old, and we only have some centuries left. But actually, we do not know this and the Day of Judgment may even be tomorrow. The tsunami came because of the multiplicity of sins committed in Aceh. It is not because God does not love us. He does love us, but the tsunami was a warning. And actually this warning did not (yet) amount to anything; it lasted only ten minutes.
>
> The *ustadz* then tells the story of the prophet Musa and the seven plagues in Egypt to explain how God sends tests and warnings and concludes that those trials were much heavier than the ten minutes of the tsunami. He finishes his lecture by saying that people have to pay attention to God's signs. When the world ends, everything you have done will be revealed. And then you will regret that you did not give money to orphans. We should not care about money, because we cannot take money with us to the grave.
>
> *Field notes, May 2009*

Ustadz Ibrahim was studying abroad during the disaster and lost most of his family members who had stayed behind in Aceh. Drawing on texts from the Qur'an, he explains the disaster as a warning. The warning is directly related to the future end of the world, since in his religious lesson one's moral behaviour now will influence one's position on the Day of Judgment. His use of the disaster to warn his listeners for committing sins echoes the many lectures and teachings of religious leaders who emphasize that through the tsunami God punished the Acehnese for their sins. As can be understood from *ustadz* Ibrahim's lecture, this explanation not only installs guilt. It also explicitly leaves room for hope. God gave the tsunami because He loves the Acehnese; He warns them, because He wants to save them. The apocalyptic message of the approach of the Day of Judgment may instil fear, but at the same time it opens up an opportunity. If only people learn from this disaster and become good Muslims, God may have mercy.

It is in this context that survivors like Ibu Wira, who was also present at the meeting, saw the disaster as an opportunity, as something from which they could learn. Another woman from her neighbourhood, who also interpreted the tsunami as an opportunity to become more pious, was Ibu Agustina. She was married, had three school-going children and came from an upper middle class family. After the tsunami she had been hesitant about returning to the totally destroyed neighbourhood, but when she saw the house being constructed she slowly started to feel like moving back. While sitting comfortably together in her big, totally reconstructed house, Ibu Agustina told me elaborately about her interpretation of the tsunami as God's will. She emphasized that many of the things she owned now were bigger and more beautiful than the ones she had owned before the tsunami. On the other hand, she argued that after the tsunami she cared less about beautiful things; it was mostly other family members, such as her husband, who chose to have these things. Nevertheless, she was happy to accept this as God's will as well, as fortune (*rezeki*).

When the tsunami hit, Ibu Agustina was visiting relatives in an inner city neighbourhood. She was hit by the water, but managed to save herself and her daughter who was with her by climbing on a house. Like many others, at that time she thought that the end of the world had come (*kiamat*):

> At the time of the tsunami, Anne, when I was safe from the water, there was only one thing on my mind: according to our religion, if we die we take our sins (*dosa*) and our merits (*pahala*) with us. The question is of which there is more, the merits or the sins. So what was on my mind was that I did not bring anything! I have many sins, but no merits. My worshipping was still irregular (*bolong bolong*, lit. 'with holes in it'), I had made many promises, my clothes were wrong, too tight.

She went on to tell me how she changed this after the tsunami. She changed her dress and prayers, but also her attitude toward other people. Now, she often felt like giving things to others and so she gave money to orphans, saying: "I am afraid that when I die my merits will be too few; that it won't be enough." However, she also said that those who died during the tsunami would be in heaven:

> We, as Muslims, think that the people who died during the tsunami will have a place in heaven in the afterlife (*akhirat*). They died as martyrs (*mati syahid*). People cry for them, but actually we should cry for ourselves who are still here. They will be in heaven, but for us it is yet uncertain. We should just surrender (*pasrah*).

Schielke (2009b) has argued that we should not only pay attention to people's ideals of pious behaviour, but also to the outcomes, the failures and tensions these ideals may cause. Ibu Agustina seemed to feel uneasy about living in a beautiful house with a huge television and a refrigerator that was much bigger and more beautiful than the one she had owned before the disaster, as this seemed to contrast with the pious position of not valuing material possessions. Although people do not necessarily have solutions in case of moral dilemmas (ibid.), in this case she did propose a solution by using the notion of *rezeki* to explain that this luxury was not her own wish. In this way she positioned herself in relation to normative religious ideas about material possessions.

Although many people said that the tsunami was meant to improve moral behaviour, they also complained about the lack of moral improvement in present society. Many Acehnese told me that apparently people were 'still not aware,' referring to shops staying open during the evening prayer (*maghrib*), young people going out late at night, and the moral danger of the internet. On the other hand, many of the same people complained about the lack of entertainment in Banda Aceh. Pious behaviour is then, as anthropologists of Islam have remarked, not the only moral framework or aim in people's everyday lives (Marsden 2005, 2009; Schielke 2009a, 2009b). Nevertheless, the enormous attention to the relation between the tsunami and personal as well as collective moral change influenced at least some people's actual behaviour, as well as post-tsunami religious institutional reform (see Feener this volume; Feener 2013; Lindsey et al. 2007; Miller 2010).

Forebodings of the Final End

Returning then to the tsunami explanations in Aceh, the sense of a final end makes both the tsunami (as a warning, punishment, or test) and present actions meaningful. Present social actions are influenced by the expectation of an end, because by their present conduct people can influence their *personal* end (on the Day of Judgment). This is what Ibu Agustina sought to establish by changing her behaviour. The sense of an ending thus establishes a relation between the individual and his or her position in the end, after death and on the Day of Judgment. If the tsunami is interpreted as an immediate consequence of past sinning, however, present *collective* conduct can also influence the (near) future of Aceh. This is the immediate conclusion from a warning that was painted in graffiti on some unused roadblocks. It said: '*awas maksiat, stunami* [*sic*] *dekat, mari kita berdoa*,' which can be translated as 'beware of sin, the tsunami is at hand, let us pray.' The assumption is clear: if people sin (again), another tsunami will come soon. Numbers in red on these same roadblocks are counting down: 3–2–1. It is not sure that the numbers are connected to the message, but if they are, their meaning seems obvious. Thus, present actions influence both the near and the ultimate future.

Like *ustadz* Ibrahim, Ibu Agustina told me that the tsunami, together with other disasters in Indonesia, was a sign that the end of the world was near. As noted above, to many people the tsunami itself seemed to be the end of the world and only when it was over they realized it was not. In the apocalypse there can be different 'ends' (Kermode 1967, 89). Next to the ultimate end of the world (that stops time), there are the great crises in human life that do not stop time (ibid.). They seem to be the apocalypse, "but the world goes forward in the hands of the exhausted survivors" (op. cit. 82). In Aceh, the great crisis of the tsunami made the final end (*kiamat*) immanent and imminent (Kermode 1967). Although the apocalyptic idea is nothing new, it is through the framework of crisis of the tsunami that it becomes imminent and immediately relevant to the present. It means that time is running out for changing one's behaviour. Moreover, frequent crises in Indonesia and abroad are interpreted as a sign that the Day of Judgment is near. While many people only in retrospect recognized that their dreams and other signs had foreshadowed the tsunami, now the tsunami itself was interpreted as a sign of the end that gives meaning to the present. The tsunami therefore made the religious temporality of an end time more present, thereby increasing the need for present and future religious improvement.

Although the end cannot be evaded, there may be hope. As we have seen above, many people interpret the tsunami as a test (*tes, cobaan*). The tsunami made many victims for whom the disaster was the personal end. But the survivors lived through this 'end' and people like Ibu Wira and Ibu Agustina see this as an explicit personal opportunity to be morally good persons and add up to their religious rewards (*pahala*). They interpret their survival as a personal second chance. Moreover, living through the tsunami and its aftermath has made them, as many people say, more aware (*sadar*) of their religious duties. Without denying that these narratives may instil guilt and fear, I would say that for many people they are primarily ways to come to terms with the terrible disaster in accordance with their most profound beliefs. As I emphasized above, different explanations of the tsunami as a test, a warning, or a punishment are not mutually exclusive. Neither are the feelings of guilt, submission, acceptance, devotion, and becoming aware of religious duties. They are all ways of making sense of the past in the present.

Hikmah

As we have seen above, the interpretation of the tsunami as given by God as part of a divine plan and as foreshadowing the end of the world, urged for people's moral improvement in the present. But many Acehnese related the certainty that the tsunami was God's will also to other kinds of post-tsunami improvements, such as the peace agreement and increased social and economic well-being. Rather than something people were urged to work upon, these improvements were seen as almost a direct effect of the tsunami. The way in which these different kinds of improvement became entangled in the interpretation of the tsunami as part of a divine plan is clearly seen in how people used the concept of *hikmah* (divine wisdom).

The concept of *hikmah*, often translated as 'wisdom' but also related to 'truth,' 'knowledge,' and 'perfection,' has been mostly elaborated in Sufi philosophy. Throughout Islamic history it has also been identified with intellectual sciences in general (Nasr 2006, 37). Since the early period of Islam, it has had a wide range of connotations and there is no single fixed meaning of the concept throughout the Qur'an (Yaman 2011, 1–4). Hikmet Yaman shows how according to early Muslim commentators, "there is a causal relationship between sincere piety and being given hikmah [...]" (2011, 3), and that according to the Qur'an, "God is the ultimate possessor of hikmah" (ibid.). The concept can be understood very broadly as "all knowledge within the reach of man" (Goichon 2011). For early Muslim mystics, "real knowledge of everything, including hikmah, is not a matter of rational "knowing," but existential "being": hikmah is a process of knowing" (Yaman 2011, 270). Nasr describes how for many early Islamic philosophers, *hikmah* meant both knowledge and the way it is practiced (Nasr 2006, 36–38).

Although exact lines of entrance of the concept of *hikmah* into Acehnese Islam have not yet been mapped, it is likely that one line of transmission was through the work of the twelfth-century scholar Al-Ghazali and later through the Sufi work of the nineteenth-century Sumatran scholar Abd al-Samad al-Palimbani.[25] Interestingly, the Acehnese descriptions of *hikmah* in the tsunami as both God's wisdom and the positive effects of this divine intervention in the world echo the close relation between *hikmah* as both knowledge and practice that is found with the early Islamic philosophers described by Nasr.

The idea that there was divine wisdom in the tsunami (*tsunami ada hikmah*) usually came up in conversations about material and social improvement; when discussing things that got better after the tsunami. By evoking the concept of *hikmah*, people suggested that the tsunami was part of God's plan to

25 R. Michael Feener, personal communication. On the work of Abd al-Samad al-Palimbani, see Kaptein (2013).

do something good for them, to bring about improvement—ranging from a religious lesson or warning to improvement of the political and economic situation.

When Pak Nazaruddin, the shop owner, and I talked in his shop about the meaning of the tsunami, he formulated two forms of tsunami *hikmah*:

> If God gives us a test, in the end there will be *hikmah* in it. [...] After what happened here, with people losing their parents and others, the Acehnese could have had *stres* now. But because they have a strong religion, a strong faith, they would think 'this test will have *hikmah*.' What that *hikmah* is? Well, for example. That young man, Tarmizi, did not have a house before the tsunami. Now he owns a house. That is *hikmah*. And then there is the second *hikmah*. Before the tsunami, there was an ongoing conflict in Aceh. That ended because of the tsunami.[26]

While the idea of the tsunami as a test through which the Acehnese should strengthen their faith was pervasive in what Pak Nazaruddin told me, his idea of *hikmah* was rather related to livelihood improvement. Significantly, this use of the concept of *hikmah* calls attention to a broader development of increasing entanglement between Islamic religious ideals and modern technologies of development (see Feener 2013). It is important to note that both Pak Nazaruddin and I knew that the young man, Tarmizi (see below), had lost many family members during the tsunami and had great difficulties in making ends meet financially. By explaining the concept of *hikmah*, then, Pak Nazaruddin obviously did not mean that the tsunami had been only good for them. Rather, it meant that the disaster was part of a divine plan and that in the long term it was meant to improve certain things. According to Pak Nazaruddin, it was this realization that kept people from going mad.

In Pak Nazaruddin's explanation, *hikmah* is both per definition part of the test that God gave to the people and can be seen in the effects of this test (such as better houses and the peace agreement). Others also spoke of *hikmah* as something people received (*dapat*) through the tsunami. As indicated above,

---

26 A discussion on Islam and grieving in post-tsunami Aceh is beyond the scope of this chapter. However, this remark of Pak Nazaruddin represents a more general idea that people did not go mad because of their faith. *Stres*, as he uses it and different from Western psychology, refers to serious mental disorder and is in this context often interchangeably used with *gila*, mad. Interestingly, this speaks not only to the pious self-identification of many people in Aceh, but also to the magnitude of the grief—without faith, going mad would be a real possibility.

this could mean material improvement in the form of houses and objects, the peace agreement, or for example the post-tsunami international attention. However, in other contexts *hikmah* could also refer to the religious lesson that people learned from the tsunami, often in relation to its interpretation of being a test or a warning as discussed above. This latter meaning of *hikmah* ties in to Sufi traditions of 'wisdom' that are imparted by religious teachers and spiritual guides.

Different imaginaries of present and future improvement are entangled in these uses of the concept of *hikmah* as divine wisdom and its practice or effects in the world. The narrative of improvement through development (including amelioration of living conditions), however, also ties in to a broad, more secular, development discourse that became very influential in the post-tsunami years.

Building Back Better

As captured in the different uses of the notion of *hikmah*, aspirations for change included a variety of ideas about personal and social improvement. Schielke (2009b, 172) argues that:

> [...] the development of global capitalism, corresponding practices of production and consumption and the aspirations of progress and a better life have become a fundamental constituent of people's expectations and experiences even in the most remote places [...]

He notices that "consumption and moral practice have become intertwined in a complex way as key modalities of aspiring to and realizing happiness [...]" (ibid.). Aspirations for both moral improvement and material development were very influential in post-tsunami and post-conflict Aceh. Both of these aspirations were created and expressed by many institutions (such as the national government, international organizations, religious institutions, and NGOs), as well as by ordinary Acehnese. Concerning the improvement narrative of socio-economic development, it was especially the younger generation that voiced their aspirations to earning a lot of money and living a middle class lifestyle.

However, both younger and older people often spoke of their hopes for Aceh as a province to become more prosperous. In this often sketched image of the future, economic prosperity went together with a strong Islamic identity. It was often in this context of a future imaginary, including Islam and prosperity, that people evoked the idea of Aceh's glorious past, in which the region was at once Islamic, prosperous, and cosmopolitan. As with the concept of *hikmah* discussed above, this is another example of how the narratives of moral improvement and socio-economic development come together. In the remainder of this section, I will discuss the latter narrative; the influential improvement narrative of socio-economic development. Before taking a look at the ideas about development and the future of Aceh in the narrative of a young man, Tarmizi, I will briefly discuss the influential institutional promotion of the development discourse and ask how and where the state's discourse on the future meets with ordinary people's expectations.

From 2005 onwards, the BRR (Badan Rehabilitasi dan Rekonstruksi, Rehabilitation and Reconstruction Agency) and many of its reconstruction partners (NGOs and other international aid agencies) started to use the slogan "Building Back Better" to argue that Aceh would not only be reconstructed, but even made much better than it ever was. The joint report of the BRR and a number of its partners that came out one year after the disaster is titled: "Aceh and Nias one year after the tsunami: the recovery effort and way forward." The one year report of the BRR (April 2006) is called "Building a land of hope." Finally, the title of the first of a series of books published at the end of BRR's term is "Tsunami: from disaster to the emergence of light" (BRR 2009). The first two reports featured pictures of children playing and smiling, and the Acehnese working hard to rebuild their houses. The latter book indeed ends with a picture of the sun shining on an Acehnese mountain. In the public statements of many humanitarian agencies and the BRR, the focus has been squarely on reconstruction and the bright future that lies ahead. Few references were made to the death and grief of the tsunami or the conflict. Often, the tsunami is even described as an opportunity and a starting point for this better future.

The optimistic message that was so often voiced by the reconstruction agency and its partners was related, of course, to their own task of rebuilding. It was a political message of a government that was unpopular during the years of conflict (and still much criticized during the reconstruction process). It was the message of a government that therefore had everything to win by focusing on the future; a bright future that in fact seemed to be beyond the official term of the BRR (which ended in April 2009) and the reconstruction projects of most international agencies. Moreover, as Anderson (1998) shows, the image of going from darkness to light as a message of social and political transition has a long history in Indonesia.[27] In Banda Aceh, this image has been given a particularly

27 See Siegel (2000 [1969], 122) on the idea of modernist Islam as 'light' after darkness in Aceh.

concrete form through the experiential architecture of the Tsunami Museum (see Samuels 2012, 171–174).

The 'building back better' narrative leaves little room for discussing failures of the past, remembering the conflict and mourning the tsunami dead. The progressive focus on rebuilding toward the future and 'the way forward' also leaves little room for discussing stumbling blocks on that 'way' and other pressing issues (such as rebuilding the local government, politics, and corruption). The continuous use of phrases such as 'building back better,' 'the way forward' and Aceh being in 'transition' evoked the idea of a 'better future' (see also Feener 2013). However, the agencies that took responsibility for the reconstruction process only stayed for a short while and would certainly be gone once that future would arrive. The narrative is thus one of continuous progress without an end point in the future—although projects through which progress should materialize had clear end points.

Importantly, different voices with different visions of improvement come with different interests. These voices are not equal in terms of power relations. Yet while Indonesian government officials may have endorsed certain improvement ideas due to particular political interests, these ideas could also gain in power because the expectation of improvement was widespread in society at large. Rather than being a one-way process of powerful institutions developing and disseminating improvement narratives that are in their own interest to an ignorant population, these narratives develop and intersect in a complex field of social relations that have evolved in Aceh over time. While state actors develop and spread their ideas about the future, they cannot prescribe how people imagine their future and interpret the present. It is precisely by looking at the ways in which ordinary people appropriate and adapt official discourses and create ideas about the present and the future in their everyday lives, that we can grasp the limits of the state.

In April 2009, the BRR's term officially ended and the assets as well as the leftover problems were handed over to a short-term transitional agency (BKRA) and the provincial government.[28] Many international humanitarian agencies and donors had left already and others were busy finishing and evaluating their projects. Only a few of them pledged to stay after 2009. In the same month legislative elections were held and for the first time local political parties were allowed to participate.[29] The province had entered another period of 'transition' facing substantial political and administrative changes.

28 See "Post-reconstruction Aceh: Leftover problems." *Jakarta Post*, 26 December 2009.

29 See Barter (2011) for an analysis of the 2009 elections.

It was at this time that I met Tarmizi. He, like so many others, was worried about the economic situation. Also, many people were concerned about the peace process; not only in light of the upcoming elections, but also because many international organizations were leaving. According to many Acehnese, their presence, even if it was for tsunami reconstruction projects, had contributed to political stability. Now that the attention of 'the world' moved to other regions and countries, uncertainty increased. Concerning the future, many people said that they hoped it would be 'better' (*lebih baik*), for Aceh and for themselves. Tarmizi's ideas resonate with many imaginaries of the future I came across in Banda Aceh's neighbourhoods. They give us an idea of what this 'better' could mean.

Tarmizi was in his early thirties and had lost his parents and many of his extended family members in the tsunami. He married less than a year after the disaster, and in 2009 he lived with his wife and his three-year-old son in a newly built tsunami-house in his old neighbourhood. Their living conditions were poor, in part because Tarmizi did not have a steady job. Despite his difficult situation, he often told me how he kept the spirits up (*tetap semangat*). He frequently connected his ideas for the future of Aceh to his hopes for the future of his son, whom he wanted to give a good education:

> Aceh has changed because of the new buildings and infrastructure, but also for example in the area of education. We have better technologies now. Schools teach more languages. Before, we used to learn English. Now they also offer Japanese, Dutch, French, and Arabic. After the tsunami, education has much improved. Every school now has a lab (laboratory) with computers. Before, I did not know how to handle a computer. Now primary school children know how to do it. There is the internet; it is a time of major change. [...] I really hope that Aceh will be more developed (*maju*) in the future. That is, in the sense of technological development and of education. We should improve Aceh in the sense of education. It is important that [our students] go to the Netherlands, to America, and to Germany to learn. Then they can bring pride to Aceh, because of their knowledge (*ilmu tinggi*). Aceh does not want to lose, does not want to retreat; it wants to go forward/develop (*maju*). Today, we see how extraordinary the world outside (*dunia luar*) is; the food and electronic products that they [people outside Aceh] can make. Aceh will also be like them.

Later, Tarmizi also sketched the relations between these 'modern' developments and 'traditional' community values:

> Together we rebuilt our neighbourhood. It is something we did together; we never lost hope, we went on struggling. [...] [I value] both the ordinary people and the modern people (*masyarakat awam dan masyarakat moderen*). In this neighbourhood we use a certain system, it is like a symbol. It means that we do not use modern languages, languages that people may not know, modern languages that they perhaps do not understand. So, because of the everyday mingling with the people, I use Acehnese, even though I do speak Indonesian and English. By using the right language in the right place, people won't feel jealous. If they do not speak Indonesian, they do not feel side-lined.

All the people I met in his neighbourhood spoke Indonesian well (like almost everyone in Banda Aceh). One could say that Tarmizi here adopts a paternalistic attitude of knowing better than his neighbours. Although that may be so, I would also argue that it points to a specific aspect of what he sees as 'modernity' and what he sees as a better future for Aceh. Modernity in this perception is associated with 'the world outside,' with things people can adopt from this world outside—predominantly knowledge and technology—and the tools to do this—predominantly language and education. 'Ordinary' language, in Tarmizi's account, is needed to keep cohesion, while 'modern' language is needed to advance, to develop. Improvement, for Tarmizi, has everything to do with Aceh's place-in-the-world (Ferguson 2006), with the 'outside world' recognizing Aceh as a 'modern' player, so that "Aceh will also be like them."

While Tarmizi's account resonates with the state's development discourse, pointing to a change toward modernity in education and language, it also reformulates this discourse in a much more globalized way, by defining modernity in terms of international relations and skills. His idea of the future of Aceh reflects his subjectivity and positioning with his background of a community broker with NGO contacts as well as his plans for his son. At the same time, it reflects an image of Aceh's past and future that was widespread among ordinary people in Aceh during the post-tsunami years. Tarmizi's reflections therefore give us a sense of how imaginaries of Acehnese futures are produced and reproduced; influenced but never totally determined by the state.

As I have argued throughout this chapter, in post-tsunami Aceh these future imaginaries were often framed in relation to the notion of the tsunami as an opportunity to improve oneself and society both morally and socio-economically. In this regard, BRR has called the tsunami a 'blessing in disguise' (BRR 2009, 95, cited in Feener 2013). Many people in Aceh would rather think of it as *hikmah*.

Conclusion

People in Aceh saw the tsunami as a starting point for improvement in different ways. As a destined event predetermined by divine wisdom, many people thought of the disaster as revealing a divine message as well as showing that they were part of God's plan. Many Muslims in Aceh understood the tsunami in an Islamic temporality, in which one's own death and the end of the world are predetermined. In this perspective, during their time in the world, people can improve themselves and society. For many, the tsunami was a God-given warning, punishment, or test that revealed the need for such improvements. The idea of the tsunami as an opportunity for moral change was for many people entangled with the idea that the disaster was a starting point for the amelioration of everyday living conditions or 'development.'

This narrative of improvement as development came to expression in a context of (inter)national attention for 'building back better' and concurrent 'expectations of modernity,' building on a development discourse framed in a temporality of linear progress. However, in everyday Aceh, it also built on an idea of Aceh and Aceh's place-in-the-world that has developed over the last century. This idea of Aceh's place-in-the-world is constituted by a temporality of nostalgia that underlies the aspiration for Aceh's 'return' to its glorious past of Islamic rule and economic prosperity. This future imaginary strongly connects improvement narratives of Islam and socio-economic development, a relation that more broadly inspires attempts of social engineering that have developed in Aceh since the second half of the twentieth century (Feener 2013).

In this chapter, I have identified another important way in which the improvement narratives of Islam and socio-economic development were brought together by my Acehnese interlocutors, namely through the Islamic concept of *hikmah* (divine wisdom). Discussing the tsunami in terms of *hikmah*, they connected the idea of the disaster as a God-given opportunity for change with expectations of and aspirations for moral *and* socio-economic improvement.

Institutional discourses are very influential in creating future imaginaries, yet they do not totally determine the dynamics of these and other imaginaries in everyday life. Throughout this chapter, I have focused on the imaginaries of the future of ordinary Acehnese and suggested that temporalities of Islam and development intersect in Acehnese understandings of the tsunami and the future in the process of the post-disaster remaking of society. They do so through narratives of improvement that are part of official policies, but also acquire their fluid forms in the fine-grained dynamics of the everyday. It is exactly in their everyday expectations and aspirations that people creatively appropriate and adapt state discourses, while imagining and shaping their own futures and the future of Aceh.

References

Abdurrahman al Baghdady. 2005. *Tsunami, Tanda Kekuasaan Allah.* Jakarta: Cakrawala Publishing.

Agamben, Giorgio. 2001. "Das Unheilige Leben." Interview by Hanna Leitgeb and Cornelia Vismann. *Literaturen* 2(1):16–22.

Anderson, Benedict. 1983. "Old State, New Society: Indonesia's New Order in Comparative Historical Perspective." *Journal of Asian Studies* 42(3):477–496.

———. 1998. *The Spectre of Comparisons: Nationalism, Southeast Asia, and the World.* London: Verso.

Appadurai, Arjun. 2004. "The Capacity to Aspire: Culture and the Terms of Recognition." In *Culture and Public Action*, edited by Vijayendra Rao and Michael Walton, 59–84. Stanford: Stanford Social Sciences.

Aspinall, Edward. 2009. *Islam and Nation: Separatist Rebellion in Aceh, Indonesia.* Stanford: Stanford University Press.

Barter, Shane Joshua. 2011. "The Free Aceh Elections? The 2009 Legislative Contests in Aceh." *Indonesia* 91:113–130.

Birchok, Daniel Andrew. 2013. "Sojourning on Mecca's Verandah: Place, Temporality and Islam in an Indonesian Province." PhD diss., University of Michigan.

Böwering, Gerhard. 1997. "The Concept of Time in Islam." *Proceedings of the American Philosophical Society* 141(1):55–66.

BRR. 2006. *Building a Land of Hope: One Year Report Executing Agency of the Rehabilitation and Reconstruction Agency for Aceh and Nias.* BRR report.

BRR. 2009. *Tsunami: From Disaster to the Emergence of Light.* Jakarta: Multi Donor Fund/UNDP.

BRR and partners. 2005. *Aceh and Nias One Year After the Tsunami: The Recovery Effort and Way Forward.* BRR report.

Buchanan-Smith, Margaret and Simon Maxwell. 1994. "Linking Relief and Development: An Introduction and Overview." *Institute of Development Studies Bulletin* 25(4):2–16.

Christoplos, Ian and Treena Wu. 2012. "Linking Relief, Rehabilitation and Development (LRRD) to Social Protection: Lessons from the Early Tsunami Response in Aceh." In *From the Ground Up: Perspectives on Post-Tsunami and Post-Conflict Aceh*, edited by Patrick Daly, R. Michael Feener and Anthony Reid, 40–56. Singapore: ISEAS.

Fanany, Ismet. 2010. "Afterword: Reconstructing the Invisible Landscape." In *Post-Disaster Reconstruction: Lessons from Aceh*, edited by Matthew Clarke, Ismet Fanany and Sue Kenny, 235–249. London: Earthscan.

Fealy, Greg and Sally White, eds. 2008. *Expressing Islam: Religious Life and Politics in Indonesia*. Singapore: ISEAS.

Feener, R. Michael. 2013. *Shari'a and Social Engineering: The Implementation of Islamic law in Contemporary Aceh*. Oxford: Oxford University Press.

———. 2011. "The Acehnese Past and its Present State of Study." In *Mapping the Acehnese Past*, edited by R. Michael Feener, Patrick Daly and Anthony Reid, 1–24. Leiden: KITLV press.

Feener, R. Michael and Patrick Daly. Forthcoming. "Religion and Reconstruction in the Wake of Disaster." *Asian Ethnology*.

Ferguson, James. 1999. *Expectations of Modernity*. Berkeley: University of California Press.

———. 2006. *Global Shadows: Africa in the Neoliberal World Order*. Durham: Duke University Press.

———. 2008. "Global Disconnect: Abjection and the Aftermath of Modernism." In *Readings in Modernity in Africa*, edited by Peter Geschiere, Birgit Meyer and Peter Pels, 8–16. Bloomington: Indiana University Press.

Gardet, L. 2011. "Kiyāma." In *Encyclopaedia of Islam*, Second Edition, edited by P. Bearman, Th. Bianquis, C.E. Bosworth, E. van Donzel, and W.P. Heinrichs. Leiden: Brill. [online access]

Goichon, A.M. 2011. "Ḥikma." In: *Encyclopaedia of Islam*, Second Edition, edited by P. Bearman, Th. Bianquis, C.E. Bosworth, E. van Donzel, and W.P. Heinrichs. Leiden. Brill. [online access].

Grayman, Jesse H., Mary-Jo Delvecchio Good, and Byron J. Good. 2009. "Conflict Nightmares and Trauma in Aceh." *Culture, Medicine, and Psychiatry* 33:290–312.

Green, Nile. 2003. "The Religious and Cultural Roles of Dreams and Visions in Islam." *Journal of the Royal Asiatic Society* 13(3):287–313.

Heryanto, Ariel. 1988. "The Development of 'Development'." *Indonesia* 46:1–24.

Idria, Reza. 2010. "Muslim Theological Perspectives on Natural Disasters: the Case of Indonesian Earthquakes and Tsunami of 2004." MA Thesis, Leiden University.

Ihsan, Sehat. 2010. "Kenduri Kematian di Kluet Aceh Selatan: Pemaknaan yang Beraneka Ragam." In *Serambi Mekkah yang Berubah: Views from Within*, edited by Arskal Salim and Adlin Sila, 253–284. Jakarta: Pustaka Alvabet and Aceh Research Training Institute.

Kaptein, Nico J.G. 2013. "ʿAbd al-Ṣamad al-Palimbānī." In *Encyclopaedia of Islam*, Three, edited by Gudrun Krämer, Denis Matringe, John Nawas and Everett Rowson. Leiden: Brill. [online access].

Kennedy, James, Joseph Ashmore, Elizabeth Babister and Ian Kelman. 2008. "The

Meaning of 'Building Back Better': Evidence from Post-Tsunami Aceh and Sri-Lanka." *Journal of Contingencies and Crisis Management* 16(1):24–36.

Kermode, Frank. 1967. *The Sense of an Ending: Studies in the Theory of Fiction.* New York: Oxford University Press.

Kloos, David. 2013. "Becoming Better Muslims: Religious Authority and Ethical Improvement in Aceh, Indonesia." PhD diss., VU University Amsterdam.

———. 2014. "In the Name of *Syariah*? Vigilante Violence, Territoriality, and Moral Authority in Aceh, Indonesia." *Indonesia* 98:59–90.

———. Forthcoming. "Images of Violence and Piety in Aceh." In *Islam, Politics and Change: the Indonesian Experience*, edited by Kees van Dijk and Nico Kaptein. Leiden: Leiden University Press.

Leland de la Durantaye. 2009. *Giorgio Agamben: A Critical Introduction.* Stanford: Stanford University Press.

Li, Tania Murray. 1999. "Compromising Power: Development, Culture, and Rule in Indonesia." *Cultural Anthropology* 14(3):295–322.

———. 2007. *The Will to Improve: Governmentality, Development, and the Practice of Politics.* Durham and London: Duke University Press.

Lindsey, Tim, and M.B. Hooker, with Ross Clarke and Jeremy Kingsley. 2007. "Shari'a Revival in Aceh." In *Islamic Law in Contemporary Indonesia, Ideas and Institutions*, edited by R. Michael Feener, and Mark E. Cammack, 216–254. Cambridge: Harvard University Press.

Marsden, Magnus. 2005. *Living Islam: Muslim Religious Experience in Pakistan's North-West Frontier.* Cambridge: Cambridge University Press.

———. 2009. "A Tour not so Grand: Mobile Muslims in Northern Pakistan." *Journal of the Royal Anthropological Institute* (N.S.):S57–S75.

Miller, Michelle A. 2010. "The Role of Islamic Law (Sharia) in Post-Tsunami Reconstruction." In *Post-Disaster Reconstruction: Lessons from Aceh*, edited by Matthew Clarke, Ismet Fanany and Sue Kenny, 29–60. London: Earthscan.

Miller, Michelle A. and Tim Bunnell. 2010. "Urban-Rural Connections: Banda Aceh through Conflict, Tsunami and Decentralization." Working paper, Asia Research Institute, National University of Singapore.

Nasr, Seyyed Hossein. 2006. *Islamic Philosophy from its Origin to the Present: Philosophy in the Land of Prophecy.* New York: State University of New York Press.

Newman, Sarah J. 2009. "Patrolling Sexuality." *Inside Indonesia* 96.

Njoto-Feillard, Gwenaël. 2012. *L'Islam et la Réinvention du Capitalisme en Indonésie.* Paris: Karthala, IISMM.

Otayek, Renee and Benjamin Soares. 2007. "Introduction: Islam and Muslim Politics in Africa." In *Islam and Muslim Politics in Africa*, edited by Benjamin Soares and Renee Otayek, 1–24. Basingstoke: Palgrave Macmillan.

Overbeck, Hans. 1929. "Shaer Ta'bir Mimpi." *Journal of the Malayan Branch of the Royal Asiatic Society* 3:338–375.

Phelps, Nicholas A., Tim Bunnell and Michelle Ann Miller. 2011. "Post-Disaster Economic Development in Aceh: Neoliberalization and Other Economic-Geographical Imaginaries." *Geoforum* 42:418–426.

Rudnyckyj, Daromir. 2010. *Spiritual Economies: Islam, Globalization and the Afterlife of Development*. Ithaca: Cornell University Press.

Samuels, Annemarie. 2012. "After the Tsunami: The Remaking of Everyday Life in Banda Aceh, Indonesia." PhD diss., Leiden University.

Schielke, Samuli. 2009a. "Being Good in Ramadan: Ambivalence, Fragmentation, and the Moral Self in the Lives of Young Egyptians." *Journal of the Royal Anthropological Institute* (N.S.):S24–S40.

———. 2009b. "Ambivalent Commitments: Troubles of Morality, Religiosity and Aspiration among Young Egyptians." *Journal of Religion in Africa* 39:158–185.

Siapno, Jaqueline Aquino. 2002. *Gender, Islam, Nationalism and the State in Aceh: The Paradox of Power, Co-optation, and Resistance*. London: RoutledgeCurzon.

Siegel, James. 1979. *Shadow and Sound: The Historical Thought of a Sumatran People*. Chicago: University of Chicago Press.

———. 2000 [1969]. *The Rope of God*. Ann Arbor: The University of Michigan Press.

Smith, Catherine. 2012. "War, Medicine, and Morality in Aceh: An Ethnography of Trauma as an Idiom of Distress." PhD diss., Australian National University.

Snouck Hurgronje, Christiaan. 1894. *De Atjehers*, Volume 2. Leiden: Brill.

Soares, Benjamin. 2006. "Islam in Mali in the Neo-Liberal Era." *African Affairs* 105:77–95.

Soares, Benjamin and Filippo Osella. 2009. "Islam, Politics, Anthropology." *Journal of the Royal Anthropological Institute* (N.S.):S1–S23.

Spyer, Patricia. 2000. *The Memory of Trade: Modernity's Entanglements on an Eastern Indonesian Island*. Durham and London: Duke University Press.

Waizenegger, Arno and Jennifer Hyndman. 2010. "Two Solitudes: Post-Tsunami and Post-Conflict Aceh." *Disasters* 34(3):787–808.

Wieringa, Edwin. 1998. "The Dream of the King and the Holy War against the Dutch: The 'Kôteubah' of the Acehnese Epic *'Hikayat Prang Gômpeuni'*." *Bulletin of the School of Oriental and African Studies* 61(2):298–308.

———. 2011. "God Speaks through Natural Disasters, but What Does He Say? Islamic Interpretations in Indonesian Tsunami Poetry." In *Aceh: History, Politics and Culture*, edited by Arndt Graf, Susanne Schröter and Edwin Wieringa, 316–333. Singapore: ISEAS.

Yaman, Hikmet. 2011. *Prophetic Niche in the Virtuous City: The Concept of* Hikmah *in Early Islamic Thought*. Leiden: Brill.

CHAPTER 3

Sinning and Ethical Improvement in Contemporary Aceh

David Kloos

> You see, David, I never wear a headscarf in front of you, even though you are not a Muslim and not close family (*muhrim*). Of course, this is a sin (*dosa*). It is said that for every single visible hair, a bundle of wood will be added to the fire in hell. And I do not even speak of all the sins which happen unnoticed.
>
> IRMA, Banda Aceh, 2010

∵

This chapter explores the ways in which Acehnese Muslims engage in personal projects of ethical improvement.[1] I will approach this topic by discussing how people deal with the problem of sin. Much has been written about techniques of formal discipline in Acehnese history, from the development of a sophisticated system of Islamic courts in the seventeenth century sultanate state (Hadi 2004; Ito 1984; Lombard 1967) to the attempts to implement a regional variation of Shari'a law in the mid-20th century (Aspinall 2009; van Dijk 1981; Feener 2013; Reid 2006; Sjamsuddin 1985) and today (Aspinall 2009; Feener 2013, this volume; Großman, this volume; Lindsey et al. 2007; Miller 2010; Miller and Feener

1 The research for this chapter has been made possible by the Faculty of Arts, VU University Amsterdam. Additional funding was provided by the Aceh Research Training Institute (ARTI) in the form of a travel fellowship in 2009–2010. I would like to thank all the participants in the conference in Leiden for the inspiring discussion. Daan Beekers and Sadiah Boonstra have commented on an earlier draft of this text, for which I am thankful. Henk Schulte Nordholt and Heather Sutherland, my PhD supervisors, have commented on my work and inspired and stimulated my research and thinking in many different ways, something for which I am extremely grateful. My co-editors, Michael Feener and Annemarie Samuels, have read through and commented on multiple versions of the text, thus helping me to improve it beyond expectation.

 | DOI: 10.1163/9789004304864_004

2010; Nur Ichwan 2007). However, apart from an earlier work by James Siegel (1969) and, more recently, Sehat Ihsan Shadiqin (2010), very little has been written about the question of how ordinary Acehnese Muslims, without much power, influence, or specialized knowledge (Peletz 1997) have shaped, judged and adjusted their own behaviour in relation to the admonitions of state and religious authorities. Elaborating further on the central theme of this volume, in this chapter I argue that the responsibility to reduce personal sinfulness, which is both generally recognized and supported by the state, offers space for interpretation and action as much as it restricts personal choices and decisions.

As in Muslim societies elsewhere, in Aceh there is a tension between individual and communal responsibilities with regard to judging bad behaviour. Most Acehnese Muslims believe that uncontrolled sinfulness has a destructive effect not only on the sinner him- or herself, but also on the harmony and integrity of the 'community of believers' (*umma*). This view is particularly salient in contexts, such as war, colonization, and natural disaster, in which a sense of moral crisis can be significantly heightened. In addition to this general consideration, moralizing practices and discourses are often (though not always) legitimized on the basis of the idea that Islamic piety and Acehnese ethnic identity are intertwined. In the construction of Acehnese ethnic identity, Islam takes centre stage.[2] That said, most ordinary Acehnese agree that the consequences of sinfulness can also be mitigated by individual Muslims' personal, long-term processes of ethical improvement, depending on the accumulation of knowledge, changes in everyday conduct and routines, and a developing sense of responsibility. Three main channels for this mitigation may be distinguished. Firstly, many Acehnese believe that God judges the behaviour of humans not only on the basis of what they do wrong, but also on what they do right. Thus, the accumulation of 'sins' (*dosa*) during one's life has meaning only in relation to the simultaneous accumulation of divine rewards (*pahala*), through the performance of good deeds or practices. The second channel is the possibility for Muslims to ask for God's mercy (*ampun*) through practices of repentance (*bertobat*) or by asking God directly for forgiveness (*minta ampun*). This means that Acehnese Muslims rarely see committed sins as isolated facts, but always in the context of a cumulative lived experience. Thirdly, one may distinguish

2 'Being Acehnese,' apart from speaking (any dialect of) the Acehnese language, following locally defined traditional customs (*adat*), and identifying with the Acehnese past, means to be Muslim. Various political and religious leaders have presented the implementation of state Shari'a law as a specifically 'Acehnese' need, paying scarce attention to the ethnically and ideologically diverse make-up of the province (Aspinall 2009, 211–212; Feener 2012, 307–309).

the factor of 'intention' (*niat*) as a component of ethical formation. As we shall see, when people in Aceh judge their own behaviour, they take into account the future as much as they consider their past and present.

Although it is tempting to view the tension between individual and communal sensibilities as a typically modern example of bodily discipline colliding with the assertiveness (and perhaps, subversiveness) of emancipated individuals, it is important to acknowledge the nuances of academic debate on this subject. In recent decades, we have seen an increasing interest in the role of ritual practices of (self-)discipline in constituting Muslim 'selfhood' (see, e.g., Asad 1993; Mahmood 2005). This chapter broadly builds on the renewed focus on ritual in anthropology (see, e.g., Tambiah 1985), particularly on the 'pragmatic turn' in the anthropology of ritual (Beatty 2000, 39–40). In addition, I seek to respond explicitly to the calls of scholars such as Michael Lambek (2000, 309–310), Magnus Marsden (2005, 26) and Anna Gade (2004, 48–49) to think beyond conceptual frameworks treating (Islamic) religion primarily as a disciplinary order. Instead, I argue that it is important to acknowledge the ways in which religious motivations are applied to address, affectively and creatively, the personal spaces and dimensions of individuality that are commonly subject to contestation, doubt, and ambivalence, rather than an unequivocal focus on a progressive and idealistic process of pious perfection. Although sinfulness seems to be pre-eminently a matter of discipline, I argue that even the basic concern of dealing with bad behaviour is, at the level of lived experiences, marked by considerable measures of flexibility and creativeness. These sensibilities, in turn, strongly influence the ways in which people approach the legalistic frameworks and moral repertoires formulated by state actors and institutions.

When I was conducting fieldwork in Aceh in 2009–2010, I was fascinated by the way in which my interlocutors explained, time and time again, and often quite eloquently, that pious expressions (or their absence) should be understood as a process. What I was observing, then, was a general persuasion to see these expressions as part of an (ideally progressive) personal project. An example is the way in which Ramadan, the fasting month, was experienced by many of my interlocutors. During Ramadan, Muslims engage in the (supplementary, but highly recommended) *tarawih* prayers, which follow on *isya* (the last of the mandatory prayers). On the first nights of Ramadan, nearly everyone joined in the *tarawih*. Numbers then steadily declined as the month progressed, only for the mosques and *meunasah* (village prayer halls) to fill up again on the last day. Some people commented on this by complaining that their fellow villagers (especially the younger ones) were lazy (*malas*). A much more common reaction, however, was the explanation that the *tarawih* was a practice to "grow into" (*membiasakan diri*). Thus, many young Acehnese actively counted and remembered the total number of days they joined in and completed the ritual, in this year and in previous years. Their main argument was that, rather than trying to be perfect, it was important to increase the number each year, or at least to have this intention.

These observations lead to a set of interrelated questions which so far have not, or hardly, been addressed in the existing literature on Aceh, namely: what role do cultural models of sinning and practices of repentance play in the construction of Acehnese' personal projects of ethical improvement? How do these ideas and practices relate to, respond to, or resist the dominant, communally-defined discourse of moral and intellectual conservatism rooted in what Nur Ichwan (2011, 2007), Lindsey et al. (2007) and Aspinall (2009) have referred to as Aceh's 'idealized' past, that is, a conception of the past in which ethical vigour and Islamic norms supposedly were 'officially' and successfully upheld? How do ordinary people negotiate the totalizing discourse of state Shariʿa in the context of their everyday lives? (Feener, this volume). And finally, how do the answers to these questions relate, in turn, to the post-conflict, post-tsunami 'moment' (Samuels 2012; Feener 2013)?

This chapter is an attempt to formulate answers to these questions. Most of the material I draw upon comes from the interactions I had with two individuals who, at first sight, seem to have very little in common. Rahmat was an elderly man, who lived in a small village about one hour from the provincial capital, Banda Aceh. Yani was a young unmarried woman, who lived in a neighbourhood that was destroyed in the 2004 tsunami. However, the comparison is prompted not by the differences between them, but by a similarity. In recent years, it has been extensively argued—as well as intensely researched—that, in this period of post-war and post-tsunami reconstruction, Acehnese society is going through a fundamental transformation. What the stories of Rahmat and Yani together demonstrate, however, is that there are also strong currents of continuity at work in the ways in which Acehnese lead their daily lives, and try to be 'good' people. As already suggested in the epigraph to this chapter, these continuities build on a conception of ethical improvement which is informed by cultural models connected to the 'knowledge' of sins.

This essay begins with a brief discussion of public discourses of sinning and moral failure in the context of Shariʿa revival. Subsequent sections discuss the lives, thoughts and practices of Rahmat and Yani. I use both cases to address a particular dimension of the way in which the problem of sinfulness is constructed. The practices and experiences of Rahmat focus on the importance of age and regret in the increasing awareness of past sinfulness, while the section about Yani dissects the relationship between social pressure and personal responsibility. In the final section, I connect this material to more general observations about the distinction between knowing and not-knowing sins. I conclude by drawing attention to the dialectical relationship between 'state Islam' and the personal project of ethical improvement.

Sinning, Social Pressure, and the Post-war, Post-tsunami Moment

Acehnese often talk about the 'test' each person will be subjected to after entering the 'world of the grave' (*alam barzakh*). This is essentially a test of faith, carried out by the two angels, Munkar and Nakir, who follow each Muslim in life, and note down their good deeds and bad deeds. The exam consists of five questions, namely: Who is your God? Who is your Prophet? What is your Book? Where is your *kiblat*? And, who are your Brothers and Sisters? After crossing the *barzakh* the deceased moves on to the hereafter (*akhirat*). Different ideas are expressed about what happens after this. Many people think that, even though every single adult Muslim who dies will be punished (*disiksa*, "tortured") on basis of his or her record, ultimately they will all go to heaven. Others think that this record decides whether someone will go to heaven or to hell. Then, there are also many positions in between. Thus, I heard people explain that there is a period in the afterlife, when 'bad' people are tortured, and 'good' people merely wait, until the Day of Judgment (*kiamat*) comes to bring the final verdict (cf. Bowen 1993, 251–272). What most people agree on, however, is that sins committed during life have serious consequences, and that this is something to worry or be concerned about.

The proposition that the Acehnese are particularly pious has a long history. Acehnese often refer to their region as the "Verandah of Mecca" (*Serambi Mekkah*) (presumably at the front of a Malay-Indonesian 'house'). Firmly attached to the *Serambi Mekkah* discourse is the politically mouldable (and arguably manipulable) claim that Acehnese Muslims, by simple virtue of being Acehnese Muslims, have a particular responsibility towards their community to engage in 'proper' Muslim conduct. There is considerable scholarly argument about the political effects this discourse entails. Equally subject to debate is the question whether, or to what extent, the implementation of Shari'a law is based on local traditions. Edward Aspinall, in his work on the conflict and the emergence in the 20th century of Acehnese nationalism, emphasized the role of the central government in Jakarta, an aligned Acehnese technocratic elite, and their joint contention that Shari'a should be a part of the solution to the conflict (Aspinall 2009). Lindsey et al. (2007, 216–222), while not denying that Shari'a was seen by Jakarta as a "political tool," argued instead that the

Shariʿa revival must be seen explicitly in the context of a "return to [Aceh's] past prosperity," an "assertion of Acehnese identity" and as a "means of re-emphasizing perceived traditional Acehnese values." A different perspective has been offered by Michael Feener (2012, 2013), who views the recent implementation of Shariʿa law as a form of "social engineering," that is, a new and future-oriented "ideal for the ordering of society," based on an institutional and ideological framework that has been decades in the making. While all of these studies have contributed greatly to our understanding of the development of political Islam in Aceh, little has been written so far about the agency of ordinary Muslims in appropriating official discourses, and the impact and complexities of state practice on the ground.

The idea that the Acehnese are a particularly pious people is an important factor in the post-conflict, post-tsunami dynamic, and the development in this context of a local formulation of Shariʿa law. The notion that the Acehnese have a special responsibility not to engage in sinful behaviour has accelerated the implementation of Shariʿa law since 2002–2003.[3] At the same time, the notion has been used to legitimise non-state practices of moral policing and vigilantism in villages and neighbourhoods (see, e.g., Feener 2013, 240–243; Human Rights Watch 2010; Kloos 2014; Newman 2009; Otto and Otto, this volume; Salim and Sila 2010; Siapno 2002, 36–39). Yet it is important to recognize that the current Shariʿa revival is not a unilinear, or even a very coherent process. Instead, it seems to be driven by a mutual reinforcement of several processes, including the increased determination of some local government agents and institutions to enforce moral regulations (whether on the basis of religious conviction, electoral opportunism, or both), the tendency of some activist groups and local communities disappointed with local government to take the law into their own hands (see, e.g., Mahdi Syihab 2010), and the competition for political power by changing alliances of ulama after the granting of 'special autonomy' in 1999 (Feener 2012; McGibbon 2006; Nur Ichwan 2011). Underlying these various processes is what I have identified elsewhere as a set of deep, as yet largely unresolved, contestations about moral authority in contemporary Acehnese society (Kloos 2014).

3 In this period, the provincial government, led by Governor Abdulah Puteh, issued a series of bylaws (*qanun*) regarding the creation of a system of Islamic courts (Mahkamah Syariah), the regulation of belief (*aqida*), worship (*ibadah*), and symbols (*syiar*), including the regulations on dress and the criminal persecution of the use of intoxicants (*khamr*), gambling (*maysir*) and illicit relations between men and women (*khalwat* and *zina*). See Feener, this volume, for a detailed discussion.

While individual Acehnese take into account the presence of the angels Munkar and Nakir, they have been increasingly confronted, through different media such as political speeches, newspaper articles and religious sermons, with the suggestion of a collective failure in Aceh to uphold an acceptable moral standard. Perceptions of the separatist conflict, as a perpetual source of "chaos" (*kacau*) and "discord" (*fitnah*), and the tsunami, as a divine "punishment" (*hukuman*), "warning" (*peringatan*), "test" (*ujian*) or "challenge" (*percobaan*), have fed this paradigm (see Samuels, this volume). Still, lively debate takes place within its boundaries. For example, I witnessed heated discussions, in Jurong and in Blang Daruet (the villages of Rahmat and Yani and my main fieldwork locations), about the relationship between the conflict and the tsunami. Some people expressed the view that it was the war (that is, the violence and the incapacity of Acehnese leaders to manage their own province adequately) that led God to intervene and bring about the tsunami. This view was appealing to some people, but angered those who protested against the implicit suggestion of separatists being blamed for the tsunami.

Finally, connected to the concern of sinfulness and the suggestion of collective failure and moral degradation, there was the awkward combination of enthusiasm and anxiety that many people felt in relation to the idea of Aceh having "opened up" to the outside world (*Aceh sudah terbuka*), the latter including everything from aid workers and non-governmental organizations (NGOs), domestic and foreign investment, non-Acehnese religious teachers, missionaries, researchers, tourists, alleged 'terrorists,' to the more intangible forces of globalization and 'westernization.' This process was perceived by most people simultaneously as a blessing and a threat. Authoritative figures who, for whatever reason, had stakes in emphasizing morality (politicians, government officials, preachers, religious teachers, members of the security forces) responded to both emotions. As set forth above, this essay sets its focus on the question of how individuals (in this case Rahmat and Yani) have judged and dealt with their own perceived sins in this (partly rhetorical) context of dramatic social and political transformation in the post-tsunami/post-conflict period.

Early Life Discipline, Older Age Consciousness: The Repentance of Rahmat

Under the house, between the thick wooden poles, stood one of the relics of Rahmat's past: an old and dusty, yellow Vespa motorcycle built in 1959. Rahmat had bought it from his boss, in the late 1960s, not long after he had moved from

Pidie to Banda Aceh to work as a trader in the market. It was not until the late 1980s, that he replaced it with a newer model, which he still used in 2010 to commute to the market and the gardens. Still, he would never get rid of that first one. It stood there motionless, and its battery was dead. But if necessary, Rahmat claimed, it would still start (*masih hidup*, "It still works!"). Standing in a dark dusty corner, covered with cloth, it was not a conspicuous object, and I may never have noticed it, were it not for the fact that Rahmat often mentioned it when he talked about the past. There were not many motorcycles in Banda Aceh in the 1960s, and fewer cars. For Rahmat, who came from a poor family, to become the owner of that Vespa was a significant achievement. At the same time, it symbolized the relationship with his boss, whom he referred to with the (marked Chinese) term *towkay*. This relationship lasted almost half a century, until the *towkay*'s death in the late 1990s. Thus, the motorcycle stood there as a quiet demonstration of Rahmat's past.

Rahmat was born in 1944 in a village in Pidie, to a family of four children, and described his youth as "very tough" (*pahit sekali*). He remembered periods in which, for days in a row, there was no rice but only fruits to eat. His parents were farmers, but they did not own the land on which they worked. To earn cash, his father sold coarse earthen kitchenware manufactured by his mother. They collected the clay themselves, and sold the pots and plates in the vicinity, at markets and in villages. Rahmat dropped out of primary school at an early age. When he was twelve years old, he was told by one of the villagers (a maternal relative) to follow him to Sigli, where the man traded in sugar and ran a distribution centre for government rations. It was the start of a long-lasting relationship, and Rahmat quickly succeeded in earning the *towkay*'s trust. On the first day, he was given a broom and told to keep the place clean. One week later, he assisted his boss in transporting the imported sugar from the harbour of Sigli to the warehouse. After a few years, he was entrusted with the task of bringing large amounts of money to Banda Aceh. For the first few years, Rahmat was allowed to stay in the village (instead of sleeping in the shop with the older workers), and he was given a bicycle to ride every day to Sigli. After about ten years, he was ordered by the *towkay* to go and work in his newly opened cloth shop in Banda Aceh, where Rahmat eventually came to work for more than three decades.

Rahmat met his wife Nurianti in the market in Banda Aceh. Nurianti, who was two years younger than him, came from Jurong in Aceh Besar. Her family was relatively well off, at least compared to most other villagers. Her father had been involved in a short military career which had taken him to North Sumatra during the Revolution. After that, he returned to Jurong and became a tailor. Nurianti was one of the few girls in the sub-district who went to Banda Aceh to study. She wanted to become a teacher. In Banda Aceh, she lived in the house of her uncle, who became a wealthy man. When her uncle decided to move to Jakarta and asked her to come along, Nurianti refused his offer. Instead, she moved into a boarding house for girls. It was in this period that she ran into Rahmat. They married in 1968, after Nurianti had finished her studies, moved back to Jurong, and found a job as a teacher in the local primary school. Rahmat moved in with her family. A few years later, they built their own place next to the old family home.

By 2008, Nurianti and Rahmat had been married for 38 years and had had five children. In that year, they performed the pilgrimage to Mecca (Hajj). Until that moment, neither Nurianti nor Rahmat had ever travelled beyond Medan, in the neighbouring province of North Sumatra. Both of them experienced the Hajj as a pivotal moment in their lives. They loved to tell the story, in which they concentrated as much on the eccentricities of Saudi Arabian society (its wealth, its crowdedness, its thieves) as on the different rites constituting the pilgrimage.[4] Both Nurianti and Rahmat expressed to me the feeling that the Hajj signified the end of a life phase, marking the beginning of their 'old age.' Having completed the last of the five pillars (*rukun Islam*), they now felt they had entered a period of reflection. The Hajj, Rahmat said, "is like a lid on my life" (*tutup hidup ayah*). It coincided, moreover, with what he called the "maximum age" for Muslims, 63, the age on which the Prophet died. Every year above this age was "extra" (*kelebihan*), which in practice meant that he should be "extra grateful" (*lebih bersyukur*), and "extra diligent in worship" (*lebih rajin beribadah*). In particular, it signified a period of "repentance" (*bertobat*).

To understand the emotional roots and implications of this shift, it is useful to give a brief impression of Rahmat's daily routines, as I observed them in this phase of his life. Rahmat was diligent in prayer, usually performing the five (mandatory) daily prayers (*salat*) at home. He woke up early every morning at the sound of the *azan* (the call to prayer), to carry out the dawn prayer (*subuh*). After prayer he ate breakfast, usually comprised of the leftovers from

---

4 Rahmat and Nurianti's experiences resonate with an old and extensive (oral as well as textual) discourse centring on the constitutive and transformative Malay or Indonesian experience in the Hejaz. A number of scholars have investigated the importance of the pilgrimage in the development of Muslim consciousness or (changes in) religious discourse and practice in Southeast Asia, producing a literature that ranges from discussions of the social and political roles of pilgrims in the colonial period (Laffan 2003; Ricklefs 2007), to collections and analyses of published memoires and other written accounts (Matheson and Milner 1984; Tagliacozzo 2013; Chambert-Loir 2013), to specific accounts of affluent middle class 'hajj tourism' (Moeslim Abdurrahman 2002).

the previous day's dinner. Not so long ago, this was the time of day at which he would leave for Banda Aceh to work. In this new life phase, he worked in the vegetable garden in the morning. He came back for lunch and mid-day prayers (*zuhur*), after which he rested or slept. Sometimes he went out again before returning for afternoon prayers (*asar*). He rarely left the village. On market days (Monday and Friday) he went to the nearby market to buy fish (Jurong is part of a cluster of eight villages centred on a small local market). On Friday, he prayed in the market mosque. Sometimes, if their youngest son felt like driving, they went on family visits. Rahmat liked to go on trips, but not alone. They had an old car, which he never drove. In the village, he mostly kept to the house. He rarely visited the shops or the coffee houses, except for buying his daily ration of cigarettes. After the sunset prayer (*maghrib*), he spent about half an hour performing *dhikr* (devotional chanting). After the evening prayer (*isya*) he liked to watch TV.

Rahmat often referred to the proximity of death, and the need to prepare for the afterlife (*akhirat*). The main purpose of old age, he said, was to ask for forgiveness (*minta ampun*) and repent (*bertobat*). Islamic repentance rituals take multiple forms, but the most routinely practiced is its standard inclusion in the daily prayers (*salat*). For Muslims worldwide, *salat* is bestowed with a variety of meanings, a phenomenon which, as John Bowen explained, is less the result of pluralism than of the fundamental absence within the ritual itself of a "single symbolic or iconic code" (Bowen 1989, 615). For most Acehnese I came to know, the essence of the *salat* lay in the individual's concentration on the personal relationship with God. Thus, young Acehnese were taught that the bodily performance (the exact movements, the careful pronouncement of the Arabic), were closely connected to the attempt to clear one's head from any thought other than that of God. This state of mind, referred to by the term *khusyuk*, is part of the standard repertoire of religious teachers, both in more formal contexts of religious education (for example in the many Islamic boarding schools, called *dayah* or *pesantren*), as well as those informal settings in which village teachers (*teungku*) show children how to pray and recite the Qur'an. The term is ingrained in Acehnese religious awareness, being regularly mentioned in sermons and opinion columns. For Rahmat, who did not have the disposal over specialized religious knowledge or skills, the importance and desirability of experiencing *khusyuk* through daily prayers seemed self-evident. Acehnese Muslims may choose to repent as a part of any prayer by uttering a formula in which they ask God for His forgiveness, either for their own sins, or for those of others. Most people believed that the better one succeeded in establishing a state of *khusyuk*, the more directly the prayer, including the request for forgiveness, was heard by God.

Repentance through worship is not the only way in which Acehnese Muslims deal with their sins. Another channel is to compensate for bad behaviour by collecting *pahala*, or divine rewards for 'good' behaviour. According to Rahmat's wife, Nurianti, there are many ways to do this, including visiting the sick, people who had given birth, or places where a disaster (*musibah*) happened. "All these places we have to go to. All of this brings us *pahala*." Most prominent, however, was visiting funeral *kenduri*, the communal meals and prayers for the deceased. For Nurianti, the act of visiting *kenduri* was as much a matter of accumulating divine rewards as it was a social obligation. When I asked her whether she visited these *kenduri* more often now than in the past, she answered: "In the past I went as well. But you need to have the time. I have more time now, since I have retired. For Muslims, it brings a lot of *pahala* [...] But it is also *adat* (custom), Acehnese *adat*. Some people don't want to go. They are just lazy." Such ambiguities aside, there was no doubt that her invigorated keenness to visit funeral *kenduri* was connected to her advanced age, and the thought that death was approaching.

Just like his wife, and in ways comparable to a certain extent to John Bowen's (1993) analysis of ritual and religious discourse in Gayo society, Rahmat connected conceptions of ritual, knowledge and faith to concerns of life phase and death. He was not afraid of death ("everyone dies, eventually"). I asked him: "So do you feel you have sufficient knowledge, you know, for the exam of the angels? (*ujian malaikat*)." He answered that he did not worry about this, because the "knowledge of life" (*ilmu kehidupan*) was surely enough. He explained: "We Muslims, we must pray (*harus salat*). We must fast (*harus puasa*). And we must not take what belongs to others (*jangan ambil yang punya orang*)." When a Muslim is conscious of this (*sadar*), he continued, the answers to the Angels' questions will appear as a matter of course. For Rahmat, this faith explained why the "knowledge of life" was more important than the "higher [religious] knowledge" (*ilmu tinggi*) taught in the *pesantren*. This did not mean that he regarded this higher knowledge as useless, quite to the contrary, but that, at his age, it was becoming less and less relevant for him personally.

Rahmat focused on the virtues contained in daily routines. For him the significance of *salat* lay partly in the fact that it was rehearsed. Prayer, he explained, "is like *sepor*" (a term referring to an old-fashioned Dutch word for gymnastics). "[It is] like a morning-run, it is all about practice (*latihan*)." This was the reason, he argued, that *salat* should be taught to children when they are young. "Children should start learning how to pray from their seventh year. Once they are seventeen, they should make sure not to neglect it anymore." If the *salat* was taught in this way, he thought, upholding the daily routine should no longer be difficult or challenging. With praying regularly from an early age, a "little clock" is developed internally (*supaya ada jam di dalam*). The clock makes sure that, if a prayer is skipped, a person will feel uncomfortable (*merasa kurang enak*). Turning to the problem of sinfulness, one could say that obligatory rituals, such as *salat* and the fast, are doubly charged. They have a function in dealing with sins, but at the same time it is considered sinful when they are not (or not adequately) performed. Rahmat stressed the importance of *salat*, emphasizing that it was not just an 'abstract' religious obligation. The bodily discipline associated with the faithful performance of the ritual, constituted for him a physical defense mechanism against the workings of the devil (Ac. *seeten*/Ar. *shaytan*). This was also the reason that he thought it was crucial to pray as soon as the call to prayer (*azan*) sounded. "If you do not pray directly after *azan*, you will make the work of the devil easier [...] The devil will make you lazy (*seeten yang melalaikan*)."

Rahmat thought that prayer also had a disciplining effect on other ('worldly') activities. He was careful, however, to make sure I understood this was not as such the *function* of the *salat*. When I suggested once, rather carelessly, whether the *salat* could also be seen as a kind of (disciplinary) training for life as a whole (*apakah salat itu juga latihan untuk kehidupan*), he immediately corrected me. The *salat*, he said, is an isolated practice, in which only the thought of God mattered. At the same time he acknowledged and valued the effect. "If you are disciplined in the *salat*, you will also be more disciplined in life (*kalau disiplin sembahyang, hiduppun begitu juga*)." The key term for him was *tenang*, which in this context may be best translated as 'composure,' or as an interplay between calmness of mind and self-control. In this way, upholding the practice of *salat* was directly connected to key challenges of life, such as making a living and preventing conflict. "If people pray, there will be peace [lit.: no chaos]. The same goes for one's earnings in life (*kalau ada sembahyang tidak ada kacau. Rezekipun juga*)."

One day, when Rahmat had talked long about his life and his youth in Pidie, I asked him what worried him most at this stage of his life. He took a long puff from his cigarette, and thought for a while. Finally he said:

> What is there still to worry about? Earning money [...] [pauses] If you do not go anywhere, then what money is there to find? [...] Now my children sometimes give me some money. In the past I gave it to them, now they give it to me [...] I cannot work anymore. My lungs hurt. But I cannot stand doing nothing either. If I do not go to the gardens for a while, I am reminded of this. If only for once I do not go, I won't feel good [...] If there was still some money left, I would like to go there again, one more time,

> you know, to Mecca. That is a thought that makes me feel comfortable (*senang*).

When I asked him whether he had any regrets, and whether he would change anything about his life, if this were possible, he answered, without thinking: "The things I neglected in the past (*yang kita melalui dulu*)." He continued: "It is only now that I think about these things (*sekarang sudah teringat*) [...] now I am close to death." When I asked him for an example, he followed with a long reflection, which came down to a fundamental regret about his own short-temperedness, and the damage he believed he had inflicted because of this. Rahmat, according to his own judgment, had been angry too often, and for too little reason. In fact, he believed that he would still be like that if he did not actively limit his movements. It was only now, after many months, that I started to understand why Rahmat no longer wished to sit with the other men at the *pos jaga* (the conflict-era 'checkpoint' at the entrance of the *kampung*), or at the coffee shop where he went daily to buy his cigarettes. "If I sit there, people might say things, and I might react, and people will get angry, and I will get angry [...] This is what I am careful about now [...] In the past I made many people angry, and what to think of my time in Banda [Aceh] with all those haughty people there! It was difficult to control myself."

This regret was not only connected to a change in daily routines, it was also a main incentive for his daily repentance. Here, the emotional climax lay in Rahmat's difficult relationship with his father, which had been characterized for Rahmat by anger, guilt and disappointment. Rahmat's anger was rooted in his early youth, and the unfairness in the way he and his siblings were treated as children. Tensions became more serious when Rahmat got older, and his father failed to bring home enough money, either because he earned too little or because of his habit of gambling away the little he had. Later, after Rahmat left his village, escaping from his family's poverty by following his *towkay* to Banda Aceh, anger was complemented by the feeling of guilt. In subsequent years he visited his family a few times per year. He gave his father a bicycle, so he could stop carrying around earthenware and sell fish in neighbouring villages instead. But the meetings were often tense, and he regularly lost his patience with his father and his father's incapacity to provide proper care for his family.

These encounters as Rahmat described them were almost incredible to me. In rural Aceh as I know it (this is Aceh Besar, but Siegel [1969] described a similar situation for Pidie in the 1960s), fathers and sons develop avoidance relationships, in which emotions are concealed and physical proximity is to a large extent avoided. In all the father-son relationships I personally witnessed in Jurong, this seemed to be the norm. Not linked particularly to father-son relationships, openly issuing reprimands or admonitions to parents is considered as very shameful behaviour in Aceh. In that sense, then, perhaps it is not strange that the memories returned to Rahmat with a vengeance. "In the past, I was often angry with my father. But I did not know I should not do this. It is only now that I think about it, and that I hear about the need to repent, in the mosque, in the sermons. It is only now that I ask forgiveness (*minta ampun*)." I asked him: "Is it just your own wrongdoings that you repent for, or do you ask forgiveness for your father too, like you said before?" He answered:

> That is just the same (*begitu juga*). What he did was not right, and so I ask for mercy. But it is also my sin. In Islam, it is a very grave sin if you become angry with your parents. This is what I regret now (*yang menyesal*), all the more when I listen to the imam when he talks about the need to repent. Perhaps, because I did not know, I can be forgiven. I said those things to my father, and this is a great sin indeed. I have only just become conscious (*itu saya baru sadar*).

Thus, Rahmat connected the way in which he dealt with his sins to a particular sense of failure, which could only be really understood by him when it was too late to improve the relationship with his father. Although he emphasized his willingness to repent, and his relationship to God, there was a discomfort there—and certainly about the possibility of mitigating particular sins—which I found specific to older people like him.

What is important to emphasize, then—and this is the point I want to stress as I move on to the next section—is that the problem of sinfulness had not always meant the same to Rahmat throughout his life. He did talk about particular rituals (such as prayer) in terms of a basic standard for a 'good life.' However this was only a part of the story. Prayer, in his view, was a condition for faith to take root. But inner enrichment—which was closely related to faith, but, interestingly, built on failure and discomfort as much as successful self-discipline—came only with age.

Rahmat's focus on personal "awareness" (*kesadaran*) and "composure" (*ketenangan*) had an impact on his attitude towards village conflicts over moral issues. Just like in other villages, privacy in Jurong was curtailed by occasional acts of vigilantism carried out by young, unmarried males (usually designated as the *pemuda kampung*, lit. 'village youth').[5] With regard to the cases I wit-

5 While in Indonesia the word 'youth' (*pemuda*) is also used in a more general sense, in this

nessed or heard about, Rahmat generally judged the *pemuda*—and especially its leaders—to be too "hot-blooded" (*darah panas*). For example, when a young couple was once accused of *khalwat* and ritually cleansed (with clean water from the tank that was used for bathing) at the *meunasah*, Rahmat concluded that the *pemuda* had gone "mad" (*gila*).[6] In his view, the *pemuda* should have involved the village leadership first, rather than to take the law in their own hands. As I just explained, Rahmat thought himself to be hot-tempered too. Thus, by constructing his judgment it seemed he was taking into account both past and present concerns.

In the next section, I turn to the life and thoughts of Yani, a young, unmarried woman living in Banda Aceh. With regard to the enforcement of social norms through acts of vigilantism, Yani was in a more vulnerable position than Rahmat. Yet, there was a conspicuous similarity in the way Yani related existing moral frameworks to her own personal process of becoming a 'better' person. Although I will focus again on the problem of sinning, here I will centralize a different perspective. In the case of Rahmat, I have been interested mostly in the question of how he engaged, consciously, in developing a form of inner spirituality. In the next section, I will ask how Yani linked her inner struggles to the contentious and sometimes sensitive challenge of developing a moral responsibility, in a place, moreover, that was still in the midst of a process of (social as well as physical) reconstruction.

---

context I refer to the institutionalized role of male-gendered young adults (roughly between 15 and 30 years old), who, according to local customs, are responsible for a number of village 'chores,' such as digging graves or preparing festivities, but also for guarding the village against 'disruptions' and bad influences from 'outside.' The latter may include thieves, but also public morality breaches. As Syihab, the 'head of the pemuda' (*ketua pemuda*) in Jurong, summarized it, the *pemuda* are those 'in front' (*di depan*), taking care of the boundary between the domain of village integrity and the 'outside world.'

6 The practice of publicly 'cleansing' (*memandikan*, or *siram*) people accused of moral (and especially sexual) transgressions is quite common in Aceh. I was personally witness to the incident mentioned above, though not from the very start (I noticed something was going on when the couple had just been taken to the *meunasah*). A couple of days after the incident I talked to Syihab, the 'head' of the *pemuda*, to learn about his view of the 'incident.' He told me that, "in Jurong, village law applies" (*hukum kampong berlaku*). It is allowed to receive guests at night, but not to meet in dark spots or in the shrubs (*semak-semak*). Syihab mentioned two reasons for the 'arrest.' Firstly, he stated that illicit behavior such as *khalwat* had "damaging" effects on the moral integrity of the Jurong residents (*merusakkan warga*). Secondly, "state law" (*hukum negara*, as opposed to *adat* law, or 'village' law) was, in his view, unreliable. Importantly, Shari'a played no role in his explanation. For an elaboration of this case, see Kloos (2014). See also Otto and Otto (this volume).

The Responsibilities of Yani

Yani was 29 years old when I first met her. She presented herself to me as an open-minded and self-proclaimed 'modern' (*moderen*) woman. She talked easily about contentious issues, such as religious persuasion, public morality, clothing and decency, friendship between (unmarried) men and women, as well as more sensitive matters like homosexuality. She liked to know 'what was going on' in Jakarta—in terms of news, fashion, trends and scandals—but if I asked her whether she felt more Indonesian or Acehnese she said: "Aceh, of course!" (*Acehlah!*) At the same time, she was ambivalent about the supposed responsibilities connected to being an Acehnese woman. Yani lived in Desa Blang Daruet, which is relatively close to the seashore, and stood no chance when the tsunami smashed into the city on 26 December 2004. The neighbourhood was completely destroyed. Apart from a few larger buildings, everything (mainly houses and shops, but also warehouses) was razed to the ground, and a staggering 75 percent of about 3,000 inhabitants died. In the following years, the neighbourhood was physically reconstructed with the help of two international NGOs, and when I went to live there in 2009 almost all survivors had been given a house. Daruet then had a total of 1,325 inhabitants, including many newcomers. Yani's family was also devastated by the tsunami. Her mother and three sisters lost their lives. Of the immediate family, only her father and a younger brother survived. In 2006, they received two neighbouring tsunami houses. Yani lived alone in one of them. The other was shared by her father, her brother, her father's second wife (whom he married in 2007) and her young son from an earlier marriage.

Yani was not born in Blang Daruet but in a bordering neighbourhood, which was also her mother's birthplace. In 1986, when she was five years old, the family moved to Daruet to build a house on the land owned by Yani's paternal grandfather. Yani's mother was a teacher at a primary school. Her father was a clerk at the civil court. For nine years (1992–2001), he was village head (*geuchik*) of Daruet. This was rather remarkable. Although the function of *geuchik* was highly unpopular in times of conflict, even in Banda Aceh, where the safety situation was incomparably better than in rural areas, it was still unusual to elect a 'newcomer' (*pendatang*) as village head. He had resigned, however, after being accused by fellow villagers of corruption. After finishing high school, Yani attended a vocational college and obtained a diploma in education. Although her family had the means to pay for university fees, she had no ambition to pursue a degree. She briefly worked in a kindergarten, but in 2009 she worked four mornings per week at the administrative office of Daruet (the Kantor Kepala Desa), doing mostly clerical work. She did not have a government contract, working instead on terms of a poorly paid apprenticeship (*honor*; something which many young people do in the hope of being promoted eventually to the position of salaried civil servant).

Yani was not married, even though most Acehnese women marry earlier, in their late teens or early twenties. She still expected to get married one day, but apparently felt that there was no need to hurry. She adored children, however, and could not imagine never having them herself. At the same time, she had clear ideas about her demands and desires regarding marriage. She desired a man with a good character (*sifat baik*), who was polite in his speech, and who would treat her right and not beat her. He should not be lazy and earn enough money. Finally, she wished for someone who was comfortable around her (*senang dengan saya*). She valued her independence and expected to keep earning her own income after marriage. But she also said she would not be rigid. If her future husband would demand that she stayed at home to care for the house and the children, she would try to seek a solution. She could demand a fixed allowance, or she could try to reach a compromise through discussion and exchanging favours and demands. Finally, she argued that there was always the powerful device of influencing a husband through "talking shrewdly" (*istri bisa ngomong pintar*).

During the course of my fieldwork, I was increasingly impressed by Yani's self-confidence with regard to marriage, economic (in)dependence, and the future more generally. There was, however, a distinct material dimension to this self-confidence. Yani had inherited land from her mother. I had never cared to ask it's worth, although according to my notes she had told me about this in one of our first conversations. The plot of land was located in her mother's *kampung*, and had been idle since the tsunami. However, in the last month of my fieldwork Yani suddenly suggested that she thought about stopping work in the *kampung* office, buying a shop house on the main road and a car, and opening a small business selling cosmetics and beauty products. She caught me by surprise, for I knew her as someone who was perpetually short of cash. When I asked where she thought to get the money, she told me she would sell her mother's land. Thus it turned out that, although well disguised by her modest lifestyle, Yani and her brother had at their disposal a gigantic capital worth up to two billion rupiah (EUR 160,000).[7] Although the possession of

7 Yani and her brother owned two plots of land. The largest, measuring around one acre, was located right next to a commercial area close to the harbor. Various people had offered to buy this land for Rp 100,000 per square meter, which would come down to a total of Rp. 1,000,000,000. However, they had also been advised to refrain from selling this land until there

this plot seemed to warrant financial independence, it would be a mistake to reduce Yani's self-confidence to the single factor of economic power. As we will see, self-conscious engagement in ritual, and the connected creative dimension of social positioning in a world of continuously changing judgments and demands, were equal building blocks of a moral order she designed for herself, and which she used to legitimise her behaviour and future aspirations.

Yani was serious about her ritual obligations, but cared little about outward appearances and even less about people telling her what to do. A male acquaintance once told Yani he was interested in marrying her. Yani did not agree immediately, but dated him for a while so they could get to know one another (*pacaran*). Other people told her that the young man's parents were "very religious" (*kuat beragama*). Her boyfriend confirmed this, and warned that, when she met his parents, she should dress differently from usual. Yani was not very conservative in the way she dressed. Since the implementation of Shariʿa law, she always wore a headscarf when going out, but she refused to change her habit of wearing tight pants or leggings, as well as high-heeled shoes.[8] In the end, she never got to the point of meeting his parents. It started with their refusal to either approve or disapprove of her boyfriend's plans, something which, according to Yani, was the result of people "talking badly" about her. But in fact, Yani saw a bigger problem in the attitude of her boyfriend. The only thing he did to try and improve the situation was to tell her that, in the end, it would probably be alright, and that it just needed time. From this Yani concluded that he chose to remain quiet rather than confront his parents and discuss the terms of the marriage. She was frustrated about his lack of courage and apparent unwillingness to defend her, and ended the relationship. The episode was typical, Yani judged: "It is always like this. People want to tell me what to do, neighbours, distant friends, family members commenting on my clothes, my headscarf, this happens almost every day." This annoyed her, especially when it came from people who were not particularly strict about "religious rules" (*aturan agama*) themselves. She called them "hypocrites" (*munafik*).

---

was more clarity about the question whether or not Banda Aceh would be granted free port status. In that case, the harbor would be expanded greatly, and the government might buy the land for double the price. The other plot was potentially even more costly, up to Rp 300.000 per square meter, but also ten times as small (1,000 square meter).

8 Yani's decision to wear a headscarf was prompted especially by the activities of the Shariʿa police (WH; See Feener 2013; Otto and Otto, this volume), which regularly patrolled some of the places Yani frequented for leisure (such as the harbor area at Ulee Lhee, and the beach at Lhok Nga). Yani had never been caught in a "raid" (*razia*, although her tight clothes certainly carried that risk), but some of her close friends had, and the possibility certainly worried her.

She was ambivalent, however, with regard to the need to defend public morality, whether voiced by agents of the state or by local village authorities. Just like in Jurong, local male youth in Daruet felt responsible for guarding the "good name" (*nama baik*) of the *kampung*. However, Yani felt very few personal ties with the local male *pemuda*, and neither did she have much sympathy for their agenda. Instead, she emphasized the role of village elders in protecting village morality (*hak orang tua kampung untuk membela moral*). At the same time, she regarded religion as a "private matter" (*usaha pribadi*), claiming that there was a certain amount of personal space she would defend. An older man, who lived in her street, occasionally reprimanded her and her friends about their clothing. His mantra, Yani said, was that "the children of Mecca's porch" (*anak Serambi Mekkah*) should "behave themselves" (*membawakan diri*) and "cover their bodies" (*tutup aurat*). For a long time she listened politely, until one day she lost her patience and told him that she "had her own values, which were her business" (*nilai punya sendiri, urusan saya saja*). The man became angry and never talked to her again.

Keeping male company was a riskier affair. Yani had male and female friends, with whom she sometimes visited popular coffee shops, made trips (for example, to the beach), or watched movies. Yani sometimes had groups of friends staying over during the night, and on rare occasions they included men. Also, whenever her younger brother Diki had friends visiting, Yani allowed them to watch TV in her house. Just as in Jurong, there were occasionally cases of neighbourhood vigilantism against *khalwat* (illicit company) or *zina* (adultery) and sometimes these turned violent, particularly if the people involved were 'outsiders' who had come to Daruet recently or stayed there only temporarily. According to most of my interlocutors, such incidents happened in the past as well, but the frequency had increased in preceding years, particularly after the tsunami.

In Blang Daruet, like in other tsunami-affected places, senses of loss and grief were accompanied by disruptive social and physical changes. Importantly, there had been an influx of 'newcomers' (*pendatang*), including relatively 'risky' categories from a public morality point of view: single people (young men and women looking for jobs, students), but also members of the state security services (police, military, and intelligence), commonly glossed by ordinary villagers as *aparat* (the "apparatus"). Compared to the situation preceding the tsunami, it had become less clear who owned what house, who lived where, for how long, and more generally 'what was going on' in the neighbourhood. While accused wrongdoers were designated as 'violators of Shariʿa' (*pelanggar syariat*), state implementation of Shariʿa law seldom served as the explanatory framework. Instead, people pointed at the changed atmosphere after the tsunami, the many newcomers, the attraction of the *kampung* for people looking for a temporary place to stay, or more specifically, for 'evil-doers' (*orang jahat*). The WH were never called in, at least not directly. Most cases were resolved internally, "according to local custom" (*melalui adat*).[9] Yani, who worked at the *geuchik*'s office, often knew the ins and outs of such cases, but cared little about this. It was people's "own business." At the same time, she regarded those who were caught as "not so smart" (*kurang pintar*). "*Adat* is strong here, and people should know that" (*adat kuat di sini sebenarnya orang tahu*). She did not believe she could ever end up in such a situation herself.

Although in Yani's view, the implementation of Shari'a constituted a significant change in Aceh, it would be a mistake to reduce questions of (outward and inward) piety to the domain of state discipline and the law. For most Acehnese, discussions about sinning and virtuousness in the private sphere (that is, concerns of individual consciousness, or matters discussed among family or friends) including debates about covering *aurat*, appeared to be more important. Take, for example, a discussion I witnessed one day when I accompanied Yani and her friend Tia to have dinner with the family of Yani's niece, Neli. Like Yani, Neli had lost her mother (though not as a result of the tsunami; this happened earlier). Neli now lived alone with her father and her younger sister. The discussion was about the question whether Tia should wear a headscarf in Neli's house (that is, in front of Neli's father). Tia asked Yani for advice, saying that she was the oldest and should know best. Yani suggested that it might be best if she did wear the *jilbab*, arguing that she was not *muhrim* (a closely related family member). I learnt later that evening that Neli's father, although widely regarded in his neighbourhood (not Daruet) as 'knowledgeable in religion' (*alim*), could not care less whether his daughter's friends chose to wear a headscarf in his house or not. Also, Yani herself was not *muhrim* either (she was related by blood to Neli's mother, not to her father) and she had never worn a headscarf in their house. When I asked Yani a couple of days later to explain the stakes involved in the discussion (or, more precisely, whom it concerned), she answered simply that "this was a question for Tia, not

9 About six months before I came to live in Daruet, a young couple (of 'newcomers') was accused of adultery (*zina*) and publicly 'cleansed' (*dimandikan*) using filthy water from the gutter. After this, village leaders contacted the authorities. The couple was taken to the police station, where they were held for a few days. After the arrival of their parents consultations (*musyawarah*) were held to discuss the way in which the case should be 'solved' (*diselesaikan*). Ultimately, the couple was married in the Blang Daruet mosque. Immediately thereafter the couple moved away from Daruet.

a general matter" (*masalah Tia, bukan hal umum*). Tia was an adult, she said, and thus expected to make her own substantiated assessment. The question was whether Tia thought she would be committing a sin if she did not wear a headscarf, and, if yes, how bad this was. I asked whether Yani ever posed this question to herself (she never wore a headscarf in front of me when I was in her house). She nodded, and simply said that she was "not perfect yet" (*Yani belum sempurna*).

Most young Acehnese I knew pondered and discussed the problem of making moral decisions that considered factors far broader than simply those set forth in formal Shari'a legislation. On Hari Raya Idulfitri (the holiday marking the end of the fasting month), one year before I came to Daruet, Yani's father had gone to Medan to visit the family of his ('new') wife. This made Yani sad, because she was confronted more than ever with the loss of her mother and sisters. Normally, in such a situation she would have visited the mosque, where at least there would be many people and a festive atmosphere. However, the problem was that she was having her menstrual period, which according to Islamic law made it *haram* (forbidden) to pray. Also, it is generally thought that, during their period, women should not even enter a mosque, as menstruation (*haid*) is regarded as contaminating (*menajiskan*) the purity (*kesucian*) of the mosque's sacred space. Caught in a dilemma, she called her father to ask his advice. He said that she could still go, if only she would remain seated at the back of the mosque during prayer and the sermon. His argument was that she was still allowed to 'socialize' (*bergaul*) even when it was prohibited to pray. But in the end, she did not go. She gave more weight to the arguments of the "religious teachers" (*teungku-teungku*), who would probably say that to enter the mosque would be a sin. Also, she was afraid of people asking why she did not pray. When I asked her which one of these two reasons was decisive, if any, she answered that it was the first, not to sin. "Actually, I was not sure who was right, my father or the *teungku-teungku*. So I decided to make the safest choice (*keputusan yang paling aman*)."

If sinning was a serious (though contentious) concern, so was the need to repent, even if for Yani this was not yet such a central concern as it was for Rahmat. During Ramadan she enthusiastically joined the daily *tarawih* prayer, because this was a month "full of forgiveness" (*bulan penuh ampunan*), and "many rewards" (*bulan banyak pahala*). It was important for her to value this opportunity granted to her by God (*kasih ampun penting dimanfaati*), especially, she exclaimed, "Because I have so many sins!" (*karena banyak dosa*). When I asked her what sins she repented, she mentioned elements from the standard repertoire (gossiping, not wearing a headscarf), but she also explained that 'designating' sins was rather pointless. "We commit sins all the time," she argued, "and most of the time we are not even aware of it" (*banyak dosa kita tidak tahu*). The main answer to this problem lay in prayer. "The *salat*," she said, "is like the pole of a house (*salat seperti tiang rumah*). If you take it away, the house will collapse."

For the same reason, Yani thought it was important to ask forgiveness for her mother and sisters, both of whom "needed her prayers" (*dia membutuhkan kita berdoa*). Unsurprisingly, the extraordinary event of the tsunami played an important role in the way in which Yani approached this personal responsibility. Like most others, she regularly thought about its meaning. Nobody could know for sure, she said, because it was impossible to know God's ways. She did, however, believe that the tsunami constituted a form of divine wisdom (*hikmah*; see Samuels, this volume, for a more extensive discussion of this concept). Thus, she wondered what the event should mean for her. In one way, the tsunami changed everything. It meant the death of her mother, her sisters, and the end of her family as she knew it. Yani had been particularly close to her mother, so her death was a crucial loss. At the same time, the relationship with her father changed. He became more strict after the tsunami, and increasingly demanded the right to know where she went and with whom. Yani gradually distanced herself from him. "There is not much I can tell my father," she said. "He gets angry easily now" (*cepat emosi beliau*). She got along adequately with her father's new wife, but did not confide in her. Her father still supported her financially, but she increasingly felt the need to become "responsible and self-supportive" (*bertanggungjawab dan mandiri*). But she also asked, rhetorically: "What kind of life is this? There is no more happiness (*sudah hilang kebahagiaan*). Life has become just ordinary (*biasa aja*), not very happy, not very terrible (*tidak senang tidak buruk*). In the family, I have no more friends (*tidak ada lagi kawan*)." But "who knows," she said, "it may be *hikmah* that I finally grow up (*supaya jadi dewasa*), and become independent (*mandiri*). After all, people say that the tsunami is a trial (*percobaan*)."

These ponderings, beyond the result of intense sadness, clearly contributed to a personal process of ethical formation, as Yani regularly oscillated between framing personal ethics in terms of the tragedies connected to the tsunami and other, more 'immediate' concerns. No one in Daruet who had experienced the tsunami up close, considered life to be the same afterwards. But in their reactions to the transformation marking the post-tsunami moment, most people built on past certainties as much as on present doubts.

Everyday Islam and State Islam: Competing Models of Ethical Improvement?

According to high-ranking Acehnese administrators, such as Al Yasa Abubakar (the first head of the State Shari'a Agency), state Islam is a tool for 'perfecting' the religious consciousness, and thereby the moral selves, of Acehnese individuals (Feener, this volume). Such totalizing views of Islam have been strengthened by the 'total reconstruction' discourses engulfing politics after the tsunami (Samuels, this volume). As I have tried to make clear, ordinary Acehnese Muslims like Rahmat and Yani are equally concerned with (individual) ethical improvement. Yet it appears that a disjunction exists between the standardizing logic of "high-modern" state Islam (Feener 2013) and the complex formations of beliefs and practices guiding ordinary Acehnese in their attempts to become 'better people.' In order to understand the nature of this disjunction, it is necessary to integrate into the analysis a distinction, emphasized by many of my interlocutors, between 'knowing' and 'not-knowing' sins. As I will try to demonstrate, this (culturally constructed and personally interpreted) distinction feeds directly into the mechanisms through which people understand, and react to, the moralizing discourses connected to the post-conflict and post-tsunami sense of renewal. While other contributions to this volume demonstrate how official policies and discourses have been adapted, diverted, or even resisted, in this final section I will focus on the individual dimension of everyday interactions with the state. As a conclusion to the chapter, I will return to Rahmat and Yani, and discuss how this distinction between knowing and not-knowing sins has influenced their view on the specific issue of state Islam and Shari'a implementation.

In her study of Qur'anic practices in Indonesia in the 1990s, Anna Gade emphasized the role of affect in ordinary Muslims' projects of personal piety. In processes of ritual learning, she argued, emotions have the capacity to generate "continued or escalated practice" (Gade 2004, 49), thus driving forward (subjective) processes of ethical improvement. Gade attached equal value to ritual practice as to power and ideology, as "organizing principles" of religious change. The "moods and motivations" associated with the revival of particular rituals can be seen as both cause and effect of the religious resurgence among Indonesian Muslims (Gade 2004, 51). For example, she argued that the memorization of the Qur'an should be understood not so much as a "technology of the self," but rather as a way for Muslims to be (or become) recognized as 'preservers' (*hafiz*, pl. *hafaz*) of Islamic tradition, thus increasing their social statuses (Gade 2004, 60). Although Gade's work forms a significant contribution to the study of Islam in Indonesia, it also leaves unanswered important questions about the ways in which individual ethical projects interact with the political importance attached to pious expressions by the state. Clearly, it remains a challenge to develop solid theoretical and methodological frameworks for linking affect and self-development to changes in public and political morality.

To some extent, this is due to the slippery concepts of 'morality' and 'ethical practice.' An interesting approach, in this respect, was formulated by Jarrett Zigon, working on post-socialist Russia. Unsatisfied with the under-theorized position of morality in anthropology, Zigon proposed to conceptually separate morality from ethical practice. Morality, in this framework, may be seen as a combination of social-intellectual 'spheres': the institutional sphere, the (non-institutional) 'public' sphere, as well as the whole of embodied, largely non-conscious, moral dispositions related to the Bourdieuan concept of habitus (Zigon 2009a, 2009b). Ethics, in contrast, denotes the conscious, reflective acts through which people cultivate their embodied capacity of morality. People experience regular, albeit often unpredictable, 'moments' of ethical consciousness (which Zigon called, somewhat awkwardly, moments of "moral breakdown"), when they become reflective and reflexive about their "moral way of being in the world." It is this "conscious acting on oneself" through which a person attempts to become a "morally appropriate and acceptable person not only in the eyes of others but also for oneself" (Zigon 2009a, 82).

In the epigraph to this chapter I quoted Irma, a middle-aged mother of three living in Daruet, who said that many sins "go unnoticed" (*tidak nampak*; lit. "do not become visible"). In similar vein, Yani explained to me that "most of the time we are not even aware of [our sins]." Although such statements constitute genuine warnings, apparently referring to quite inflexible notions of discipline and divine punishment, I gradually realized that there was also a different charge to such comments. Ultimately, these expressions reflected the everyday nature of sins. At the same time, the distinction between knowing and not-knowing sins connects closely to the notions of awareness (*kesadaran*) and responsibility (*tanggung jawab*) emphasized by Rahmat and Yani when explaining their personal moral developments. It was on the basis of such ideas that they decided to 'act on themselves.' But there is more to it. Knowing sins, as well as the understanding of what this knowledge effectuates, partly depends on experiences associated with the transitions between particular (self-perceived) phases of life. In some occasions, these are physical transitions or culturally determined rites of passage, like puberty (*akil baligh*), which marks the start of the angels Munkar and Nakir's judging and documenting of good and bad behaviour (and thus the onset of moral responsibility for one's actions). Equally important, however, are the more extended processes of personal development, connected, for example, to the gradual accumulation of knowledge, maturity, and character formation, of which it is often unclear when they start and when they end.

Compared, for example, to the categories of gender and class, the role of age, life-phase, and generational interaction in the development of Muslim personhood still constitute a highly underdeveloped terrain (see Kloos 2012, 2013 for more extensive discussions of this). Still, it is clear that the kind of transitions mentioned above are important. One reason for this is a view shared by many Acehnese, namely that the more knowledgeable a person becomes, the more responsibilities he or she acquires, and the more likely (or grave), his or her sins become. A good example of the relationship between moral judgment and the transitions between life phases is the act of learning to perform rituals, such as prayer. Children learn how to pray by following the example of their parents, the *teungku meunasah*, or the people they see praying in the *meunasah*. This process of imitating does not stop when children become adults. Adults who are uncertain about the way they perform the ritual may still look at the imam, or at people sitting in front of them, in order to improve their own movements and utterings. There is, however, a social tension in this type of interaction. People who feel that they have become more knowledgeable, or 'more aware' (*lebih sadar*), may become careful, or even hesitant, to imitate others.

For example, Eri, a young man in Daruet who had studied in a Jakarta *pesantren*, regularly complained to me about the 'poor' standard of religious learning among the *kampung* and mosque leadership. He had learned to recite a large part of the Qur'an by heart, and upon his return to Daruet recognized certain mistakes in the congregational prayers led by *kampung* elders. For the people who did not have the knowledge to hear these mistakes, he argued, it did not matter at all (*kalau orang nggak tahu salah itu, bukan masalah ikutnya*). But for him it created a dilemma (*tapi kalau saya tahu, ikutnya dosa*). To keep on participating consciously (or 'knowingly') in these communal prayers would mean to sin, at least according to his own judgment. Thus, whenever the problem arose, Eri would sit quietly at the back of the mosque and pray for himself, or even decide to pray at home instead. The reverse also applied. I was told by several people, and in different contexts, that setting one's self up as an example to others (for example by accepting the responsibility to lead the prayer) was a risk for those who did not consider themselves to be sufficiently knowledgeable to bear the responsibility.

Another example of the distinction between knowing and not-knowing sins, is the way in which my interlocutors experienced the fasting month (*puasa*). Generally, *puasa* was perceived by my interlocutors as a "month of forgiveness" (*bulan penuh ampun*), in which the "door to God" was opened (*pintu Tuhan dibuka*). This led, typically, to reflections on acts of self-discipline through an emphasis on controlling one's own passions (*mengontrol nafsu sendiri*). This challenge (and of course the failure to live up to it) is occasionally connected to emotions like fear (*takut*) and shame (*malu*). However, what emerged from many conversations was not so much that people were afraid to sin, but rather of failing to put to good use the opportunities associated with *puasa*. I once asked my seventeen-year-old neighbour, Santi, whether the thought of sinning weighed more heavily on her during *puasa*. She thought about this for a moment, and then decided: "No, that is not the point. Many of our sins we do not even know [...] It is just that this is a month of seeking divine rewards (*cuma ini bulan cari pahala*)." Like many of my other interlocutors, Santi believed that *puasa* constituted an opportunity for dealing with unknown sins. Like prayer, it constituted a 'gift' from God, or a fixed "time of blessing" (cf. Feener 2006, 146) provided by God to deal (among other things) particularly with this problem.

The distinction between knowing and not-knowing sins, and its connection to the subjective experience of (sudden or elongated) transitions between life phases, is an important factor in explaining ordinary Acehnese flexibility in legitimizing individual behaviour. This becomes particularly clear when taking into account ordinary Acehnese' reactions to the Shari'a revival. One of the channels through which Rahmat was confronted on a regular basis with the notion of state Shari'a, was the sermons of religious teachers, in the village or in the market mosque. He was generally critical of these sermons. In the past, he argued, religious teachers taught villagers "what was right and what was wrong, without additional (monetary) interests (*tanpa bunga*)." Today, what they cared about most, at least according to Rahmat, was money. This does not mean that he did not care about their messages at all. He once returned from the market mosque on Friday and spoke enthusiastically about the sermon. The preacher had talked about repentance, and about the importance of asking forgiveness from other people for past wrongdoings. "This is very important!" he stressed. "Imagine that someone dies. No regret could be shown, and no forgiveness could be given. The sin would remain (*tetap dosa*)." This was something Rahmat worried about, much more than the ways of addressing sinful behaviour by implementing new government laws. About the state implementation of Shari'a, he showed himself rather indifferent. Once when I asked his opinion about it, he said: "If they do this, they should do it properly." Government laws, he argued, were not designed to apply to important people (*orang besar*). If the courts would start cutting off hands, perhaps, corrupt and hypocritical politicians would be made to adhere to the law. However, when I asked him whether he supported politicians who endorsed Shari'a, he replied: "I am already old. This is something for young people to solve."

One of those young people was Yani, who was more straightforward in her judgment of state Shari'a than Rahmat. Her life (and that of other young women) was directly affected by the new morality rules:

> In Jakarta women are free to wear a tank top, or a short top. Here, in Aceh, this is not allowed (*di sini tidak diperbolehkan*). If people have the [religious] intention (*niat*) to wear a headscarf outside the house, they can, but they can wear whatever. Here it is different [...] I think it would be better if people were not forced (*menurut Yani kalau bisa jangan memaksa*), it should be people's own wish (*keinginan sendiri*). Actually I did not yet have this wish to wear a headscarf. But because Shari'a has already been implemented, and the headscarf is obliged, we wear it.

In line with these comments, it is not so strange that she detested the Shari'a police (WH), which carried out raids (*razia*) on the streets and near beaches to lecture people (especially women) accused of breaking Shari'a regulations. She complained that they were too strict, inspecting women on "everything, including tight clothes." Using a common formula, she argued that "we [the Acehnese] are not ready yet" (*kita belum siap*). She preferred going to the beach without covering up her whole body, but because she had little desire for "being humiliated" (*dipermalukan*), she chose to comply (*kami ikut saja*, "we just follow [the rules]"). If it was in her own neighbourhood, she was prepared to stand her ground, but she was genuinely afraid of the raids. At the same time, the practice of wearing a headscarf itself did not cause Yani much trouble. On the contrary, she was rather positive about it, explaining that, once she got used to it, she felt "more tidy" (*rapi*), "clean" (*bersih*) and "comfortable" (*senang*), even if this did not change her opinion that expressions of piety should "come from the heart" (*dalam hati*).

Rather than simply rejecting or adopting state and public discourses, Rahmat and Yani actively selected and appropriated 'official' moral discourses of state Shari'a in order to make decisions, assess emotions, or justify behaviour. In this sense, there is considerable overlap between their experiences and the ideas about internalization theorized by Gade. At the same time, it should be noted that the powerful affective qualities of individual ethical improvement provide ordinary Muslims with considerable agency regarding the judgment and adaptation of the standardized models propagated by the state. It is in this dialectic that Zigon's theory of ethical practice becomes particularly applicable to the Acehnese context of Islamic morality.

The interplay between expressed beliefs, emotion, and power may be further refined by addressing what Michael Lambek (2000) and Fredrik Barth (1993) have called 'concerns.' According to Lambek (2000, 312–313), within the conceptual domain of religion, power is always confronted with human concerns, and thus "counterposed" to morality. "What distinguishes the anthropology of religion from other fields of inquiry," he argued, "is that it cannot rest with power but must contextualize the very conception and production of power within a wider cultural order, one which will equally contain alternatives to power in its repertoire of ends and means" (ibid.). The crucial element, then, is his reminder that morality implies agency.[10] Rahmat and Yani were not very enthusiastic about the state Shari'a project. At the same time, it would be wrong to understand their reactions primarily or exclusively in terms of defiance, resistance, or even discipline. Rather, they were able to exercise their moral agency as they appropriated some elements in these discourses, while rejecting, ignoring, or rendering irrelevant other elements. For them, as for many of my other interlocutors, the state represented a repertoire for individual moral action as much as disciplining force (cf. Barker and Van Klinken 2009). The logic undergirding this routine of selecting and appropriating, and the associated stance of ambivalence toward the role of the state more generally, was driven by processes of ethical improvement which they interpreted as life-long, fragmented, and in the end, highly personal.

References

Asad, Talal. 1993. *Genealogies of Religion: Discipline and Reasons of Power in Christianity and Islam*. Baltimore, MD: The John Hopkins University Press.

Aspinall, Edward. 2009. *Islam and Nation: Separatist Rebellion in Aceh, Indonesia*. Stanford, CA: Stanford University Press.

Barker, Joshua and Gerry van Klinken. 2009. "Reflections on the State in Indonesia." In *State of Authority: The State in Society in Indonesia*, edited by Gerry van Klinken and Joshua Barker, 17–46. Ithaca: Southeast Asia Program Publications, Cornell University.

10 "If religion is inevitably bound up with the naturalization of power and the legitimation or sanctification of the world it construct or inherits, it also enables (and directs) meaningful agency. Contemporary discussions remain merely cynical if they do not delineate the capacity and means for virtuous action as well as the limitations placed upon it." (Lambek 2000, 309).

Barth, Fredrik. 1993. *Balinese Worlds*. Chicago: University of Chicago Press.

Beatty, Andrew. 2000. "Islamic and Non-Islamic Prayer in Java." In *Islamic Prayer Across the Indian Ocean: Inside and Outside the Mosque*, edited by David Parkin and Stephen C. Headly, 39–62. Richmond: Curzon Press.

Bowen, John R. 1989. "*Salat* in Indonesia: The Social Meanings of an Islamic Ritual." *Man* 24(4):600–619.

———. 1993. *Muslims through Discourse: Religion and Ritual in Gayo society* (Princeton: Princeton University Press).

Chambert-Loir, Henri. 2013. *Naik Haji di Masa Silam, 1482–1964* (3 vols.). Jakarta: Kepustakaan Populer Gramedia.

Dijk, van Cornelis. 1981. *Rebellion under the Banner of Islam: The Darul Islam in Indonesia*. Leiden: KITLV Press.

Gade, Anna M. 2004. *Perfection Makes Practice: Learning, Emotion, and the Recited Qur'an in Indonesia*. Honolulu: University of Hawai'i Press.

Feener, R. Michael. 2006. "A Javanese Muslim Life of Learning: Professor Dr. Haji Mohamad Koesnoe." In *Muslim Voices and Lives in the Contemporary World*, edited by Frances Trix, John Walbridge, and Linda Walbridge, 137–148. New York: Pelgrave MacMillan.

———. 2012. "Social Engineering through Shari'a: Islamic Law and State-directed Da'wa in Contemporary Aceh." *Islamic Law and Society* 19(3):275–312.

———. 2013. *Shari'a and Social Engineering: The Implementation of Islamic Law in Contemporary Aceh*. Oxford: Oxford University Press.

Hadi, Amirul. 2004. *Islam and State in Sumatra: A Study of Seventeenth-Century Aceh*. Leiden: Brill.

Human Rights Watch. 2010. *Policing Morality: Abuses in the Application of Sharia in Aceh, Indonesia*. New York: Human Rights Watch.

Ito, Takeshi. 1984. "The World of the Adat Aceh: A Historical Study of the Sultanate of Aceh." PhD diss., Australian National University, Canberra.

Kloos, David. 2012. "Piety, Aspiration and Everyday Life in Muslim Southeast Asia. Review article." *Bijdragen tot de Taal-, Land-, en Volkenkunde* 168(2–3):325–336.

———. 2013. "Becoming Better Muslims: Religious Authority and Ethical Improvement in Aceh, Indonesia." PhD diss., VU University Amsterdam.

———. 2014. "In the name of *Syariah*? Vigilante violence, territoriality, and moral authority in Aceh, Indonesia." *Indonesia* 98:59–90.

Laffan, Michael F. 2003. *Islamic Nationhood and Colonial Indonesia: The Umma below the Winds*. London: RoutledgeCurzon.

Lambek, Michael J. 2000. "The Anthropology of Religion and the Quarrel between Poetry and Philosophy." *Current Anthropology* 41(3):309–320.

Lindsey, Tim and M.B. Hooker, with Ross Clarke and Jeremy Kingsley. 2007. "Shari'a revival in Aceh." In *Islamic Law in Contemporary Indonesia: Ideas and Institutions*, edited by R. Michael Feener and Mark E. Cammack, 216–254. Cambridge, Mass.: Harvard University Press.

Lombard, Denys. 1967. *Le Sultanat d'Atjéh au Temps d'Iskandar Muda, 1607–1636*. Paris: Ecole francaise d' Extrême-Orient.

Mahdi Syihab. 2010. "Penegakan Syariat: Etnografi Aksi Razia Santri Dayah di Aceh Utara." In *Serambi Mekkah yang Berubah: Views from Within*, edited by Arskal Salim and Adlin Sila, 57–91. Tangerang: Pustaka Alvabet and Aceh Research Training Institute.

Mahmood, Saba. 2005. *Politics of Piety: The Islamic Revival and the Feminist Subject*. Princeton NJ: Princeton University Press.

Marsden, Magnus. 2005. *Living Islam: Muslim Religious Experience in Pakistan's North-West Frontier*. Cambridge: Cambridge University Press.

Matheson, Virginia and Anthony C. Milner. 1984. *Perceptions of the Haj: Five Malay texts*. Singapore: Institute of Southeast Asian Studies.

McGibbon, Rodd. 2006. "Local Leadership and the Aceh Conflict." In *Verandah of Violence: The Background to the Aceh Problem*, edited by Anthony J.S. Reid, 315–359. Singapore: Singapore University Press.

Miller, Michelle A. 2010. "The Role of Islamic law (Sharia) in Post-tsunami Reconstruction." In *Post-disaster Reconstruction: Lessons from Aceh*, edited by Matthew Clarke, Ismet Fanany, and Sue Kenny, 29–60. London: Earthscan.

Miller, Michelle A. and R. Michael Feener. 2010. "Emergency and Islamic Law in Aceh." In *Emergency Powers in Asia*, edited by Victor Vridar Ramjaj and Arun K. Thiruvengadam, 213–236. Cambridge: Cambridge University Press.

Moeslim Abdurrahman 2002. "On Hajj Tourism: In Search of Piety and Identity in the New Order Indonesia." PhD diss., University of Illinois.

Newman, Sarah J. 2009. "Patrolling Sexuality." *Inside Indonesia* 96.

Nur Ichwan, Moch. 2007. "The Politics of Shari'atization: Central Governmental and Regional Discourses of Shari'a Implementation in Aceh." In *Islamic Law in Contemporary Indonesia: Ideas and Institutions*, edited by R. Michael Feener and Mark E. Cammack, 193–215. Cambridge, Mass.: Harvard University Press.

———. 2011. "Official Ulema and the Politics of Re-Islamization: The Majelis Permusyawaratan Ulama, Shariatization and Contested Authority in Post-New Order Aceh." *Journal of Islamic Studies* 22(2):183–214.

Peletz, Michael G. 1997. "'Ordinary Muslims' and Muslim Resurgents in Contemporary Malaysia: Notes on an Ambivalent Relationship." In *Islam in an Era of Nation-States: Politics and Religious Renewal in Muslim Southeast Asia*, edited by Robert W. Hefner and Patricia Horvatich, 231–273. Honolulu: University of Hawai'i Press.

Reid, Anthony J.S., ed. 2006. *Verandah of Violence: The Background to the Aceh Problem*. Singapore: Singapore University Press.

Ricklefs, Merle C. 2007. *Polarising Javanese Society: Islamic and Other Visions, c. 1830–1930*. Leiden: KITLV Press.

Salim, Arskal and Adlin Sila ed. 2010. *Serambi Mekkah yang Berubah: Views from Within*. Tangerang: Pustaka Alvabet and Aceh Research Training Institute.

Samuels, Annemarie. 2012. "After the Tsunami: The Remaking of Everyday Life in Banda Aceh, Indonesia." PhD diss., Leiden University.

Sehat Ihsan Shadiqin. 2010. "Kenduri Kematian di Kluet Aceh Selatan: Pemaknaan yang Beraneka Ragam." In *Serambi Mekkah yang Berubah: Views from Within*, edited by Arskal Salim and Adlin Sila, 253–284. Tangerang: Pustaka Alvabet and Aceh Research Training Institute.

Siapno, Jaqueline A. 2002. *Gender, Islam, Nationalism and the State in Aceh: the Paradox of Power, Co-optation, and Resistance*. London: Routledge.

Siegel, James. 1969. *The Rope of God*. Berkeley: University of California Press.

Sjamsuddin, Nazaruddin. 1985. *The Republican Revolt: A Study of the Acehnese Rebellion*. Singapore: Institute of Southeast Asian Studies.

Tagliacozzo, Eric. 2013. *The Longest Journey: Southeast Asians and the Pilgrimage to Mecca*. Oxford: Oxford University Press.

Tambiah, Stanley J. 1985. *Culture, Thought and Social Action*. Cambridge, Mass.: Harvard University Press.

Zigon, Jarett. 2009a. "Morality and Personal Experience: The Moral Conceptions of a Muscovite Man." *Ethos* 37(1):78–101.

———. 2009b. "Within a Range of Possibilities: Morality and Ethics in Social Life." *Ethnos* 74(2):251–276.

CHAPTER 4

Women's Rights Activists and the Drafting Process of the Islamic Criminal Law Code (*Qanun Jinayat*)

Kristina Großmann

The contested process of drafting a comprehensive code of Islamic Criminal Law (*Qanun Jinayat*) has played a prominent role in the project of Shari'a social engineering, as well as Aceh's political, socio-cultural and legal transformation more broadly (Feener 2013, see also Jauhola 2013).[1] Between 2005 and 2008, a broad alliance of activists, state actors, academics, and religious scholars promoted a just and future-oriented vision of Islamic law, to be implemented under the framework of Special Autonomy in post-tsunami/post-conflict Aceh. One part of this group was comprised of local Muslim women's rights activists, who demanded a just and 'gender-sensitive' Islamic Criminal Law and the full equity of women and men in the public and private spheres. Their demands were based on female Islamic scholars' new exegeses of the Qur'an and hadith.[2] They were able to exert influence within the ongoing negotiations of the drafting process of Islamic legislation in Aceh by participating in amendment groups and expert meetings aimed at drafting the *Qanun Jinayat*. Some of their demands, such as the inclusion of language mandating adherence to international conventions concerning human and women's rights, as well as provisions dealing with sexual harassment and rape, were successfully accommodated during the early stages of the drafting process. However, this process experienced a set-back on 14 September 2009, when the Acehnese provincial parliament (DPRA) passed a version of the *Qanun Jinayat* bill that side-lined the inclusion of many of the aforementioned demands by women's rights activists, and added new provisions reflecting Islamist interests, including the criminalization of homosexuality and a penalty of death by stoning (*rajam*) for convicted adulterers.

---

1 I wish to thank Michael Feener, David Kloos and Annemarie Samuels for their helpful comments and sustained support on earlier drafts of this chapter. Additionally I am grateful to Antje Missbach, Gunnar Stange, Roman Patock and Susanne Schröter, who provided me with valuable information and constructive comments on the topic.

2 Although some male activists work on issues of women's rights, I focus on female activists since they are the most prominent people working on those issues in Aceh.

 | DOI: 10.1163/9789004304864_005

This chapter discusses the experiences of women's rights activists with drafting the *Qanun Jinayat*, with a focus on the aims, strategies, modes of participation, successes, frustrations, and failures of women's rights activists in the process. In particular, it will follow the experience of Khairani Arifin, one of the key people representing civil society actors concerned with issues of women's and human rights in the state implementation of Islamic law in Aceh. In doing so, I will use the term 'scopes of acting' rather than a concept of agency here, as the latter is heavily loaded by decades of discussions focusing on the power and 'resistance' of marginalized persons or groups. The concept of agency has been criticized for its western-centric view of actors as individualistic, intentional agents, and is not necessarily applicable in other cultural contexts (Comaroff and Comaroff 1992, 36; Mahmood 2005). It has also received criticism for providing romanticized and cultural relativistic descriptions of female subjectivities and realms of power within social and religious practice, for its lack of contextualization and its promotion of explicitly feminist agendas (Bangstad 2011, 18). Intending to avoid these connotations, I use the term 'scopes of acting,' more as an analytic tool than as a concept of resistance or individual power. In this sense, I define 'scopes of acting' by referring to Ahearn's definition of agency as the culturally mediated capacity to act (Ahearn 2001, 112), and I include realms of politics, history and the understanding of the multifocality of power.[3]

The drafting process of the *Qanun Jinayat* has a long and complex history, which began in 2003, soon after the implementation of provincial Shariʿa legislation, or *qanun*, in the framework of Aceh's contemporary Islamic legal system (see Feener, this volume). To mark the significant points of this process, I will concentrate on the three versions drafted from 2006 onwards: A) the first draft *Qanun Jinayat* (2007), B) the redrafted (*Rancangan*) *Qanun Jinayat* (2008) and C) the *Qanun Jinayat* (2009). I will analyse the last draft in greater detail, contextualizing and thickly describing the passing of this particular formulation of the bill by the provincial parliament DPRA.[4] By concentrating on the scopes of acting of female Muslim women's rights activists, I point out a remarkable but scarcely researched phenomenon: the participation of women, who are neither part of the state apparatus nor of the religious elite, in the drafting process of Islamic legislation. Through this empirical approach, I seek to complement

---

3 For an extended discussion of the concept 'scopes of acting' as extension of agency, see Großmann (2013).

4 The research results presented in this chapter are based on three periods of fieldwork, carried out in 2009, 2010, and 2011, with a duration of eleven months in total, in Banda Aceh and Lhokseumawe (North Aceh).

studies of Islamic law in contemporary Aceh by showing that the implementation of Shariʿa has not only been shaped by state actors but also by non-state actors, both women and men alike.

Controversies over the Implementation of Islamic Law

Discussions of why Islamic law has come to be implemented in contemporary Aceh comprise at least four tightly interwoven lines of argument. The first is found in the history of Islam in Aceh.[5] This is closely linked to the second argument, namely the centrality of Islam, and the importance attached to Islamic law, in the construction of an Acehnese ethnic identity.[6] The third argument stems from the hope to end the secessionist conflict and restore trust in the central government.[7] Finally, there was the intention of social transformation through Islamic law, which has taken on new dimensions after the catastrophe of the tsunami (Feener 2013).

The implementation of Islamic law in contemporary Aceh was connected to the hope that it would facilitate broader goals of peace, reconstruction and reconciliation. This hope was strengthened by the suggestion that Indonesia's national legal system had rarely delivered justice for the Acehnese. However, the initial expectation of Shariʿa as a panacea, which would eliminate political, economic and social problems and produce an egalitarian society, was soon

5 Supporters of this argument point to the historical existence of institutions associated with the implementation of Islamic law under the pre-modern sultanate, such as the office of *qadi* (Husein 2008; Ismail 2008; Lindsey et al. 2007).

6 Because of its long history as a Muslim sultanate, a population renowned for its piety and the important social and political role of *ulama*, many Acehnese claim to possess a distinctive Islamic identity, which is tightly connected to the implementation of the state Shariʿa (Salim 2004). Therefore, supporters of the introduction of Islamic criminal law justify its re-implementation as something that Aceh had always sought and fought for. Critically examining the notion of a homogeneous, resilient and self-conscious Acehnese identity, Edward Aspinall points out that the complex process of building "the" Acehnese distinctive identity, which includes Islam as a the main point of reference, was a product of the colonial encounter (Aspinall 2009).

7 Although the decision to grant autonomy to Aceh in 1999, including provisions for the state implementation of Shariʿa, was driven by the aim to support a political solution to the Aceh conflict, it did not actually lead to the end of the armed conflict. See Miller (2009) for further information about the widespread implications of the legislation on decentralization and special autonomy for conflict resolution (cf. Feener, this volume; Miller and Feener 2010).

tempered.[8] Furthermore, the state implementation of Islamic law seems to have given rise to its own issues of justice and equity. Public canings have been conducted in Aceh since 2005. On 10 June 2005, the governor issued a decree that delineates the process and method of caning. The first caning was executed on 24 June 2005 in Bireuen. Eighteen persons were sentenced for violating the prohibition on gambling and were lashed in public between four and eight times. My own gender-specific examination of executions of canings between the years 2005 and 2011 show that men were caned more often and received more lashes than women, because in most cases this kind of punishment is handed out after violations of the laws on gambling and alcohol consumption, which are committed mostly by men (Großmann 2013, 108 ff.).

During the first caning mentioned above, opening addresses were delivered by the president of the Supreme Court of Indonesia (Mahkamah Agung Republik Indonesia; read by the president of the provincial Islamic court, Mahkamah Syariah), by the highest attorney in Indonesia (Kepala Kejaksaan Agung Republik Indonesia; read by the highest attorney in Aceh), and by the national chief of police (Kepala Kepolisian Republik Indonesia; read by the provincial chief of police). All speeches emphasized the important symbolic effect of caning (Abubakar 2007, 1). Until now, canings have been carried out publicly in front of mosques, mostly after the Friday prayer, where onlookers can take pictures and videos that are frequently published online.

Although the success of the attempt at creating a new legal order and restoring the confidence in the legal system has been less than impressive, the state implementation of Islamic law has a significant impact on some aspects of social life, including the activities of women in urban public spaces (Feener, this volume). In 2009, the WH (Wilayatul Hisbah, 'Shari'a Police') reported 2689 cases regarding breaches of the Islamic dress requirements that are stipulated in Qanun No. 11/2002 (Human Rights Watch 2010, 22). In this category, the overwhelming majority of the cases concerned women.[9] Methods to enforce the Islamic dress code include public shaming and large-scale raids (*razia*) that target mostly young Muslim women riding motorbikes on the street. During some of these raids, hundreds of women were stopped, instructed about the right way to dress modestly, and required to present identification and to have their personal information recorded by WH officers.[10] Beyond these provincial laws

---

8 For more information about the Shari'a as a 'panacea,' see Husein (2008, 4).

9 Interview with Effendi, Head of the WH, Banda Aceh, 18 February 2010.

10 Human Rights Watch (2010, 53) and personal interviews with women who were checked in controls in Banda Aceh, March 2009 and February 2012.

that disproportionately impact the lives of women, there are also some district-level Shariʿa by-laws such as the prohibition for women to wear trousers and other tight clothing implemented in 2009 by the Head of the West Aceh district, Ramli Mansur. He authorized the WH to stop women wearing trousers, confiscate 'inappropriate dress' immediately, and hand out skirts to wear instead. For this purpose, the district government allegedly ordered 20,000 skirts (Kurniawati 2010).

Most women I spoke to during my stay in Aceh neither wore an Islamic headscarf (*jilbab*) nor followed modest clothing before the implementation of the new requirements for 'modest Muslim dress' as set forth in Aceh's Shariʿa legislation.[11] One female school teacher told me that she dressed with knee-length skirts and short-sleeved blouses while teaching and never wore a *jilbab*. Other women told me about their meetings at the public beaches in North Aceh, where they wore bathing suits and sometimes bikinis. If women—prior to the official requirements for 'modest Muslim dress'—decided to wear the *jilbab*, it was to express their piety. However, meanings ascribed to the headscarf as an expression of personal religiosity changed with the compulsion to wear an Islamic headscarf in public spaces. Thus, among some groups and individuals the headscarf has become a more contested symbol.

Yet, the control of female Islamic dress did not start with the introduction of the legal foundation of Islamic dress requirements that are stipulated in Qanun No. 11/2002 and the attempts by the WH to enforce it. Even before the state Islamic legal system was established, vigilante groups were taking unofficial measures to impose more stringent conceptions of Shariʿa morality. In April 1999, violent attacks occurred against women, who, in the eyes of the attackers, were not dressed according to Islamic dress requirements. Within so-called large-scale 'headscarf raids' (*razia jilbab*), groups of men forced women to dress according to their understanding of an Islamic dress code, even though there was no legal obligation to wear 'Islamic dress.' Women were stopped on the streets and in some cases physically attacked, after which they got their—allegedly too tight—trousers cut or their heads shaven in case they were

11 Here I refer not only to women's rights activists, but also to women whom I spoke to during the 11 months of my fieldwork. During my stay in Aceh, I lived with three local families of activists, joined women's rights activists in their daily work (for example in seminars, meetings and public events), and conducted participant observation in several workshops, trainings und discussions, as well as internal meetings of civil society organizations. When I refer to 'women' here, I therefore mean activists, members of their families, friends, participants of seminars, workshops and trainings and women I met during public events.

not wearing a headscarf.[12] Much speculation took place about the identity of the attackers. The activist Cut Nurdin, who interviewed several victims of the 1999 *razia jilbab*, told me that some perpetrators had said that they belonged to the Free Aceh Movement (GAM), while some others said they belonged to Islamic groups. Rumour had it that the perpetrators were disguised members of the Indonesian military who claimed to be GAM, in order to defame the separatists and to destabilize the situation, thus justifying military interventions.[13] The important point here is not so much the identity of the group members, but the fact that within the *razia jilbab* men could—with the tacit acquiescence of significant segments of society—attack women who did not dress according to their expressed understanding of Islamic dress code. Cut Nurdin stated in her interview with me, that the *razia jilbab* was the beginning of forced veiling for women by men in Acehnese history, which has also been pointed out by Jacqueline Siapno (2002, 37). After the implementation of the legal foundation for the WH in 2002, the latter not only conducted official 'raids' (*razia*), but at times even turned a blind eye toward vigilantism.[14]

Most women I spoke with explained that the *jilbab* had ceased to be a voluntary expression of personal piety, and had instead for them become a symbol of male dominance and patriarchal state power. The understandings and perceptions of Islam have changed insofar that modes and contents of religious beliefs and Islamic conduct, and therefore also standards of 'modest Muslim dress' and Islamic head-covering for women, are no longer viewed primarily as a private affair, but have been politicized. Moreover, women have been instrumentalized in the pursuit of the interests of politicians, military and religious authorities. This is comparable with the processes of technocratic religious reform in neighbouring Malaysia, to which resistance is constrained by a range of factors (Feener, this volume; Peletz 2002, 232 ff.). It could thus be argued that the obligation of the Islamic dress code, especially the compulsion to wear a *jilbab* for women, which is rigidly enforced through state sanctions and through pressures from local communities and family members, increases the vulnerability of women and limits their mobility as well as their self-confidence in public spaces.

---

12 See, e.g., "Razia Jilbab: Sejumlah Wanita Dipangkas," *Serambi Indonesia*, 18 September 1999; "Hentikan Kekerasan dalam Razia Jilbab," *Serambi Indonesia*, 5 May 1999; "Tentara Liar Merazia Wanita di Aceh Utara," *Harian Suara Bangsa*, 29 April 1999; Cf. Bowen (2003, 232); and Siapno (2002, 36 ff.).

13 Cut Nurdin, personal interview, 24 February 2009, Banda Aceh.

14 In other cases, however, the WH actually took action to take people beaten by village vigilantes into protective custody. See Otto and Otto (this volume).

Against the background of restrictions on women's public dress and comportment, there is a small number of Muslim women who almost never wear the *jilbab* in Aceh. They circumvent the obligation to veil in as many situations as possible. However, in their handbags they always carry a *jilbab* that they can put around their neck or over their head when necessary, for instance when controls of the WH occur, people on the street make comments, or when the risk of their behaviour being judged negatively is too high. To justify the transgression of requirements for women to wear the headscarf, some have developed situation-specific applicable lines of argument. To mention a few examples, external influences such as the weather, or the presence of Western people are sometimes successful justifications of non-compliance. The persuasiveness of their arguments and, accordingly, the self-confidence and the courage of women play an important role.

A number of recent studies have emphasized aspects of empowerment and signification in processes of identity-formation of women who wear Islamic dress.[15] These works complement examinations in which the *jilbab* is presented primarily as a symbol of male dominance.[16] The development of formal legislation and measures for the state enforcement of standards for modest Muslim dress have significantly changed local understandings of the *jilbab* and its public symbolism in Aceh. Since 1999, some women have come to feel compelled to wear a headscarf in Aceh because they experienced physical or verbal abuse for not doing so. Even those who have not experienced any repressive measures directly now feel exposed without a headscarf in public and therefore vulnerable.

Compared to earlier periods, when it was mostly women themselves who decided the timing and form of donning the *jilbab*, the power of definition of Islamic dress has changed to their disadvantage. Since 1999, state institutions have increasingly defined and in some cases violently enforced the format of the Islamic dress code for individual Muslim women. Moreover, with the implementation of the legal basis for Islamic dress requirements that are stipulated in Qanun No. 11/2002, state employees are authorized to define and control the dress of women in public and therefore the female body. Groups that were already marginalized in the public sphere, such as women, the poor, as well

15 For information about veiling in Indonesia as a symbol of Islamic modernity, national resistance and identity-building, see, e.g., Brenner (1996); Lindquist (2004); Parker (2007; 2008); Smith-Hefner (2007).

16 See, e.g., Chandranigrum (2007); Feillard (1999); Kamaruzzaman (2004, 2005); Munir (2004); Nordin (2002) for critiques of the inclining discrimination and constrains of women in public spaces as justified by Islam.

as people who did not comply with popular understandings of Shariʿa morality, such as artists and musicians, have also become targets of vigilante justice (Idria, this volume; Jauhola 2013).[17] Therefore, the seemingly positive peace and democratization processes in Aceh have also been accompanied by considerable restrictions on women and members of other marginalized groups in public spaces. Similar developments have also been observed in the democratization processes of other Muslim-majority countries, as noted by Claudia Derichs (2008).

The use of force, both by the state and by vigilantes, has sparked criticism of Aceh's state Shariʿa project from various sectors.[18] International, national, and local human and women's rights activists have criticized the way in which the implementation of Islamic law has resulted in the creation of multiple injustices by ignoring women's concerns and promoting male-dominated policies.[19] However, attempts to critically discuss topics that are related to Shariʿa potentially result in dangerous accusations of heresy, defamation and exclusion. Thus, most Acehnese human and women's rights activists do not articulate demands for the abolishment of Islamic law in Aceh. In fact, most are convinced that, if Shariʿa were to be implemented properly, in ways that emphasized justice, welfare and gender-sensitivity, it would actually improve Aceh's economic, political, and socio-cultural conditions (see also Afrianty, this volume).

---

17 Cf. Nur Ichwan (2007, 208ff.); Salim (2003, 224ff.; 2009, 5ff.) for further information on the problematic state implementation of Shariʿa laws in Indonesia.

18 The disappointment with the implementation of Islamic law also becomes clear from the results of the SMS polling with almost 800 participants on the implementation of Islamic law in Aceh, which was conducted by the Acehnese civil society organization Yayasan Insan Cita Madani (YICM) in 2007. Results of the poll showed that only 36% replied that they know and understand enough regarding the conceptualization of the Shariʿa. 81% stated that the Shariʿa does not meet their needs and hopes, and 82% pointed out that in their view governmental performance has not improved after the state implementation of Islamic law. Since 2004, YICM has focused its activity on issues of state Shariʿa in Acehnese society. Efforts involved inviting all members of the community to take part in focus group discussions, workshops and training sessions on issues that affect their communities (Interview with a program manager of YICM, 18 December 2008, Banda Aceh).

19 Cf. Crisis Management Initiative (2006); Gender Working Group (2007); Kamaruzzaman (2004; 2008, 143); Komnas Perempuan (2005; 2007, 30ff.); Munir (2004); Nordin (2002).

Women's Rights Activists in the Drafting Process of Islamic Criminal Law

Legal anthropologists understand law as a textual, institutional, and discursive product.[20] Legal codes are not treated simply as written documents but as "performances of values and authority," created in a particular time and place and aimed at specific audiences (Hussin 2007, 789). Indonesia is known for its range of interpretations of Islamic law existing within the broader framework of the nation-state (Feener and Cammack 2007). In the study of Indonesia's post-New Order era as well as Aceh's transformation process, the concept of 'dynamic legal pluralism' is becoming increasingly popular.[21] This concept helps to clarify the constant reconstruction and hybridization processes in which different actors negotiate the terms of Islamic law.[22]

The expert groups involved in the drafting process in Aceh, although dominated by male religious scholars, are open to Muslim women's rights activists in certain circumstances. Pieternella van Doorn-Harder has described a similar phenomenon, concerning the engagement of female scholars, teachers or activists in reinterpretations of *fiqh* texts on modern women's issues, amongst circles connected to the Nahdlatul Ulama (NU) and the Muhammadiyah, the two largest Islamic organizations in Indonesia (van Doorn-Harder 2006; 2007). She points out that in Indonesia "the reinterpretation of the Qur'an and the body of jurisprudence (*fiqh*) concerning certain topics is not limited [...] to an elite group of male scholars" (van Doorn-Harder 2007, 27). Michael Feener has also described the increasing involvement of women's rights activists with a NU or Muhammadiyah background in the development of gender justice agendas in Indonesian society (Feener 2007, 184 ff.).

In the Acehnese context of drafting Islamic Criminal Law, one of these actors is the women's rights activist Khairani Arifin.[23] She was general secretary of the civil society organization Relawan Perempuan untuk Kemanusiaan (Women

20 Franz and Keebet von Benda-Beckmann (2006, 13) argue that law is a "generic term that comprises a variety of social phenomena [...] at different levels of social organisation."

21 For a more detailed examination of legal pluralism, see von Benda-Beckmann (2006, 14 ff.).

22 See Arskal Salim (2007) for a deeper analysis of the process of dynamic legal pluralism concerning the position and influence of Aceh's Shari'a Courts.

23 The following information regarding Khairani Arifin is based on personal interviews with her on 19 May 2011, 3 November 2010, and 14 December 2009 in Banda Aceh and the unpublished report by Khairani Arifin (n.d.) *Hasil Penelitian: Perspektive Kesetaraan dan Keadilan Qanun Kompilasi Hukum Jinayah.*

Volunteers for Humanity/RPuK) from 2001 until 2009. Khairani Arifin graduated with a master's degree in Islamic law from Syiah Kuala University in Banda Aceh and currently holds a position as a lecturer there. Although her academic degree forms the basis of her knowledge in jurisprudence, it is neither the crucial factor for her expertise on topics about women and Islam, nor a justification for her participation in legal drafting. She gained the technical knowledge that justified her participation in these discussions mainly through seminars and discussions with Acehnese religious scholars. Acehnese women's rights activists started to work on Islamic legal issues after an increase in violent assaults on women, ostensibly justified by the Shari'a, from 1999 onwards.[24]

Women's rights activists participated in seminars in which they were trained in topics concerning gender, Islam and legal issues that were mostly financed by national and Western donors. The Fahmina Institute in Cirebon or the International Women's Rights Action Watch Asia Pacific in Kuala Lumpur are prominent places in which women's rights activists are trained in topics concerning women, Islam and the implementation of CEDAW (Convention on the Elimination of All Forms of Discrimination against Women). In addition, women's rights activists organized seminars in Aceh and were strategic in their choice of speakers to invite. As Suraiya Kamaruzzaman, co-founder of the NGO Flower Aceh, describes:

> First we invited female activists of other NGOs; then we invited male activists from other NGOs; in a next step we invited female religious scholars and then we were ready to invite male ulama to have discussions with them.[25]

In that way, women's rights activists in Aceh achieved several objectives. They further educated themselves, autodidactically, in the fields of Qur'anic exegesis and *ijtihad* (independent legal reasoning). More importantly, the seminars provided a protected space in which both activists and Islamic scholars (ulama) could temporarily bracket some of their mutual prejudices and engage in substantial dialogue. Step by step, activists overcame their lack of self-confidence

---

24 For more information about the increase of discrimination and violence against women that is justified with reference to the Shari'a, see Duguay (2008); Gender Working Group (2007); Human Rights Watch (2010); Kamaruzzaman (2004); Komnas Perempuan (2007); and UNIFEM (2008).

25 Suraiya Kamaruzzaman, personal interview, 19 May 2011, Banda Aceh. For more on Flower Aceh, see Afrianty (this volume).

and started to have critical discussions with male ulama. Moreover activists enhanced their recognition as actors in the drafting process of Islamic legislation in Aceh amongst ulamas, enabling potential further cooperation. Additionally, the ulama who were invited in their seminars opened up possibilities for exclusive meetings with other religious scholars. Once activists gained access to these spaces, the reception of their arguments was positive. As Suraiya Kamaruzzaman points out: "The problem is not that ulama are not willing to listen to our arguments, but that we have few opportunities to speak with them."[26]

Khairani Arifin's main overarching aim in the implementation of Islamic law is to improve justice and to contribute to the solution of Aceh's complex social and political problems. She and her colleagues argue that the Islamic legal system should in this sense be 'gender-sensitive' and future-oriented, include human as well as women's rights, guarantee equality before the law, and represent the interests of all citizens. The ideas and strategies formulated by these Acehnese activists show similarities to the approach of so-called 'Islamic feminists,' who aim to enhance the social status of women by reinterpreting parts of the Qur'an and the hadiths in a 'gender-sensitive' way.

Proponents of this transnational theological and political project, including members of the Malaysian based organization Sisters in Islam, fight for democracy, women's rights and tolerance in the Muslim world by advancing a holistic, historically embedded, and 'gender-sensitive' exegesis of the Qur'an (Schröter 2010). Acehnese activists appropriate aims and strategies of these global discourses on Islamic feminism through processes of translating, transferring or modifying non-local norms, values or laws in local contexts. One reason for the need for appropriation is the urge to explicitly dissociate themselves from Western paradigms, in order not to be branded as heretical or perceived as tools of 'Christian' or 'Western' interests financed from abroad. Such insults and allegations against women's rights activists being *kafir* (infidels) have sometimes provoked defensiveness and exclusion, as I will describe in the section below about the passing of *Qanun Jinayat* in 2009.

Most activists I spoke with are also very much aware of possible problems that may arise if they focus too much on international discourses about gender and Islam, instead of the needs of local women at the grassroots level. Issues that are important for members of international women's movements might not necessarily be the same as those of ordinary women in Aceh. Problems with representation can thus emerge, and they could face challenges

26 Suraiya Kamaruzzaman, personal interview, 19 May 2011, Banda Aceh.

with implementing their agendas due to the lack of support from local communities.[27]

Cooperation between Women's Rights Activists and the State Shari'a Agency

One crucial factor of Khairani Arifin's participation in the drafting process of Islamic legislation was the personal contact and cooperation with Alyasa Abubakar, the founding director of the State Shari'a Agency (Dinas Syariat Islam/DSI).[28] Since the beginning of 2000, he has been one of the leading academics at the State Institute of Islamic Studies (IAIN, presently UIN) Ar-Raniry, Banda Aceh, in the field of advocacy for and consultation about the formalization of Islamic law. In 2002 he assumed control of the newly established State Shari'a Agency and became, by virtue of his position, responsible for and personally committed to the (re)drafting of the three contested pieces of Islamic legislation (*qanun*) Nos. 12, 13, 14/2003 into one unified Shari'a criminal code, which was to be referred to as the '*Qanun Jinayat*.'[29] Khairani Arifin's and Alyasa Abubakar's conception of the aim and normative framework of Aceh's state Shari'a system is similar to the extent that both of them seek to make Aceh a more just society and to improve its social and political system. Despite these

27 The importance of the local dimension in the work of Muslim women's and human rights activists, particularly in developing awareness of global discourses and agendas into the culture of local Islamic schools (*pesantren*) is emphasized by Michael Feener (2007, 186 ff.). Pieternella van Doorn-Harder (2006, 35) describes the aim of Muslim scholars and activists as "to translate feminist thinking into an Indonesian model acceptable to mainstream Muslim believers" within their effort to fuse their early grassroots work with academic thinking about women and Islam from the Middle East, Pakistan, India and Malaysia.

28 Alyasa Abubakar was born in Takengon, and studied Islamic law at Al-Azhar University in Egypt. He has published extensively on Islamic law and inheritance law. For more on his role in Aceh's state Shari'a system, see Feener (2013, 205 *et passim*).

29 On 15 July 2003, the governor signed, after their passing through the DPRA, Qanun No. 12/2003, which deals with the consumption and sale of alcoholic beverages (*minuman khamar dan sejenisnya*), Qanun No. 13/2003, which deals with gambling (*maisir* or *perjudian*) and Qanun No. 14/2003, which deals with the illicit relationships and interactions between unmarried men and women (*khalwat* or *mesum*) (Feener, this volume). The punishment of infringing these laws ranges from three to forty strokes of the cane (*uqubat cambuk*) in public, imprisonment or fines, depending on the nature of the crime, but also on the interpretation of the law enforcers.

convergences on the normative level, their demands concerning the practical implementation of Islamic law differ widely. In particular, they promote different definitions of offences and punishments, as I will discuss in more detail below.

However, on the basis of their shared interest in developing a just and future-oriented Islamic legal system, Khairani Arifin and Alyasa Abubakar established a practical working relationship. Toward this end, state Shariʿa officials and Muslim women's rights activists discussed the role and status of women in Islam and in Acehnese society, including specific considerations of issues such as sexual harassment, rape and child protection under Islamic law. Activists emphasized the openness of Alyasa Abubakar in listening to their comments and criticism of B) the redrafted *Rancangan Qanun Jinayat* in 2008. In their personal meetings, he openly supported aspects of gender equality. On the other hand, he did not proactively argue in favour of their aims, particularly when he imagined that they might be controversial. Alyasa Abubakar tried to keep the balance between the interests of human and women's rights activists on the one hand and conservative ulama of rural *dayah* on the other. In fact, however, he never publicly disagreed or argued with Islamic religious authorities that took a different stance.[30]

As mentioned earlier, the implementation of the state Shariʿa in Aceh has been controversial since its inception. The content of Qanun Nos. 12, 13, and 14/2003 on gambling, alcohol and illicit relations between the sexes (*khalwat*) was publicly contested before the tsunami occurred and revisions have been proposed several times since. It was in this context that Khairani Arifin and Alyasa Abubakar, in cooperation with the members of several human and women's rights networks,[31] initiated a number of seminars and workshops to formulate recommendations concerning the redrafting. At this point, the three *qanun* mentioned above were still separate by-laws.

---

30 The way in which disputes are avoided can also be illustrated by the answer of the former MPU (Ulama Council) chairman Muslim Ibrahim to the question of the former director of the women's rights organization Balai Syura, on whether he would submit a request to the MPU to pass a fatwa concerning the legitimacy of women to take leading positions. He explained to her that he could not directly ask the members of the MPU because this would immediately cause them to be defensive. His opinion was that Balai Syura should release an article in a daily newspaper concerning that issue, so that he would have an opportunity to suggest a discussion on that topic (Activists, FGD, 22 March 2011, Banda Aceh).

31 For example JPuK (Jaringan Perempuan untuk Kebijakan) or JMSPS (Jaringan Masyarakat Sipil Peduli Syariah), which is formed by 16 local civil society organizations.

By 2005, momentum had been built for a thorough revision of these three *qanun*. At that time, activists, intellectuals, academics, religious scholars, official representatives of state Islamic institutions, and politicians published comments and suggested amendments to reword, systematize, and consolidate the three *qanun*. The fragile political and socio-cultural situation after the tsunami, the end of the secessionist war, and the enactment of the Law on the Governing of Aceh (LoGA) in 2006 induced the formulation of a broad spectrum of demands. These ranged from critiques of an overly rigid implementation of Islamic law (for example, that the canings violate national laws and international conventions), to calls for the strengthening and expanding of the state Shariʿa system, by introducing more severe physical punishments, including amputation.

Personal Contacts: Access to the First Draft *Qanun Jinayat* (2007)

In May 2007, then Governor Irwandi Yusuf ordered the State Shariʿa Agency to draft a unified Islamic Criminal Law Code (*Qanun Jinayat*) that should replace the three existing separate *qanun* on gambling, alcohol, and *khalwat*. Each of the three *qanun* consists of two parts: one in which the criminal offence is defined and another, often repetitive, part that goes into the specifics of the criminal procedure in greater detail (*Qanun Hukum Acara Jinayat*). Alyasa Abubakar pointed out that the main reason for the syntheses was to avoid repetition in the descriptive parts of the procedures (Abubakar 2007, 3 ff.).

Irwandi Yusuf then formed an expert committee (Tim Perumus Qanun), which was composed mostly of professors and lecturers from the IAIN in Banda Aceh and members of the Council of Ulama (Majelis Permusyawaratan Ulama, MPU), to prepare the A) first draft *Qanun Jinayat* (2007). The State Shariʿa Agency handed the draft to the provincial Bureau of Legal Affairs (Biro Hukum).[32] Women's rights activists Samsidar[33] and Khairani Arifin had a good relationship with the former head of the Biro Hukum, Hamid Zein, through whom they got access to the draft. When they read it, they were shocked. It was obviously prepared in a hurry, for many paragraphs showed internal inconsis-

32 The Biro Hukum, established in 2007, is a provincial office that deals with litigations and legal disputes. The office is also responsible for preparing, reviewing and rewording the *qanun* for submission to the parliament.

33 Samsidar was special rapporteur for Aceh of the national organization Komnas Perempuan in 2006.

tencies and were not in compliance with national laws and international conventions. For example, the draft stated that caning children was legitimate. Samsidar asked Hamid Zein to amend the A) first draft *Qanun Jinayat* (2007) again. In reaction to his answer that the Biro Hukum had no financial resources left for any redrafting, Samsidar acquired funds from the international organization UNIFEM to employ the Acehnese human rights organization Yayasan Insan Cita Madani (YICM), and its director Roy Valefi, to initiate a further process of reviewing the A) first draft *Qanun Jinayat* (2007).[34] "This organization was brave enough to critically examine the implementation of Shari'a and to discuss it with members of the MPU," Samsidar stated.[35]

The Redrafted *Rancangan Qanun Jinayat*: Participation in the Amendment Group and Expert Meetings

The participation of civil society organizations in the drafting process of *qanun* is legally mandatory according to the procedural law 3/2007.[36] To critically review the A) first draft *Qanun Jinayat* (2007) and to ensure the accommodation of the concerns of human and women's rights activists, a 'revision team' (*Tim Revisi*) was assembled. This team was formed through consultation between Governor Irwandi Yusuf, Biro Hukum, and the Acehnese rights organization YICM. This group included leading IAIN academics, such as Prof. Dr. Alyasa Abubakar and Prof. Dr. Syahrizal Abbas, the head of the MPU, Prof. Dr. Muslim Ibrahim and the Islamic scholar and human rights activist Teungku Danial,[37] as well as women's rights activists Ria Fitri and Khairani Arifin. On the one hand, the activists criticized the composition of the group, because women comprised only 33 per cent of representatives, thus not in proportion to their share of the general population. On the other hand, Khairani Arifin stated that in practice the numerical under-representation of women was com-

34 Samsidar, personal interview, 12 March 2009, Banda Aceh.

35 Samsidar, personal interview, 12 February 2011, Banda Aceh.

36 This law states that, within the drafting process of every *qanun* public participation (*ruang partisipasi publik*) has to be assured. Civil society organizations have the right to give oral and written recommendations through seminars, focus group discussions and public hearings. The contents of these statements have to be included in the substance of the draft-*qanun* or at least be recognized by the legislative or executive within seven days.

37 At the time of writing Teungku Danial was lecturer at the Malikussaleh University in Lhokseumawe and involved in the progressive Islamic organization Rabitah Taliban.

pensated by their frequent presence at meetings.[38] Nonetheless, the activists who participated had little specific expertise in Islamic theology or knowledge of *fiqh*, and this made it difficult for them, certainly at the beginning, to engage in substantial discussions.[39] However, the members of the group were very committed, and Khairani Arifin and Alyasa Abubakar in particular worked closely together and published several texts in which they formulated their critiques concerning the current implementation of the Shari'a, suggesting a just and future-oriented Islamic Criminal Law and proposing amendments.

At the same time and in addition to the discussions of the 'revision team,' three so-called 'expert meetings' took place, which were initiated by different institutions. These meetings were attended by representatives of civil society groups, religious institutions, state offices and academic committees and members of the specific group for the *qanun* drafting team (*Tim Perumus Qanun*) of the State Shari'a Agency (DSI). The *Tim Perumus Qanun* convened the first expert meeting, which included representatives from human and women's rights organizations. As the activists had very little expertise, the meeting was more like a seminar in which the participants questioned the representatives of the DSI, resulting in hardly any controversial discussion. The second expert meeting, also initiated by the *Tim Perumus Qanun*, was composed of representatives of the government, parliament, academics, activists, ulama and *adat* leaders. This meeting was characterized by a vibrant discussion and critical questions. The third expert meeting, initiated by the women's rights organization Balai Syura and UNIFEM, was composed of members of the *Tim Perumus Qanun* and activists who were trained in the field of the implementation of the CEDAW (Convention on the Elimination of All Forms of Discrimination against Women). In this meeting, significant points concerning the compatibility of human rights and the draft of the *Qanun Jinayat* were introduced, discussed and recommendations were submitted to the governor and to Biro Hukum. Subsequently, Biro Hukum reviewed A) the first draft *Qanun Jinayat* in 2007, and B) the revised draft *Rancangan Qanun Jinayat* at the end of 2008.[40]

38 Prof. Dr. Alyasa Abubakar attended 90% of the meetings, Khairani Arifin 80%, Ria Fitri 50%, Tgk. Danial 35%, Prof. Dr. Syahrizal and Prof. Dr. Muslim Ibrahim only about 25%.

39 Interview with Khairani Arifin, 25 February 2010, Banda Aceh.

40 The revised draft was termed *Rancangan Qanun tentang Kompilasi Hukum Jinayah Aceh Tahun 2008* or in abbreviated form *Rancangan Qanun Jinayat*.

The Role of Western Donors in the Drafting Process

The 2004 tsunami was followed by one of the largest humanitarian interventions in history. Well-endowed international and non-governmental organizations implemented emergency and reconstruction aid programs with massive material, personal and ideological effort. Although foreign aid interventions were criticized as ineffective,[41] the internationalization after the tsunami brought immense support to the financial, structural and personnel assets of Acehnese and national human and women's rights organizations and thereby increased their bargaining power. At the same time, the rapid internationalization of Aceh that came after the tsunami evoked forces of Islamic 'revitalization' that were less sympathetic, or even opposed, to the concerns of women's rights activists,[42] as they strengthened the demand for what was perceived as a distinctly Acehnese, and thus strongly 'Islamic,' model of political, socio-cultural and moral order. Conservative Muslims characterized funding from Western sources as infiltration from 'outside'—although they did not do so equally with reference to support from Islamist groups from the Middle East (Feener 2007, 184ff.). Particular segments of the Acehnese political and religious elite also asserted Acehnese autonomy concerning sensitive topics, such as religious matters, thereby keeping Western advisers and development programs at a distance from the implementation of Islamic law.[43]

Although the international community was formally excluded from negotiations concerning the Islamic legal system, representatives of the EU, for example, in personal conversations with members of the executive and the leg-

---

41 For example, some critics argued that reconstruction programs deepened existing socio-economic cleavages, prevented an effective and fast reconstruction because of the lack of coordination, reduced participatory efforts from the Acehnese through paternalistic approaches, and disrupted middle and long term development through the separation of emergency and development aid (Pennels 2008; Soelaksono 2009; Völz 2005; and personal interviews with activists). For more information about critical perspectives on the reconstruction efforts after the tsunami, see various contributions in Daly, Feener, and Reid (2012).

42 Public presence and the perceived paternalistic approaches of Western aid institutions after the tsunami were interpreted by many men and women in Aceh as a threat. Some of these fears were framed within conspiracy narratives, focused on alleged attempts by predatory neo-liberal interests and fundamentalist Christian groups to take advantage of the Acehnese at a point at which they were most vulnerable.

43 For example, the German Technical Cooperation (GTZ), which met with the governor as part of its good governance program, was excluded from discussions about two issues: state Shari'a and the *wali nanggroe* (the symbolic 'head of state').

islative pressed the point that Islamic law should not violate international conventions. John Penny, the envoy of the EU, pointed out to local politicians that the rigid implementation of Islamic Criminal Law, including public canings, would result in negative publicity that could hinder the peace and democratization processes and discourage future foreign investment in Aceh.[44] This argument was not only prominent on the international level but also within the national discourse of Aceh's reconstruction process. For example, Kuntoro Mangkusubroto, the head of the former reconstruction office BRR, expressed the fear that Aceh's economy would be weakened through the implementation of Shariʿa.[45]

Members of the Acehnese government, in other words, were under pressure from Western consultants to include local and national human and women's rights organizations in the drafting process. The involvement of the Acehnese human rights organization Yayasan Insan Cita Madani (YICM), funded by UNIFEM, was one response to this. On the national level, the National Commission on Violence against Women, Komnas Perempuan, was one of the few women's rights organizations sufficiently capable, well-funded and legitimized to cooperate with state officials and Islamic religious leaders in the drafting process of the *Qanun Jinayat*.[46]

Contents of the *Rancangan Qanun Jinayat* (2008)

The B) *Rancangan Qanun Jinayat* (2008) included four pages of explanatory notes (*penjelasan*) that defined the philosophical and ideological foundation and the 'contextual' model of interpreting Islamic law advocated by the head of the State Shariʿa Agency, Alyasa Abubakar. These explanations provide a theoretical basis for Aceh's Islamic legal system. Khairani Arifin was successful in having a preamble, stipulating adherence to human (including women's) rights conventions included in the draft. However, the substance of these rights was not sufficiently integrated in the more specific points of the legislation.

Other demands of women's rights activists that were successfully accommodated included the addition of provisions deterring sexual harassment and rape

44 John Penny, envoy of the EU in Aceh, personal interview, 24 March 24 2011, Banda Aceh.

45 "Sangat Menyakitkan Kalau Syari'at Islam Jadi Alasan Hambat Investor," *Waspada Online*, 1 October 2007 (Accessed 20 October 2012).

46 Komnas Perempuan published several reports, comments and recommendations on the Islamic legal drafting process in Aceh (Komnas Perempuan 2005 and 2007).

(but only outside of marriage) in the B) *Rancangan Qanun Jinayat* (2008). Furthermore, DNA evidence was acknowledged as one possible form of proof in the case of rape (as in the Indonesian national compilation of criminal law/Kompilasi Undang Undang Hukum Pidana). Another success was the enhancement of the protection of children through the definition of criminal responsibility from the age of 18, and an aggravation of the penalties in cases of crimes against children. Women's rights activists were, however, unsuccessful in their attempts to abolish corporal punishment, such as caning, generally, as well as their demand to exclude *khalwat* as a criminal offense.

Various points of criticism from both activists and religious scholars that were addressed in the B) *Rancangan Qanun Jinayat* (2008) dealt with issues of determining penalties (for example, one stroke of the cane is equal to 20 grams of gold and one month in prison) and with the role and legitimatization of the WH, which was more precisely defined. Furthermore, the total number of Shari'a criminal offenses covered under Aceh's legislation was to be increased from three to seven in the new draft. These acts now included *zina* (fornication), *qadzaf* (accusation of *zina* without providing sufficient proof, including four witnesses), and *ikhtilath* (physical affection and/or sexual intimacy between an unmarried couple). These extensions were demanded by Alyasa Abubakar, who argued that *zina* and *ikhtilath* are directly connected to *khalwat* (Abubakar 2007, 9).

Khairani Arifin was more critical, and demanded to exclude *khalwat* from the Islamic Criminal Law altogether, but she also agreed that, if *khalwat* was included, *zina* and *ikhtilath* should be included as well. The classification of a homosexual relationship as a crime is mentioned in the B) the *Rancangan Qanun Jinayat* (2008), but not precisely described. Knowing that some ulama supported the introduction of the death penalty by stoning as the severest penalty, Khairani Arifin and Alyasa Abubakar initiated the inclusion of a provision determining that the death penalty should not be codified in this draft and that the maximum punishment in the case of a *hudud* offense should be 100 strokes of the cane in the case of *zina* (fornication).[47] The content of the B) *Rancangan Qanun Jinayat* (2008) shows many amendments that went considerably beyond the provisions of the three existing *qanun* covering gambling, alcohol, and *khalwat*. This included the definition of new crimes to be covered by Aceh's Shari'a legislation, as well as the formal introduction of new penalties. The proposed changes occasioned much heated debate, and were criticized by

---

47 *Hudud* refers to the class of punishments that are fixed for a limited number of crimes as defined under Islamic law.

a number of different parties. The local legislature consequently refused to pass the bill in 2008, and sent it back for further redrafting.[48]

Re-drafting the *Qanun Jinayat*

During the next stage of re-drafting that began in 2009, two legal expert teams, one composed by the legislative and one by the executive, were established. The first group appointed by Governor Irwandi Yusuf included Alyasa Abubakar, Syahrizal Abbas, the two women's right activists Khairani Arifin and Samsidar and a conservative Islamic scholar as an additional representative of the State Shari'a Agency. According to some activists, this scholar followed a literalist interpretation of the Qur'an and demanded a more rigid implementation of Islamic criminal law. Therefore, his perspective and aims were diametrically opposed to those of Khairani Arifin and Samsidar on a number of major issues. Furthermore, he promoted his stance quite aggressively, which made it very difficult for activists to cooperate with him. The activists were under the impression that the governor was pressured by the conservative members of the MPU into appointing this conservative Islamic scholar to the committee in order to prevent progressive voices from dominating the team.[49]

This strategy was successful, insofar as Samsidar left the expert team. The reasons were, firstly, that she felt intimidated and insulted by the conservative scholars on the team and, secondly, that she did not want to be responsible for the team's decisions, as there no longer was any consensus among the members.[50] Certain conservative religious leaders regularly insulted women's rights activists, or accused them of being lesbians or *kafirs* (infidels) (see Jauhola 2013). Progressive Islamic scholars were also attacked or became victims of defamation. In the end, Khairani Arifin was the only activist left in the expert team. As a result, many of the amendments demanded by women's rights activists, for example the abolishment of corporal punishment, were not accommodated in the revised version of B) the *Rancangan Qanun Jinayat* in 2008. Still, the bill did not yet, at this point, contain the death penalty through stoning (*rajam*).

48 See IDLO (2008) for more information about the revision of the *Qanun*.

49 Interview with activists, 19 May 19 2011, Banda Aceh.

50 Interview with Samsidar, 12 May 2011, Banda Aceh.

Dominance by Proponents of Stoning in the Parliamentary Session

The redrafted version was submitted to the local legislature and discussed in three sessions. In the first, members of the DPRA debated with experts on the general philosophical bases of the proposed law, while in the second session they discussed the legal principles of the Islamic criminal law. The third session, in which the final 2009 draft of the C) *Qanun Jinayat* was discussed, was held on 14 October 2009. Khairani Arifin explained that before this session, there had been other meetings on the aims and contents of the final draft, to which she was not invited. One crucial point of debate in these meetings was the issue of the introduction of the death penalty through stoning (*rajam*) in the case of adultery.

One of these meetings was initiated by the Aceh Justice Resource Center (AJRC) and took place on 9 October 2009 with leaders of the 'Special Committee' (*Pansus*—consisting of academics, religious leaders and intellectuals) in order to discuss sensitive future content of the draft, including *rajam*. According to Arskal Salim, participants in this meeting criticized the potential addition of the stoning penalty, but most of them did not, out of principle, reject it (Salim 2009, 15). Rusjid Ali Muhammad, a professor of Islamic law at the IAIN in Banda Aceh, argued that "in any case, much would have to be done before it could be applied, including improving knowledge of Islam in the Acehnese community generally."[51]

The third parliamentary session was held on 14 September 2009, two weeks before the end of the term for many outgoing legislators, who had then just lost local parliamentary elections. In that session, the definition of provisions newly introduced into the bill including, for example, the criminalization of homosexuality and new penalties such as stoning, were formally discussed. Alyasa Abubakar and Syahrizal Abbas did not participate in this meeting. Khairani Arifin, however, did attend the session in which the final 2009 version of the *Qanun Jinayat* was passed, and described the discussion there as follows:

> There was very little consideration of building consensus in this session. At the beginning I could still successfully promote the inclusion of the compliance to national laws and international conventions, like the CEDAW, in the preamble. In the subsequent discussion I argued for the abolishment of corporal punishment. I said it would not be in compliance

51 Quoted in Salim (2009, 15).

> with the international conventions to which the legislature had agreed just minutes earlier. But I got little consent and support from the other participants. The discussion of the fifth paragraph of the draft *Qanun Jinayat* about *zina* (fornication) and the option of stoning as a penalty became very emotional and controversial. Subsequently, the speeches of religious leaders and members of the Islamist parties PKS and PPP, who promoted the inclusion of stoning, changed the mood and successively even members of the Golkar party and the representatives of the provincial police supported the inclusion of stoning in the Qanun Jinayat. As I realized that I could not prevent that step, I left the session. I called the governor, Irwandi Yusuf, and announced my withdrawal from the expert team.[52]

Khairani Arifin's anger and disappointment about this DPRA session resulted from the aggressive and uncompromising attitude and behaviour of rhetorically well-trained politicians and Islamic authorities who supported stoning (*rajam*). They dominated the session and succeeded in winning the support of members of the legislature, who were still unsure about the inclusion of *rajam*. Moreover, the majority of the legislators in the session seemed unqualified and unprofessional, in the sense that they were sensitive to the manipulation of proponents of *rajam*, who, at this very significant moment in time, did not refrain from politicizing Islam for their own interests.

Khairani Arifin pointed out that she was unable to counter this dominance, as she was the only person of the former alliance who had promoted a more moderate vision of the Shariʿa present at the session. Although she was able to ensure the accommodation of her demands in the beginning of the session, resulting in the inclusion of the international conventions in the preamble of the final 2009 text of the *Qanun Jinayat*, in the subsequent discussion about the inclusion of *rajam* she felt that her arguments were no longer heard and she could not successfully argue against its inclusion. It was this realization that led Khairani Arifin to leave the session in despair after stoning was included in the law, and to withdraw from her position in the 'revision team.'

The paradoxical final version of the C) *Qanun Jinayat* that was passed by the DPRA in 2009 includes provisions stipulating adherence to international conventions, such as the CEDAW, the Convention against torture and other cruel, inhuman or degrading treatment or punishment, the Universal Decla-

---

52 Khairani Arifin, personal interview, 19 May 2011.

ration of Human Rights, and the national convention on the protection of children in its preamble. However, this compliance with international conventions lacked integration in the substantive legal text, as strikingly evident by the inclusion of the penalty of death by stoning and the definition of homosexual relationship as a crime. The final version of the text of the C) *Qanun Jinayat* may therefore be regarded as a juxtaposition of different formulations and regulations that are legally incompatible. The intended harmonization of local law, national law, and international conventions has not been achieved.

The passing of the *Qanun Jinayat* by the legislature in 2009 was a shock for many human and women's rights activists. Many members of the human and women's rights network JMSPS (Jaringan Masyarakat Sipil Peduli Syariah) rallied in front of the DPRA building, demanding the implementation of the *Qanun Jinayat* to be postponed in order to do further redrafting. Their main point of criticism was the inclusion of the *rajam* penalty. The new criminalization of homosexuality was hardly mentioned. It was not only the human rights organizations that spoke out against the death penalty for adultery; then Governor, Irwandi Yusuf also criticized the bill and refused to sign it. He rejected the introduction of death by stoning and demanded the Shariʿa to deal with more urgent problems faced by the Acehnese society, such as poverty and unemployment. He also feared national and international reactions if the law were to be put into effect (Karni 2009).

According to the national Law on the Governing of Aceh (UU 11/2006), when a bill passed by the legislature is not signed by the governor within 30 days, it automatically becomes law and can be enacted through publication in the law gazette (*Lembaran Daerah Aceh*). However, this happens only if the *qanun* is mutually agreed upon by the DPRA and the governor, which was not the case when the final text of the C) *Qanun Jinayat* was passed in 2009. As long as it is not signed by the governor and not published in the law gazette, it remains effectively a dead letter.

Political Dimensions in the Passing of the *Qanun Jinayat* (2009)

The passing of the *Qanun Jinayat* can be explained, to a large extent, in terms of politics. The Aceh Peace Monitoring Update (APMU) of 2009, published by the Center for Peace and Conflict Resolution studies at Syiah Kuala University in Banda Aceh, argued that the passing of the *Qanun Jinayat* was a political move of the former outgoing parliament legislators, indicating a peak of tensions between these legislators on the one hand and the executive branch and the incoming parliament members on the other.[53] The former parliament (DPRA) was dominated by members of non-religious national parties and it aimed to weaken the new incoming legislature, which was to be dominated by members of the non-religious local party Partai Aceh as well as Governor Irwandi Yusuf (Center for Peace and Conflict Resolution Studies 2009, 5 ff.).

According to this line of argument, the contestation over the implementation of more severe *hudud* penalties is a manifestation of political power struggles. This is supported by the fact that the majority of the members of the former DPRA voted for the inclusion of *rajam*, even though this step was not backed by the majority of leading religious scholars in Aceh. Although most ulama supported the introduction of *rajam*, they criticized the fact that legislators of a secular parliament designed such laws and passed them in a rush without consulting religious scholars (Center for Peace and Conflict Resolution Studies 2009, 6).

The emphasis on the political dimension of the passing of the *Qanun Jinayat* in 2009 should, however, not lead to an underestimation of the demand and willingness to extend and strengthen Islamic Criminal Law in Aceh, which is widespread amongst members of the Acehnese religious and political elite. The implementation of the full range of *hudud* penalties has been discussed since 1999, even if it has not been fully implemented, and the punishment of caning applies only to transgressions of *syi'ar* (Islamic conduct) or violations of the prohibition of *khamar*, *maisir*, and *khalwat*.

In 2007, Moch. Nur Ichwan emphasized that many religious scholars and intellectuals in Aceh saw harsh punishments as a violation of national law and international conventions. However, he also pointed out that this would not prevent the authorization of harsher punishments in the future (Nur Ichwan 2007, 211 ff.). His prediction turned out to be right. As the passing of the *Qanun Jinayat* shows, in certain circumstances, key persons who strongly demand the fast and total implementation of Shariʿa, including all kinds of *hudud* punishments, are able to push through their agenda, at least on the level of formal legislation. Although they might be a minority, as Nur Ichwan points out, they have successfully asserted the power to either circumvent, silence, or defeat oppositional voices.

Before the signing of peace in August 2005, most GAM representatives had also emphasized the political dimension in the formalization of the state Shar-

53 The APMU is supported by the World Bank and The Asia Foundation. It is a continuation of the Aceh Conflict Monitoring Updates that were published by the World Bank from August 2005 through February 2009.

i'a and called it an 'unwanted gift' from the central government (cf. Missbach, this volume). However, in spite of their influential role in the provincial legislature from 2009 onwards, ex-GAM intellectuals, government members and members of the political wing of the ex-GAM, Partai Aceh, undertook no serious steps to prevent the criticized implementation of the Shari'a. Partai Aceh dominates the newly elected parliament as they gained 48% of the votes in the 2009 parliamentary election, and therefore 33 of the 69 seats in the DPRA. Therefore the rejection and subsequent redrafting of the C) *Qanun Jinayat* (2009) would have been a relatively straightforward process, were it not for the fact that, for a long time, the issue was not placed on the agenda for parliamentary discussion. The executive and legislative branches have long avoided further treatment of the sensitive topic of Islamic criminal law in Aceh, leaving it off the list of 'urgent topics' to be discussed in the DPRA.

Limits of the State in Drafting an Islamic Criminal Law

Muslim women's rights activists, as non-state actors who are neither part of the state apparatus nor of the religious elite, were able to participate in the drafting process of Islamic legislation in Aceh to enhance their aim of creating a just and 'gender-sensitive' Islamic legal system. The amendment teams and legal expert groups, which were formed by civil society organizations and the governor to be the driving force within the process of drafting the *Qanun Jinayat*, although dominated by male religious scholars, were open to women's rights activists in certain circumstances. Within the formulation process of the *Qanun Jinayat*, activists, who were until then not allowed to enter the exclusive and technical realm of Muslim jurisprudence (*fiqh*), were able to gain access to, and participate in, the process, at least in the earlier stages. This was due to the internationalization of Aceh after the tsunami, as women's rights groups were able to benefit from emancipative objectives of international organizations and received both material and non-material support in order to increase their capacities.

Through personal contacts between activists and state actors, such as the head of the Biro Hukum, women's rights activists had access to relevant information about the drafting process and the content of A) the first draft *Qanun Jinayat* in 2007. They were therefore able to push forward the further reviewing of the contested draft. The affirmative cooperation with Islamic scholars and state Shari'a officials, especially with Alyasa Abubakar, strengthened their position and ability to submit recommendations expressing their aims of a more 'gender-sensitive' vision of the Shari'a to the governor and the Biro Hukum.

Limits of Muslim Female Women's Rights Activists' Scopes of Acting

In contrast to the earlier drafting process of the *Qanun Jinayat*, however, its further reviewing and the passing by the provincial legislature in 2009 was not an inclusive and open matter. The new composition of the expert team caused significant changes in the dynamics of team member interactions, which added to the ascendance of more reactionary voices on the committee. The leading figures of this more conservative faction then went on to intimidate and insult women's rights activists on the committee, causing them to withdraw. Moreover, during the 2009 legislative session in which a version of the *Qanun Jinayat* was passed, the lobbying of proponents of the implementation of the death penalty by stoning dominated the debates among members of the legislature, and these issues were driven to the fore more by political than by legal concerns. The final version of the C) *Qanun Jinayat* passed in 2009 includes the death penalty by stoning and makes homosexual relations a criminal offense. This, despite the fact that the women's rights activists had successfully demanded the inclusion of provisions stipulating adherence to international conventions in the preamble as well as the ensuring of child protection, and the inclusion of rape and sexual harassment as a criminal act.

To summarize the scope of acting of Muslim women's rights activists within the drafting process of the Islamic Criminal Law in Aceh, I argue that they have successfully decelerated the coming about of a potentially harsh Islamic Criminal Law until 2009. Additionally, Muslim women's rights activists could make the *Qanun Jinayat* seemingly unworkable by including provisions stipulating adherence to international conventions in the legal texts which are incompatible with the inclusions of the death penalty by stoning and homosexual relations as a criminal offense.

The passing of the *Qanun Jinayat* indicates a turning point for the alliance promoting a vision of Islamic law sensitive to the concerns of gender justice and human rights. As a result of the passing of a version of the bill that included provisions for stoning and other 'hard-line' positions, most activists became frustrated and have either retreated or ignored the further developments of the *Qanun Jinayat*. Religious scholars who were previously active in the legal expert teams have returned to the academic sphere.[54] Currently, the activists

54 At the time of writing, Alyasa Abubakar was the director of the postgraduate school at the IAIN and Syahrizal Abbas was the director for international affairs, vice president of the university and member of the academic senate of the IAIN.

Khairani Arifin and Samsidar do not work in programs dealing with Islamic legislation.[55] At present, there are only a few individual activists who actively observe the further process of the *Qanun Jinayat*. Khairani Arifin hopes that if there is a further re-drafting process initiated at some point, the alliance will be reactivated, and reconfigured to include more supporters of a vision of Islamic law that addresses the needs and concerns of Muslim women in Aceh.

References

Abubakar, Alyasa. 2007. *Beberapa Catacan Akademik atas Rancangan Perubahan Qanun Provinsi Nomor 12,13 dan 14 Tahun 2003 dan Penggabungannya Menjadi Satu Qanun*. Unpublished report.

Arifin, Khairani. (n.d.) *Hasil Penelitian: Perspektive Kesetaraan dan Keadilan Qanun Kompilasi Hukum Jinayah*. Unpublished report.

Aspinall, Edward. 2009. *Islam and Nation: Separatist Rebellion in Aceh, Indonesia*. Stanford: Stanford University Press.

Ahearn, Laura M. 2001. "Language and Agency." *Annual Review of Anthropology* 30:109–137.

Bangstad, Sindre. 2011. "Saba Mahmood and Anthropological Feminism After Virtue." *Theory, Culture, Society* 28(3):28–54.

Benda-Beckmann, Franz von, and Keebet von Benda-Beckmann. 2006. "The Dynamics of Change and Continuity in Plural Legal Orders." *The Journal of Legal Pluralism and Unofficial Law* 53–54:1–44.

Bowen, John. 2003. *Islam, Law, and Equality in Indonesia. An Anthropology of Public Reasoning*. Cambridge: Cambridge University Press.

Brenner, Suzanne. 1996. "Reconstructing Self and Society: Javanese Muslim Women and 'the Veil'." *American Ethnologist* 23(4):673–697.

Candraningrum, Dewi. 2007. "Unquestioned Gender Lens in Contemporary Indonesian Shari'a Ordinances (Perda Syari'ah)." *Al-Jāmi'ah Journal of Islamic Studies* 45(2): 289–320.

Center for Peace and Conflict Resolution Studies. 2009. *Aceh Peace Monitoring Update*, 1 July–31 August 2009. Banda Aceh: Syiah Kuala University. http://www.conflictanddevelopment.org. (Accessed 5 May 2010).

55 At the time of writing, Khairani Arifin worked as program director for political participation of women and community development at the Australian organization Logica. Samsidar was a 'Gender Specialist' supporting the Aceh Police Reform funded by the International Organization for Migration (IOM), Indonesia.

Crisis Management Initiative (CMI). 2006. *The Aceh Peace Process*. http://www.cmi.fi/files/Aceh_involvement_of_women.pdf (Accessed April 4, 2007).

Comaroff, Jean, and John Comaroff. 1992. *Ethnography and the Historical Imagination*. Boulder: Westview Press.

Daly, Patrick, R. Michael Feener and Anthony Reid, eds. 2012. *From the Ground Up: Perspectives on Post-Tsunami and Post-Conflict Aceh*. Singapore: ISEAS Press.

Derichs, Claudia. 2008. "Frauen als Akteurinnen politischen Wandels in islamischen Transformationsstaaten." In *Mehrheit am Rande? Geschlechterverhältnisse, globale Ungleichheiten und transnationale Handlungsansätze*, edited by Heike Brabandt, Bettina Roß and Susanne Zwingli, 217–232. Wiesbaden: Verlag für Sozialwissenschaften.

Doorn-Harder, Pieternella van. 2006. *Women Shaping Islam: Reading the Qur'an in Indonesia*. Urbana and Chicago: University of Illinois Press.

———. 2007. "Reconsidering Authority: Indonesian Fiqh Texts about Women." In *Islamic Law in Contemporary Indonesia: Ideas and Institutions*, edited by R. Michael Feener and Mark E. Cammack, 27–43. Cambridge, Mass.: Harvard University Press.

Duguay, Philip. 2008. "The Struggle for Women's Rights in Nanggroe Aceh Darussalam Province: A Look at History and Emerging Legislation." *Singapore Law Review* 26:1–30.

Feener, R. Michael. 2007. *Muslim Legal Thought in Modern Indonesia*. Cambridge: Cambridge University Press.

———. 2013. *Shariʿa and Social Engineering: The Implementation of Islamic Law in Contemporary Aceh, Indonesia*. Oxford: Oxford University Press.

Feener, R. Michael, and Mark E. Cammack, eds. 2007. *Islamic Law in Contemporary Indonesia: Ideas and Institutions*. Cambridge, Mass.: Harvard University Press.

Feillard, Andrée. 1999. "The Veil and Polygamy: Current Debates on Woman and Islam in Indonesia." *Moussons* 1:5–28.

Gender Working Group. 2007. *Evaluation on Woman in Aceh in 2006*. http://www.aceh-eye.org/data_files/english_format/analisys/analysis_others/analysis_others_2007_03_08.pdf (Accessed 22 April 2007).

Großmann, Kristina. 2013. *Gender, Islam, Aktivismus: Handlungsräume muslimischer Aktivistinnen nach dem Tsunami in Aceh*. Berlin: Regiospectra.

Human Rights Watch. 2010. *Policing Morality: Abuses in the Application of Sharia in Aceh, Indonesia*. New York: Human Rights Watch. http://www.hrw.org/sites/default/files/reports/indonesia1210WebVersionToPost.pdf (Accessed 21 August 2012).

Husein, Mustabsyirah M. 2008. "Memahami Peran Politik Perempuan dalam Syariah Islam: Sebuah Wacana untuk Kebangkitan Perempuan Aceh." In *Perempuan Aceh Bicara*, edited by Sri Lestari Wahyuningroem, Zubaidah Djohar and Sarah Fortuna, 3–14. Bangkok: UNIFEM.

Hussin, Iza R. 2007. "The Pursuit of the Perak Regalia: Islam, Law, and the Politics of Authority in the Colonial State." *Law & Social Inquiry* 32(3):759–788.

———. 2008. "The Politics of Islamic Law: Local Elites, Colonial Authority and the Making of the Muslim State." PhD diss., University of Washington.

International Development Law Organization (IDLO). 2008. *Review on the Revisions being made to the Three Qanun on Jinayah*. http://www.aceh-eye.org/data_files/english_format/issues/issues_women/women_2008_11_01.pdf (Accessed 13 February 2009).

Ismail, Nurjannah. 2008. "Penerapan Syari'at Islam dan Kehidupan Perempuan di Aceh." In *Perempuan Aceh Bicara*, edited by Sri Lestari Wahyuningroem, Zubaidah Djohar, and Sarah Fortuna, 23–34. Bangkok: UNIFEM.

Jauhola, Marjaana. 2013. *Post-Tsunami Reconstruction in Indonesia: Negotiating Normativity through Gender Mainstreaming Initiatives in Aceh*. London and New York: Routledge.

Kamaruzzaman, Suraiya. 2004. "Women and Syariah in Aceh." *Inside Indonesia* 79. http://www.insideindonesia.org/edition-79-jul-sep-2004/women-and-syariah-in-aceh-2607223 (Accessed 8 February 2010).

———. 2005. "Women's Position, Role and Rights in Aceh. Women under Armed Conflict, under Syriah Law and After Tsunami." http://www.susanne-schroeter.de/pdf/suraiya.ppt

———. 2008. "Gerakan Perempuan di Aceh Pasca Tsunami: Sejauhmana Tantangan dan Peluang?" In *Perempuan Aceh Bicara*, edited by Sri Lestari Wahyuningroem, Zubaidah Djohar, and Sarah Fortuna, 139–151. Bangkok: UNIFEM.

Karni, Asrori S. 2009. "Al Yasa' Abubakar Tolak Hukum Rajam. Rajam Setitik Ganjal Qanun Sepasang." *Laporan Khusus, Gatra Nomor 52/XV 11 November 2009*. http://www.gatra.com/2009-11-02/majalah/beli.php?pil=23&id=131839 (Accessed 16 May 2011).

Komnas Perempuan. 2005. *Kertas Kebijakan Materi Dialog Kebijakan Komnas Perempuan tentang Pelaksanaan Syariat Islam di Aceh, Draft III/10 Oktober 2005*, Jakarta: Komnas Perempuan. http://www.komnasperempuan.or.id/wp-content/uploads/2009/01/analisis-terhadap-qanun-nangroe-aceh-darussalam.pdf (Accessed 23 November 2011).

———. 2007. *Experiences of Acehnese Women: Seeking and Accessing Justice from One Era to the Next*. Jakarta: Komnas Perempuan.

Kurniawati, Dewi. 2010. "West Aceh District Chief Says Shariah Law Needed or There Will Be Hell to Pay." *Jakarta Globe*, 18 August.

Lindsey, Tim, and M.B. Hooker, with Ross Clarke and Jeremy Kingsley. 2007. "Shari'a Revival in Aceh." In *Islamic Law in Contemporary Indonesia: Ideas and Institutions*, edited by R. Michael Feener and Mark E. Cammack, 216–254. Cambridge, Mass.: Harvard University Press.

Lindquist, Johan. 2004. "Veils and Ecstasy: Negotiating Shame in the Indonesian Borderlands." *Ethnos* 69(4):487–508.

Mahmood, Saba. 2005. *Politics of Piety: The Islamic Revival and the Feminist Subject*. Princeton/New York: Princeton University Press.

Miller, Michelle A. 2009. *Rebellion and Reform in Indonesia: Jakarta's Security and Autonomy Policies in Aceh*. London and New York: Routledge.

Miller, Michelle A., and R. Michael Feener. 2010. "Emergency and Islamic law in Aceh." In *Emergency Powers in Asia: Exploring the Limits of Legality*, edited by Victor V. Ramraj and Arun K. Thiruvengadam, 213–236. Cambridge: Cambridge University Press.

Munir, Lily Z. 2004. *Islam, Gender and Formal Shari'a in Indonesia*. http://www.law.emory.edu/IHR/worddocs/lily2.doc (Accessed 7 June 2007).

Nordin, Edriana. 2002. "Customary Institutions, Syariah Law and the Marginalisation of Indonesian Woman." In *Woman in Indonesia: Gender, Equity and Development*, edited by Kathryn Robinson and Bessell Sharon, 179–186. Singapore: ISEAS Press.

Nur Ichwan, Moch. 2007. "The Politics of Shari'iatization: Central Government and Regional Discourses of Shari'a Implementation in Aceh." In *Islamic Law in Contemporary Indonesia: Ideas and Institutions*, edited by R. Michael Feener and Mark E. Cammack, 193–215. Cambridge, Mass.: Harvard University Press.

Parker, Lyn. 2007. "Of Faith and Feminism: Imagining Discursive Feminist Space for Muslim Women." *Outskirts: Feminisms along the Edge* 17(1).

———. 2008. "To Cover the Aurat: Veiling, Sexual Morality and Agency among the Muslim Minangkabau, Indonesia." *Intersections: Gender and Sexuality in Asia and the Pacific* 16, 1–76.

Peletz, Michael G. 2002. *Islamic Modern: Religious Courts and Cultural Politics in Malaysia*. Princeton/Oxford: Princeton University Press.

Pennels, L. 2008. Mission Report: "Gender Outcomes & Reflections—Aceh." Office of the Resident Coordinator/Humanitarian Coordinator—OCHA—Indonesia. Jakarta.

Salim, Arskal. 2003. "Epilogue: Shari'a in Indonesia's Current Transition." In *Shari'a and Politics in Modern Indonesia*, edited by Arskal Salim and Azyumadi Azra, 213–234. Singapore: ISEAS Press.

———. 2004. "'Shari'a From Below' in Aceh (1930–1960): Islamic Identity and the Right to Self-Determination with Comparative Reference to the Moro Islamic Liberation Front (MILF)." *Indonesia and Malay World* 32(92):80–99.

———. 2007. "Dynamic Legal Pluralism in Modern Indonesia: The State and the Sharia (Court) in the Changing Constellations of Aceh." Paper presented at the First International Conference of Aceh and Indian Ocean Studies, Banda Aceh, Indonesia, 24–27 February.

———. 2009. *Politics, Criminal Justice and Islamisation in Aceh*. Islam, Syari'ah and Governance Background Paper Series, University of Melbourne. http://www.lindseyfederation.law.unimelb.edu.au (Accessed 2 February 2011).

Schröter, Susanne. 2010. "Feministische Re-Interpretationen des Qur'an und der Sunna. Entwürfe für eine geschlechtergerechte Ordnung in der islamischen Welt." In *Frau,*

Gender, Queer: Gendertheoretische Ansätze in der Religionswissenschaft, edited by Susanne Lanwerd and Márcia Elisa Moser, 46–54. Würzburg: Verlag Königshausen und Neumann GmbH.

Siapno, Jaqueline A. 2002. *Gender, Islam, Nationalism and the State in Aceh: the Paradox of Power, Co-optation, and Resistance*. London: RoutledgeCurzon.

Soelaksono. 2009. *NGO and Donor Coordination To Speeds up Reconstruction and Avoid NGO Competition*. http://www.disaster-response.cc (Accessed 9 February 2010).

Smith-Hefner, Nancy. 2007. "Javanese Women and the Veil in Post-Soeharto Indonesia." *The Journal of Asian Studies* 66(2):389–420.

UNIFEM. 2008. *Perempuan Aceh Bicara*. Bangkok: UNIFEM

Völz, Carsten. 2005. "Humanitarian Coordination in Indonesia: An NGO Viewpoint." In *Forced Migration Review. Tsunami: Learning from the Humanitarian Response*, 26–27. http://www.fmreview.org/FMRpdfs/Tsunami/11.pdf (Accessed 2 February 2012).

CHAPTER 5

Local Women's NGOs and the Reform of Islamic Law in Aceh: The Case of MISPI

Dina Afrianty

Introduction

When Islamic law was introduced in 1999, many Acehnese saw this as a way to return Aceh to its past glory and to restore people's sense of morality. However, as the state Shari'a system took shape, some were disappointed to find that the enforcement of Islamic law was largely focused on regulating women's behaviour, with women being apprehended and/or publicly humiliated for offenses such as wearing tight jeans or not wearing a headscarf. Some women have even been subjected to caning as a form of punishment for infractions against local legislations regulating public morality. Recently, some local leaders have introduced new local regulations that aim to limit women's freedom and mobility even further, including regulations banning women from performing traditional dances, and from straddling motorbikes (Pasandaran 2013; Saragih and Hotli Simanjuntak 2013). These regulations make Acehnese women the subject of an unprecedented amount of attention at both national and international levels. In the face of such developments, Acehnese women's movements have challenged the local government and demanded law reform. Women's organizations call upon religious leaders and local authorities to revise current Shari'a legislation, arguing that the 'true teaching' of Islam does not discriminate against women.

In general, since the turn of the twenty-first century, opportunities for Acehnese women's wider participation in public policy-making have increased. Law No. 44/1999 on Acehnese autonomy granted the province the right to organize and manage its own religious, cultural and educational affairs, giving religious leaders a larger role in policy-making (Miller 2004, 333). The 2001 Special Autonomy law, moreover, allowed the Acehnese to directly elect their local leaders. These political reforms provided Acehnese men and women with much broader opportunities to take part in local politics. In addition, the signing of the Helsinki Peace Agreement in 2005 and the subsequent passing of the Law on Governing Aceh in 2006 also increased opportunities for Acehnese women to participate in local politics.

 | DOI: 10.1163/9789004304864_006

During my ethnographic fieldwork in 2007–2009, MISPI (Mitra Sejati Perempuan Indonesia, 'The True Partner of Indonesian Women') was one of the local women's NGOs that played a leading role in working with government and religious leaders in attempts to reform Islamic law (Afrianty 2015).[1] As will be elaborated below, MISPI worked together with offices of the local government, even as it criticized the enforcement of Islamic law. MISPI was founded in 1998 by a group of former student activists from Syiah Kuala University in Banda Aceh. At the time of my fieldwork, the organization was led by one of its founders, Syarifah Rahmatillah. In pursuing its mission, MISPI chose to skillfully frame its criticisms and call for a law reform by negotiating its demands with the state and local religious leaders, instead of confronting and opposing them. The leaders and members of MISPI believe that Aceh's customs (*adat*) and culture are strongly Islamic. While rejecting some of the ways in which Islamic law has been implemented in Aceh, particularly where it discriminates against women and the poor, MISPI members also maintain that Shariʿa is not in itself problematic. Rather, in ways that echo the voices of other critics of state Shariʿa in Aceh, they argue that the problems result from particular modes of implementation.

MISPI is a particularly interesting example of women's activism in relation to Shariʿa implementation, because of its combination of strong Islamic credentials, its roots in the national-level Islamic organization HMI (Himpunan Mahasiswa Indonesia, Indonesian Students Organization), its collaboration with the Indonesian state, and its appeal to international women's rights and Islamic feminism. In this chapter, I will explore how MISPI navigated between these

1 This chapter is based on ethnographic research conducted from 2007 to 2009 in Banda Aceh, as part of my PhD research on Acehnese women's responses to the introduction of Islamic law. Fieldwork was conducted during a total period of six months, divided into three visits. My fieldwork primarily involved participant observation. During my visits, I stayed in three different places: the central town of the provincial capital Banda Aceh, a village, and a student dormitory located in the university campus area. All are in the district of Banda Aceh. However, I also travelled occasionally to Pidie and Lhokseumawe, on the Acehnese North coast, to observe the implementation of Islamic law there. During my stay, Banda Aceh was inundated by seminars, workshops and public discussions on issues pertaining to Shariʿa implementation. I attended many of these events that were organized by NGOs or by campuses and I listened to what people said about the by-laws, about particular institutions such as the Shariʿa Police (WH), and about particular issues such as the discrimination against women. I spent most of my time sitting at MISPI's office, where I became friends with the staff, and attending the workshops they organized with their stakeholders, male and female religious leaders, members of district legislatures, and women's Qur'anic reading groups (*majelis taklim*).

different spheres of influence by defending women's rights from an Islamic perspective, in the midst of debates about Shari'a implementation. The chapter begins with a discussion of the background and the establishment of MISPI, drawing attention to the central role of its leader, Syarifah Rahmatillah. From there, I move on to examine MISPI's strategic position and role within the wider local women's movements between 2004 and 2009. The chapter concludes with a discussion of the ways in which MISPI responded to the state Shari'a system, explaining how it managed to work within a markedly Islamic framework, while at the same time challenging the conservative practices and viewpoints of the state and religious leadership.

MISPI's Background

MISPI was founded just three months after the fall of President Suharto in 1998. The founding of MISPI was triggered by the dramatically transformed political situation in Indonesia after the fall of the New Order regime, which sparked the emergence and growth of a number of civil society movements, both in Aceh and elsewhere in Indonesia (Afrianty 2015; Daly, Feener and Reid 2012). The organization was formed by former members of the Acehnese branch of KOHATI (Korps HMI-wati), the women's wing of HMI. MISPI's leader Syarifah Rahmatillah had formerly been a leader of KOHATI. In order to understand the particular position of MISPI, it is therefore important to provide some insight into the background of HMI first.

HMI is a national-level Islamic student organization known to be both strongly Islamic and supportive of Indonesian nationalism. It was established in Yogyakarta in 1947. At that time, Indonesia was in the midst of its struggle for independence and had to fight against the Dutch colonial government, which sought to resume its control over the country after the Second World War and the Japanese occupation (Azra 2004, cited in Muhktar 2006, 2). Ever since its founding, HMI has been one of the most important student organizations in the country. Many former HMI members have reached high positions within the national government and politics. Usually based at university campuses, the organization has branches in almost all Indonesian provinces.

During the New Order period, HMI was one of the Muslim groups that "took a less pessimistic view" of the government, and one of its prominent leaders, Nurcholish Madjid, argued that Indonesia needed an organization that could win the moral sympathies of all Indonesian Muslims (Hefner 1997, 79; see also Hefner 1993, 5). In the first years of its existence, HMI maintained close ties to the Islamic political party Masjumi, sharing its orientation of both reformist Islam and a strong commitment to Indonesian nationalism (Feener 2007, 82–133). With regard to Aceh, it concurred with the view that "Islam was a point of commonality, not difference, between Aceh and Indonesia" (Aspinall 2007, 247). The Acehnese branch of HMI has therefore not been keen on seeing Aceh separate from Indonesia.

Considering its HMI background, it is not surprising that from the beginning MISPI's programs have been characterized by a strong Indonesian nationalist and Islamic character. According to former HMI activists and other civil society activists involved in the founding of MISPI, the creation of a strong nationalist orientation was very important in the context of growing demands for a referendum and independence from Indonesia after 1998. At the time, HMI activists were afraid that, if not handled cautiously, the situation could lead to a disruptive civil war within Acehnese society and that this would, again, adversely affect women. Former HMI activists I talked with acknowledged the injustices and human rights violations perpetrated by the Indonesian military, but at the same time the idea of independence, with Aceh ruled by the 'Free Aceh Movement' (Gerakan Aceh Merdeka/GAM), frightened them even more. They argued that people in Aceh did not want civil war and that many still preferred Aceh to remain part of the Republic of Indonesia.

At the time of MISPI's foundation, political reform at the national level was directed toward the goal of ending the state of military emergency in Aceh. Local organizations started to demand justice and investigation of the gross human rights violations committed by both GAM and the Indonesian military (TNI). However, these demands for justice did not receive an immediate response from Jakarta and fueled further resentment among Acehnese (Bertrand 2004, 175). GAM perceived this situation as a political opportunity to generate more support for their cause of Acehnese independence. However, there were also Acehnese who did not support GAM's cause for independence. Some Acehnese elders, for example, wanted Aceh to become a 'federation' so that its rights were better guaranteed (Siegel 2000, 337). Yet the public support for independence was huge and those opposed were reluctant to express their opinion (ibid.). MISPI is an example of a local organization that did not support the cause for independence, yet it chose not to express its views openly.

The development of MISPI has been closely linked with the personality of its leader, Syarifah Rahmatillah. Daughter of a civil servant, born and raised in Banda Aceh, Syarifah started her activism while she was taking a law degree at Syiah Kuala University. While at university, she became involved in the Student Association (Badan Executive Mahasiswa/BEM), the Faculty of Law Student Senate and the University Student Senate. Later, she joined KOHATI and was elected as the head of the organization. Her experience as a KOHATI leader during her time at the university equipped Syarifah with negotiating skills that she would later use in her work for MISPI.

After graduating in 1997, Syarifah continued her activism by joining ICMI (Indonesian Union of Muslim Intellectuals).[2] She then married the former leader of HMI Banda Aceh who, in 2004, was elected as a member of the local legislature representing Partai Bulan Bintang (PBB), an Islamic political party. In the meantime, she had become a civil servant at the National Land Agency (Badan Pertanahan Nasional) in Banda Aceh. During the time leading to the 2004 general elections, she became a member of the General Election Commission (Komisi Pemilihan Umum/KPU). Although she was a public official, her enthusiasm for social activism did not stop, since, apart from her activism at MISPI, she became active in the Aceh Women's Congress (Duek Pakat Inong Aceh), being first elected to its Steering Committee, and later to its Board.

Many former members of HMI hold important positions in government, and Syarifah's connections to these circles were useful in facilitating MISPI's work. She used her HMI and KOHATI networks to develop the organization, for which she recruited only women with KOHATI backgrounds. Her position at the General Election Commission further enhanced her access to government officials at different levels. All these links added to Syarifah's credentials, and advanced her leverage among other local women activists. Certainly, all of these connections have further enhanced her effectiveness and she is well known for her ability to work with various parties in Aceh, including government officials, members of the local legislature and ulama. Few other women activists in Aceh enjoy such a central position within these networks.

Syarifah told me that it was the political situation that inspired her and her colleagues to organize themselves to work for the needs and concerns of Acehnese women. They considered it a crucial time for Acehnese women to express their views within broader civil movements and they aimed to represent the voices of women who did not want to see Aceh separated from Indonesia. The name 'MISPI' was carefully chosen to express this view. Syarifah and her colleagues called their organization Mitra Sejati Perempuan Indonesia

2 ICMI was established in Malang in December 1990 by Muslim members of the urban Muslim middle class partly as a response to what they perceived as the continuing social and economic marginalization of *pribumi* ('indigenous') Muslims. They argued that Islam provided an alternative ideal in becoming a modern nation (Hefner 1993). Hefner has argued that the creation of ICMI, which received the support of President Suharto in 1990, was a sign of a 'deepening Islamisation of Indonesian State and Ideology' (Hefner 1993). For more discussions of the background of ICMI, see Azra (2004); Hefner (1993; 1997, 75–77); Ricklefs (2001, 393).

('The True Partner of Indonesian Women') to show to the rest of Indonesia that many Acehnese women were committed to having Aceh remain part of Indonesia in the future, and that it was too simple to label all Acehnese as 'rebellious.' By naming their organization 'MISPI,' they hoped that Indonesian women would perceive them as 'their true friends' and not question Acehnese women's 'Indonesian-ness' (*ke-Indonesiaan*).

While some women, like the members of the women's wing of GAM (*Inong Balee*),[3] were eager to see Aceh become an independent state, many others disagreed. According to Syarifah, many Acehnese women were actually forced to support one view over the other, even though, in fact, many women felt that both sides, the Indonesian military and GAM, perpetrated violence against women. Yet it was very difficult to publicly express such views at that time. Many women were targeted by both parties. Siegel (2000, 388–389), for example, observed that some Acehnese women were targeted by GAM only because their physical appearance closely resembled that of the Javanese, the ethnic group associated most strongly with the Indonesian military. Siapno showed that women were exploited by both the Indonesian military and GAM (Siapno 2002).

Syarifah's views on this issue were formed through direct experience. For example, she described how both GAM and the Indonesian military physically targeted her after the Humanitarian Pause was agreed in 2000. Both sides were suspicious that she supported one side over the other. She recalled that she had to hide many times to avoid being kidnapped by either one of the warring parties and she imagined that other Acehnese women had similar experiences, especially after the declaration of martial law in 2003. Despite these threats, Syarifah continued to develop her new organization, during a period in which issues of women's rights did not figure prominently in public discourse.

Rather than choose sides, then, MISPI looked for other ways to garner support from the community. Syarifah believed that all Acehnese women were victims of the political situation, and therefore she and her colleagues argued that they should be able to work with the conflicting parties in order to advance Acehnese women's rights and to gain national recognition. Crucial in this respect was MISPI's approach to the implementation of Shari'a law. If the former women's wing of GAM strongly rejected the idea of Shari'a being formally

---

3 *Inong Balee* was the name first given to female warriors who took up arms against the Portuguese, during the reign of Sultan Alauddin (1596–1604), after being widowed in an earlier battle against the Portuguese in 1511. Laksamana Malahayati is known as the first leader of *Inong Balee*, and has been claimed to lead as many as 2,000 women (Aceh Magazine, June 2007).

implemented in Aceh by arguing that it was another form of Jakarta's oppression of the Acehnese, MISPI along with other civil society activists chose not to show a strong rejection of Shariʿa. According to MISPI, there were indeed Acehnese women who wanted to see Shariʿa introduced in Aceh. Their point then was not to reject the idea of state Shariʿa implementation per se, but to critique and advocate reform of some of the particular ways in which it was being applied and enforced. The widening opportunities for political participation in the post-tsunami/post-conflict period enabled MISPI to use democratic means to voice these criticisms.

By the time the 2004 tsunami struck Aceh, MISPI was considered one of the most established local women's organizations among a rapidly growing number of NGOs.[4] Both national and international donor institutions that worked in Aceh valued MISPI for its efforts in promoting women's rights in the context of the implementation of Islamic law and their support for individual women who struggled to achieve their social and political rights. For example, MISPI employed a lawyer and paralegals to help women who experienced violence to bring their cases to the civil and religious courts. At the same time, MISPI was a leading organization in terms of promoting law reform and influencing policy making through its activities in women's networks or its lobby to both the local bureaucracy and local parliaments.

Since 2004, MISPI along with other local women's organizations such as Balai Syura Inong Aceh, Flower Aceh, LBH Apik Aceh, Putro Kande, RPUK, An-Nisa and the Center for Women's Studies at the IAIN (State Institute for Islamic Studies, presently UIN) Ar-Raniry, has advocated the need to reform the *qanun* (by-laws) as well as the implementation of these laws in a gender-sensitive way. In 2004, several local women's organizations, including MISPI, created the Women's Policy Network or JPUK (Afrianty 2011). Women activists from these organizations emphasized the importance of cooperation in demanding reform. MISPI played a central coordinating role in the establishment and the activities of this network.

Along with these other organizations, MISPI expressed the concern that the limited number of women in both the local bureaucracy and the local legisla-

4 MISPI was established around the same time as several other women's organizations in Aceh, including Yayasan Pengembangan Wanita, KKTGA (Kelompok Kerja Transformasi Gender Aceh, Aceh's Working Group on Gender Transformation in Aceh), LBH-APIK (Legal Aid of APIK), and RPUK (Relawan Perempuan untuk Kemanusiaan/Women's Volunteers for Humanities). While these organizations focused mainly on human rights violations during the military conflict between GAM and the Indonesian army, MISPI concentrated on broader issues of women's empowerment and policy.

ture was a significant contributing factor to the discrimination against women in Aceh. In one of the initial attempts to support women's political participation, MISPI organized legal drafting and gender awareness workshops for policy makers at district and provincial levels. The significance of MISPI's work with JPUK became apparent during several events. First, JPUK played a significant role during the process of drafting the *qanun* on the election of local leaders in 2005, by demanding that the word *perempuan* or 'women' be deliberately mentioned. The draft *qanun* used only non-gender specific words (*setiap orang*, everyone) which JPUK considered as too vague, and therefore it demanded the article to deliberately mention both women and men (*perempuan dan laki-laki*) (Afrianty 2011, 48). Eventually this became Qanun No. 7/2006 on the Election of Local Leaders. The JPUK further demanded that the requirement for local political parties to have a female membership of at least 30 percent would be guaranteed in the Law on Governing Aceh (LOGA/Law No. 11/2006). The demand was met and currently local political parties are obliged to meet this requirement. JPUK also played a role in the preparation of the drafting of a by-law on women's empowerment and the protection of children, which resulted in Qanun No. 5/2007 as well as the creation of the Bureau of Women's Empowerment and the Protection of Children in 2008. The fact that these measures were successfully integrated into the legislation is evidence of the accomplishments of MISPI and its networks in promoting women's rights in the province.

Until 2009, MISPI's office was located at Banda Aceh's central roundabout (Simpang Lima), at a walking distance from the landmark Baiturrahman Grand Mosque and close to the central market of Banda Aceh. Its previous office had been destroyed by the tsunami. At the time, MISPI employed seven professional staff members. Three of them performed administrative functions, while three others were responsible for running MISPI's programs. One staff member was a lawyer who provided legal aid and advice to women who were seeking justice. MISPI also employed four part-time staff members who provided litigation advice and support for women facing legal problems. Most of the staff at MISPI had undergraduate degrees in law. Some were graduates of the Law Faculty of Syiah Kuala University, and some of the Shari'a (Islamic law) Faculty of IAIN Ar-Raniry. At that time, MISPI experienced steady growth in its professional capacity, and compared to other local women's organizations it employed more local volunteers and professional staff.

Consistent with MISPI's KOHATI-HMI background, the atmosphere of its office and its routine activities were infused with an air of Islamic piety. All staff members performed the mandatory prayers. Like most other Acehnese women, they dressed in a modest Muslim fashion—wearing a skirt, blouse, tunic, and headscarf (*jilbab*). MISPI officers were aware that their choice of dress could affect their organization's reputation, especially since they regularly worked with religiously conservative people in Acehnese society, such as the ulama and the *dayah* community (the traditional Islamic educational institutions over which the ulama preside).

During my fieldwork, public discussions of Shari'a often focused on the need for women to cover their bodies, referring to specific regional regulations (*qanun*) related to acceptable forms of modest dress. The dominant discourse was that good women were those who wore proper Muslim dress and covered their hair. Therefore, a failure to dress properly could make it difficult for MISPI to engage with their intended constituencies and collaborators. According to Syarifah, while advocating for the needs of Muslims in Aceh, her team should maintain an image of wearing what she considered 'proper' Muslim dress and head covering. This, she argued, meant that they should not just drape a shawl over their shoulders without covering their hair, because this was something the 'Shari'a Police' (Wilayatul Hisbah/WH) would disapprove of. One staff member told me that Syarifah often spoke with staff members who did not wear proper Muslim dress. This attention to proper ways of dressing was not merely a 'strategic' choice on the part of MISPI. It also reflected Syarifah's personal and professional view. The strict adherence to Muslim dress set her apart from most other women activists at that time.

It was in this particular context that MISPI carried out its work of advocating women's rights. Before I move on to discuss some of MISPI's activities in advocating the reform of Shari'a implementation, I would like to briefly elaborate on the implementation of Islamic law itself and the women's movement's response to this process.

The Implementation of Islamic Law and Women Activists' Responses

The major players in the development of Aceh's state Shari'a system have been the ulama and the provincial government. Since 1999, several bylaws have been implemented that aim to enforce Islamic law. Two of these, namely Qanun No. 11/2002 that regulates (among other things) Muslim dress, and No. 14/2003 on *khalwat* or close proximity between unrelated members of the opposite sex, have been of particular concern among many Acehnese activists. The activists especially resented the discriminatory ways in which these regulations have been applied, as enforcement has primarily targeted women and the poor. Article 1 (20) of Qanun No. 14/2003 defines *khalwat* as: "Any activity carried out by two or more individuals of opposite sex who are not related by family nor legally bound under marriage."

Ever since this *qanun* has been enacted, there have been stories of couples apprehended by the WH and/or attacked by vigilantes for being in close proximity or for having sexual relations outside marriage (see Otto and Otto, this volume). At the time of my research, stories about couples caught being in close proximity and accused of violating the *qanun* and community standards of Shari'a morality, often reached the headlines of local newspapers (see, e.g., Heryanto 2008). In both urban and rural areas across Aceh, different kinds of people, including villagers, students, government officials and even members of the local legislature were accused of offenses against modesty and sexual immorality.

Khalwat is most generally understood as illicit relations outside marriage. The reality in Aceh is that *khalwat* is interpreted to mean anything from sexual activities outside marriage to a situation where a man and a woman who are not kin are in close proximity, whether in public or private space. Some of the violators of this particular *qanun* have been tried and punished by caning, but in other cases, perpetrators have managed to negotiate with the authorities to effect a different outcome. Most often, cases are not brought to court at all, but settled more informally by the community (often after calling in family members and sometimes after publication of the couple's names and pictures in the newspaper) according to custom (*adat*), which can cover a wide range of responses, from reprimand to violence and public shaming (see Feener 2013, 219–250; Kloos 2014; Otto and Otto, this volume). In the case of unmarried couples, religious leaders often encourage their parents to have them married. However, there have also been cases in which couples caught by villagers have been paraded through the village to humiliate them in public. This practice is believed to be a form of punishment as they will feel humiliated (see Kloos 2014).

Despite particular definitions of *khalwat*, there is an ongoing discussion and contestation in Aceh about what behaviour exactly falls under *khalwat* and *zina* (fornication). During my research, many people in Aceh felt that the laws discriminated against the poor. For example, they would say that an Acehnese man and woman riding a motorbike together could become an easy target of the WH, while a man and woman who sit in the car probably would not be harassed or get caught. The head of the WH field office in Banda Aceh explained this discrepancy to me in a way that had less to do with relative wealth but more with the interpretation of the categories of *khalwat* and *zina*. He said that when a man and a woman ride together on a motorbike, with the woman sitting on the back of the bike with her arms around his waist, they could easily commit *zina* (illicit sexual activities outside of marriage) as their bodies touch.[5] He further explained that when two people of the opposite sex are in physical contact they could easily fall under the influence of the devil (*syaitan*) and commit unlawful acts of fornication (*zina*). Therefore, men and women sitting together on a motorbike may be considered by the WH as committing *khalwat*, a state in which they may be tempted to commit sins. On the other hand, the head of the WH said that those who were sitting together inside a car were not considered as engaging in behaviour tempted by *syaitan* because there is no physical closeness. The issue advanced by critics of the law, then, was that it was easier to target poor people (using motorcycles) than rich people (driving cars).

Another controversial regulation is Qanun No. 11/2002, which regulates, among other things, specific standards of modest Muslim dress and the mandatory attendance of Friday communal prayer for men.[6] When I visited the WH office in Banda Aceh in 2009, I was shown a list of 593 incidents in 2006 and 2,034 incidents in 2007, in the district of Banda Aceh alone. Although there are no reports of women who have been caned for failing to comply with Qanun No. 11/2002 on Muslim dress, activists consider this *qanun* to be the most unpopular of the Shariʿa regulations. For an important part, this has to do with the raids carried out by the WH in the streets of Banda Aceh and near the beach, during which alleged wrongdoers (most of whom are women) are lectured in public.

Activists and women's NGOs voiced their concerns to the ulama, the legislature, and the local government, and took care to thereby work within the Islamic framework. To do so, they faced the challenge of combining Islamic teachings and Aceh's cultural values with international norms, in particular women's rights. Many of the Acehnese women I talked to viewed the official definition of modest Muslim dress, and in particular the mandated form of head covering (*jilbab*), as something that was actually rather new to Aceh.

---

5 Interview, Banda Aceh, 9 July 2009.

6 According to officials at the WH and the State Shariʿa Agency (Dinas Syariat Islam/DSI), women must cover their hair by wearing a certain kind of veiling popularly known as *jilbab*. The rest of their dress should consist of a long skirt and a loose dress or tunic or a type of *baju kurung* that will not show a woman's 'body shape.' Hence, the WH consider women who wear tight pants, jeans and t-shirts as violating the *qanun* on Muslim dress. In terms of formal legislation, Article 13 (1) provides that: "All Muslims are obliged to wear Islamic dress" (defined as "clothes that cover one's *aurat* and may not shine through, and which do not show the shape of the body") and article 21 (1) stipulates an obligation for men to perform the Friday prayer.

Some even claimed that the *jilbab* is an 'Arabic' way of covering the hair of women, arguing that in their understanding it is enough for women to just cover their hair with a shawl.[7] Syarifah and many of the activists at MISPI shared these views, saying that while in the past Acehnese women already dressed modestly and covered their heads, they did so in a variety of local styles. Thus, wearing a traditional *selendang* (scarf or thin veil) to cover one's hair and wearing trousers was considered appropriate for women.

Such forms of Islamic dress can be seen in popular images of historical figures. Siapno (2002, 26) observed that the most popular representation of Cut Nyak Dhien, an Acehnese heroine in the war against the Dutch, "portrays her wearing [...] a *selendang* (a thin veil) half-covering her head (in the Muslim fashion)." Other popular images include pictures of Aceh's seventeenth century queens, as shown in the Aceh Museum in Banda Aceh, wearing only a *selendang* or a shawl draped loosely over the head and shoulders. While, as Siapno notes, many of these images are idealized, we know that, traditionally, Acehnese women wore "black trousers called *luweu tham asee* or 'dog chasing trousers'" with a traditional loose type of long sleeve top that goes to the knees (Siapno 2002, 26). This tradition can still be seen in wedding rituals as brides often wear trousers as part of their traditional wedding costumes. One reason for this type of clothing is that Acehnese women have always worked their paddy field together with their husbands, or performed other jobs that require them to move easily. Syarifah explained that the way Qanun No. 11/2002 has been enforced, therefore, has changed the meaning of appropriate women's clothing and head covering, which, to her, differed in many ways from past cultural practices.

Many women's activists argued that the specific text of the *qanun* was problematic. According to Soraya Devy,[8] the explanation in the *qanun* about covering one's *aurat* and concealing the shape of the body was confusing. How, for example, could women be sure that their body shapes would not be visible if their clothes were pushed by the wind? Other arguments focused on women's freedom of movement. In the post-conflict context, women in Aceh have enjoyed greater mobility. Yet according to many activists, the sort of clothing the WH officials envisioned as in keeping with state Shari'a regulations would only limit their movements. They argued that forcing women to always wear skirts would be difficult, because motorbikes are one of the main forms of transportation for women in Aceh. As one of my interlocutors told me, "wear-

7 Interview, Suraiya Kamaruzzaman, Banda Aceh, 24 December 2007.

8 Interview, Banda Aceh, 5 March 2007.

ing long and big skirts on motorbikes is not only ineffective but most of all it is not safe, as the skirts can get caught in the bike's machinery."[9] Interestingly, in other Muslim societies, Muslim dress and especially head covering is often seen as enabling women's mobility rather than restricting it. This difference exemplifies the local variety of understandings of Shari'a and the effects of its implementation on local gender relations.

Although the phrase 'Muslim clothing' in the *qanun* pertains to both men and women, during my fieldwork public discussions of 'Muslim clothing' mainly focused on women's dress. This might be because, at the time, the WH did not focus on men's clothing in their raids. Activists and female students in Banda Aceh thus asked why men who wore short pants were not targeted by the WH, even though the *qanun* requires men to cover their *aurat* by wearing trousers that cover their knees. There were lots of jokes circulating among activists and in society at large addressing the question of what the appropriate uniform for Aceh's male soccer team would be if they were required to be consistent with the *qanun*.

According to women activists, Qanun No. 11/2002 on Muslim dress has been used by some conservative Acehnese men to justify their control over women's dress and bodies. Some male students from traditional *pesantren* or *dayah*, for example, believe that they have the right to check on women's clothing, and to approve or condemn it. Authorities such as security guards at mosques judge a woman's religiosity from her dress. For example, when I visited the Baiturrahman mosque on 30 January 2008, a male guard stopped me and my female Acehnese friend from entering through the gate by pointing his rattan cane to my knee. He did not say anything but instead waved his cane to me, moving it up and down, indicating that my loose tunic blouse should have covered my knees. Although I told him that I brought my prayer clothing, he insisted that I should leave the mosque.

Such examples of enforcing Islamic law have made women activists argue that the religious *qanun* and their implementation provided opportunities for conservative religious leaders to return society, and women in particular, to patriarchal interpretations of Islam. They showed that the way in which the *qanun* has been implemented has promoted authoritarian control over what women wear, how women behave, and how women observe their religion more than it has for Acehnese men. Finally, apart from the discriminatory implementation of these *qanuns*, MISPI was highly concerned about the corporal punishment of caning, which has been practiced in Aceh since

9 Interview, Banda Aceh, 20 March 2007.

2006, and which, along with other civil society organizations, it considered to be a violation of human rights.[10]

Another target of MISPI's criticisms was the WH. Like many other NGOs in Aceh, it has called attention to what it perceives as the WH's lack of adequate knowledge of Islamic law and current legislation, as well as of proper professional training—leading to incidents in which basic rights were violated (Afrianty 2015). Women's activists told me that, as a result of this, in the initial years of implementation there had been cases in which WH officers cut women's hair if they did not wear proper headscarves, as they did not know the proper procedures of handling such cases. More recently, WH officers have been accused of even more serious abuse. In January 2010, three officers in the district of Langsa raped a woman they caught and detained in their office for a *khalwat* offense (Mardira 2010). It has been argued that the lack of support from the local government for the work of the WH, including the poor recruitment process, has contributed to their poor performance and flawed legitimacy (Feener 2013, Otto and Otto, this volume). It is not only the work of the WH that shapes public perceptions of Shari'a implementation in Aceh, however. The sometimes brutal punishments under *adat* (customary law) also influence popular and media perceptions of the enforcement of Islamic law in contemporary Aceh. As Kloos (2014) points out, these village level outbreaks of vigilante violence "in the name of Shari'a" are indicative of the deeply contested nature of moral and political authority in contemporary Aceh.

In negotiating the combination of these sets of norms and values, some organizations have followed the example of women's movements in other Muslim societies, such as Sisters in Islam (SIS) in Malaysia and Fahmina Institute in Cirebon, West Java, that have promoted the rereading and interpretation of Islamic texts to further equality. As I will show in the next section, translocal and transnational connections have also been important for MISPI, which has framed its strategies to reform the *qanun* and to demand justice in the implementation of Islamic law in part through its networking with national and international NGOs such as UNIFEM and The Asia Foundation. Thus, I will argue that the activities of MISPI cannot be seen apart from developments at the national level and in other parts of the Muslim world.

10 On the specifics of the implementation of caning, see Feener (2013; this volume) and Großmann (this volume).

MISPI and the Reform of Islamic Law

As I have argued in the previous sections, MISPI was one of the organizations that tried to influence government policies relating to women. According to Syarifah, the problems and disputes that emerged upon the implementation of Islamic law were the result of a number of factors. Firstly, there are different perspectives among the Acehnese on how the primary sources of Islamic law (the Qur'an and the Sunna) should be interpreted and translated to specific *qanun*. Secondly, *qanun* that regulate Acehnese religiosity are almost exclusively based on the interpretation of those sources by male political leaders, legal authorities and the ulama whom she views as having been insufficiently sensitive to gender issues.[11] Thirdly, the implementation of the *qanun* has not been adequately supported by effective government institutions.[12]

Against this background, MISPI has offered several approaches to address the shortcomings in the implementation of Shari'a law. Firstly, MISPI argued that there was a serious need for Acehnese ulama, academics, policy makers, and civil society activists to go back to the sources of Islamic law, to reread and reinterpret Shari'a in the context of Aceh, and to use democratic means in drafting the law. According to MISPI, in this process of rereading the Islamic texts, women should be included, so that women from all segments of society would come to have a better understanding of the message of the Qur'an. MISPI expected that these approaches would generate a new form of religious interpretation, which later could be formalized into *qanun* that would be more gender-sensitive and promote justice and equality. Secondly, although at the time of my research the implementation of Islamic law was still in an early stage, MISPI argued that the government had to support the implementation of Shari'a by providing adequate facilities and resources to the institutions responsible for overseeing the implementation.

To reach these goals MISPI employed various strategies. For example, Syarifah, in her capacity as MISPI leader and prominent women's rights activist, was regularly invited by the local legislature to sit in on their meetings. In those meetings, she advocated the need for reformulation of the *qanun* among local members of the local legislature and government bureaucrats. MISPI emphasized the importance for women activists to work with religious communities, most importantly with the *dayah* and the ulama, in particular the female

11 An exception concerns the initial drafting of the *Qanun Jinayat*, in which women were included (Großmann, this volume).

12 Interview, 8 March 2007.

ulama, and with academics. One key strategy concerned the rereading of the sources of Islamic law to uncover the egalitarian messages of Islam that MISPI members saw as contained in the Qur'an and the Sunna. In carrying out its programs, MISPI worked together with both national and international partners. While advocating the importance of considering local context, MISPI also acknowledged the need for women's NGOs and women activists to collaborate with Muslim intellectuals.

As I have explained, maintaining Islamic credentials and solidarity with the local community has been one of the key means utilized by MISPI in pursuit of its agenda of responding to the implementation of Islamic law. Even though Syarifah disagreed with the way in which Qanun No. 11/2002 on Muslim dress was enforced, she chose to adhere to the regulations of the WH (see below). It is important to point out, however, that this appeal to Islam was not merely a 'strategy' to advance women's interests. The HMI background of MISPI as well as Syarifah's personal views attest to a strong commitment to an Islamic way of life as well as to the implementation of Shari'a in Aceh. What makes the case of MISPI so interesting, is exactly that it is from within this Islamic framework that the organization tried to advocate women's rights. MISPI's Islamic credentials proved important in gaining support from the male-dominated government institutions and the ulama. Syarifah explained that she could call key people in these institutions and discuss any issue with them and she expected that this would enable her to influence legal reform and policy-making. Indeed, while ulama and members of the local legislature often saw other activists as being corrupted by foreign influences, some of them told me that they would rather listen to Syarifah's views on issues pertaining to women and Shari'a (Afrianty 2015).

One of MISPI's central goals was to raise awareness of what it understood to be Islam's teachings on gender equality. Before giving some examples of the activities that MISPI was involved in, it is important to clarify MISPI's views in relation to gender equality, for its position shows a complex navigation of values inspired by Islam, feminism and gender equality discourses. Interestingly, MISPI activists tried to avoid using the term 'gender equality' (I. *kesetaraan gender*) in disseminating its ideas about equality to women's Qur'anic reading groups. Instead, they used the Indonesian phrase 'relational equality between men and women' (*kesetaraan hubungan antara laki-laki dan perempuan*) and stressed that this was mainly about 'relations' (*hubungan*) of equality. MISPI activists were careful with these phrases because they were aware that female members of Qur'anic reading groups might be suspicious of, or even hostile to, foreign terms. In fact, ulama and government officials were also hostile toward the term 'gender equality' (Afrianty 2015). MISPI was careful not to make the

Qur'anic reading groups feel that they were being taught 'foreign' values. To many Acehnese women, the word '*kesetaraan*' or 'equality' implies a situation in which men and women become the same, so that women, for example, must be able to do men's jobs and vice versa. Such a position is considered highly problematic since it is opposed to deeply-held notions that the woman is tasked to be a wife, daughter, and mother, while men must be husbands, fathers, and brothers.

To deal with this sensitive issue, MISPI carefully explained that while Islam requires women to fulfill particular social roles, it does not prohibit them from doing other things outside the home, such as obtaining an education and working. To underscore this, MISPI made references to the lives of the Prophet's wives, such as Khadija, who was a successful businesswoman, and Aishah, who led the Muslim forces to war and became an important political figure after the death of the Prophet. As a result, it is argued, women actually carry a burden that is heavier than that of men, because if they take up public roles they are also still responsible for the care for their children and husband. In explaining this to their female audiences, Syarifah used herself as an example of someone brought up in a family where she was allowed to be active outside the home, while at the same time learning to be responsible for the household. As women activists at MISPI refer to the Qur'an for arguments that support gender equality, it is clear that they engage to some extent with Islamic feminist discourses. However, MISPI activists themselves are reluctant to acknowledge that their activism is inspired by 'feminism,' as they consider this a foreign concept. The reluctance to acknowledge that their work is inspired by feminism can be understood as a part of a broader Acehnese resistance to ideas coming from the West.

In their efforts to reach Acehnese women, MISPI activists specifically targeted groups at two levels: women policy-makers (such as female members of the local legislature, women in the bureaucracy, female academics, and female ulama), and women at the grassroots level, whose voices are rarely heard by policy-makers. Apart from advocating an Islam-inspired view of gender equality among these women, Syarifah also hoped that MISPI's program would create links between these two groups. This was important, she argued, because existing democratic mechanisms had not been able to bring these two elements of society together, thus contributing to the failure of the government to produce gender-sensitive policies. MISPI organized two programs; one for women in villages and another for female Islamic leaders who regularly attended workshops at MISPI's office or other locations.

For women at the grassroots, MISPI developed a program through which they could gain a better understanding of the Qur'an and the Sunna. MISPI sought out women who were members of Qur'anic reading groups or *majelis taklim*, since these groups were considered to have strong bases in the villages. MISPI hoped that, once *majelis taklim* members were introduced to issues of equality and women's rights, they would then share these understandings with their family members and broader society. MISPI focused on Qur'anic reading groups in Banda Aceh and its surrounding areas. Syarifah explained that the decision to work with women's Qur'anic reading groups was based on MISPI's perception that these groups were widely considered to be apolitical.[13] In most of the villages where MISPI worked, *majelis taklim* were held on a weekly basis, with attendees listening to a female preacher and reciting the Qur'an. In these sessions, MISPI introduced interpretations of the Qur'an and Sunna that highlight messages of gender justice.

The second program was for leaders of *majelis taklim*, who regularly participated in meetings organized by MISPI. These meetings took place in different places. Sometimes they were organized at MISPI's office or at one of the *majelis taklim* around Banda Aceh. Shariʿa was explained in these meetings as a divine teaching derived from the Qur'an and the Sunna. At one of the workshops I attended, on 8 March 2007, one of the speakers argued that since Shariʿa is divine law, it cannot limit women's freedom. This view was based on readings of particular verses of the Qur'an that emphasize the equality of men and women, in particular verse 2:228, which reads "… and women have the rights similar to those against them in a just manner." At this occasion, another verse was quoted, which emphasizes that God created men and women of different nations, but what differentiates them is only their good deeds for God, as written in the Qur'an (49:13).

> Oh human kind, We created you from male and female and made you into nations and tribes so that you might know one another. Verily the most noble of you in the sight of God is the one with the most *taqwa*.[14]

During the meetings, participants of the women's Qur'anic reading groups also learned that God's revelation in the form of the Qur'an and the Sunna has been interpreted by ulama in their works of jurisprudence (*fiqh*).

At one point during my fieldwork, in 2008, MISPI organized a training session for *majelis taklim* leaders from around Banda Aceh and Aceh Besar, which

13 Indeed during the conflict, these groups had proved to be relatively safe from both warring parties, being able to continue regular meetings at local *meunasah* or village mosques.

14 This verse is quoted from Wadud (1999). *Taqwa* is a key Qur'anic term that refers to a person's moral integrity and commitment to the teachings of Islam (Wadud 1999).

was meant to help female members of *majelis taklim* better understand Islamic scripture and Shariʿa as well as *fiqh* and the *qanun*. The material of this training covered several themes, such as the meaning of the verses in the Qur'an, preaching ethics (*akhlak*) within the family, understanding Islamic texts, Shariʿa, and *fiqh*, and a discussion on women's and men's roles in family, as well as in society at large. More than 20 women from different *majelis taklim*, as well as the leaders of the women's wings of Muhammadiyah and Nahdhlatul Ulama, participated in this event. Speakers included Nurjannah Ismail, a respected female lecturer of the Shariʿa Faculty at IAIN in Aceh who has extensive knowledge of the subject of Islamic law and gender, and Roosmawardani, a female judge working for an Islamic Court (Mahkamah Syariah). There were also male leaders speaking at the event, most importantly the leader of the Ulama Consultative Assembly (Majelis Permusyawaratan Ulama/MPU).

MISPI considered *fiqh* to be a topic that needed to be better understood by women at the grassroots. In this meeting for *majelis taklim* members and leaders, Nurjannah Ismail argued that women should understand that if there is discrimination and oppression of women, this is not the result of Islam, but of patriarchal interpretations of Shariʿa that can and must be challenged. She also mentioned that most of the problems with discrimination and oppression related to the fact that the ulama who interpret Shariʿa are mostly men. She pointed out that throughout history, the work of interpreting the Qur'an and hadith has been dominated by men. Yet, she said, Aisha, the Prophet Muhammad's youngest wife, was an important transmitter of *hadith*. Thus, in her contribution to the training, she was saying that the interpretation of Islamic law had to some extent neglected women's interests.[15]

Having identified Qur'anic teachings about the basic equality of men and women, and the question of how to understand Shariʿa and *fiqh*, female *majelis taklim* leaders were subsequently taught about the process of creating *qanun* in Aceh. This was important because the general understanding among Acehnese was that the *qanun* are the same as what is written in Islamic texts, including the Qur'an and *hadith*. Thus, it was explained that, unlike Shariʿa, *qanun* can always be changed because they are not divine law but rather interpretations of Islamic law made by Acehnese ulama, political leaders and the government.

---

15 Her discussion at that training was similar to the explanation of scholars such as Ziba Mir-Hosseini (2006, 632): *Fiqh* is the science of jurisprudence which is part of the human endeavor to discern and extract legal rules from the sacred sources of Islam that include the Qur'an and the *Sunna*. If Shariʿa is sacred, universal and eternal, *fiqh* is "human and like any other jurisprudence it may change over time" (Mir-Hosseini 2006, 632).

To emphasize this last point, a session in the *majelis taklim* gatherings led by MISPI was dedicated to explaining how the *qanun* were drafted and ratified.

The training discussed above equipped Acehnese women not only with religious knowledge but also with knowledge about the relationship between Shari'a implementation and local politics in Aceh. The important positions of the speakers in Acehnese politics show MISPI's attention to the political context in which Shari'a implementation took place. It also shows that MISPI worked together with government institutions, despite its criticisms of them, and that at least some elements in these institutions shared with MISPI particular goals in terms of educating women.

Through the grassroots activities and the workshops for *majelis taklim* leaders, MISPI not only provided opportunities to women from Qur'anic reading groups to obtain new knowledge, but also encouraged them to interact with other women in a new environment. Most importantly, women were taught how to express their own perspectives, and to raise their voices in a forum, even on occasions where men were also present. MISPI taught the female participants about the need to be critical of the constructed social values that were produced by male patriarchal authorities. While this was done by a range of NGOs that were active in Aceh at the time, what made MISPI special was its particular emphasis on the Islamic framework in which all these activities were situated.

Conclusion

In response to the implementation of Islamic law, women's organizations in Aceh have demanded that regional regulations (*qanun*) be reformed to become more sensitive to gender concerns and the specific cultural contexts of Aceh. In their efforts to promote equality and women's rights, MISPI has worked within, not outside of, an Islamic framework. The organization has been highly critical of the way in which Shari'a law has been enforced. Yet, instead of opposing the authorities, it managed to work closely with government institutions such as the State Shari'a Agency, the Islamic Court system (Mahkamah Syariah), and the provincial legislature in advocating the reform of the *qanuns* that deal with Islamic law, so as to stop discrimination against women and the poor. In addition to their advocacy with government institutions, MISPI has engaged with local communities to increase their understanding of the teaching of Islam and the Islamic texts that are at the basis of Shari'a law in Aceh. Working with these different groups in society, those with political and religious authority and the people whose lives would be most strongly affected by the implementation of Shariʿa, MISPI tried to influence processes of policy-making that related to Islamic law. It did so by advocating the need for the reinterpretation of Islamic texts and doctrines.

From MISPI's work, it is clear that Acehnese women have created a space to involve themselves in discussions of what Feener (2013) calls "Shariʿa and social engineering." Women activists, including those at MISPI, invited both society and the government to engage in a discussion on the question of how Shariʿa should be implemented in Aceh. More importantly, this movement was to a large extent enabled through the work of national and international organizations working in Aceh during the post-tsunami reconstruction period.

In this chapter, I have given an overview of the ways in which one particular organization, MISPI, responded to and acted upon the implementation of Shariʿa in Aceh. The material presented here shows that MISPI was distinctive in three fields. First of all, in its activities it brought in considerations of local history and culture. Given its Islamic background and good relations to a wide range of prominent people and institutions in local politics and bureaucracies, MISPI was able to bring together women from various backgrounds and influence policy makers on different levels. Secondly, apart from having this strong local base, MISPI managed to appeal to broader national and international norms and networks in support of its causes. This was in part fostered by the influx of funds and international organizations after the tsunami. Yet, as I have argued in this chapter, MISPI's networks also had strong pre-tsunami roots. Finally, while advocating for change, MISPI was also involved in a close collaboration with the Indonesian state and with national-level Islamic organizations such as HMI. Its Indonesian nationalist roots as well as its Islamic background made MISPI stand out in a landscape of organizations that were perceived of as being sympathetic to the Free Aceh Movement (GAM).

MISPI collaborated with the state, even while criticizing some of its policies. The organization argued for the implementation of Shariʿa in Aceh but demanded reforms that would guarantee women's rights and more equality between men and women, as well as between rich and poor, in the implementation of the law. As a civil society organization engaged with local women at the grassroots level as well as with important figures in Acehnese society, MISPI worked both with the state and outside its limits. Therefore, MISPI gives us another view on the roles of civil society in demarcating the 'limits of the state' in the implementation of Shariʿa in Aceh. Its advocacy of the reconciliation of Shariʿa and women's rights, and the appeals it made to various sectors of state and society to reach these goals, demonstrate that these limits are fluid, contested and negotiated by civil society actors like Syarifah and her organization.

References

Afrianty, Dina. 2011. "Local Women's Movement in Aceh and the Struggle for Equality and Justice: The Women's Network for Policy." *Review of Indonesia and Malaysia Affairs* 45(1/2):37–68.

———. 2015. *Women and Sharia Law in Northern Indonesia: Local Women's NGOs and the Reform of Islamic Law in Aceh.* Abingdon and New York: Routledge.

Aspinall, Edward. 2007. "From Islamism to Nationalism in Aceh, Indonesia." *Nations and Nationalism* 3(2):245–263.

Azra, Azyumardi. 2004. "Political Islam in Post-Suharto Indonesia." In *Islamic Perspectives on the New Millennium*, edited by Virginia Hooker and Amin Saikal, 133–149. Singapore: Institute of Southeast Asian Studies.

Bertrand, Jacques. 2004. *Nationalism and Ethnic Conflict in Indonesia.* Cambridge: Cambridge University Press.

Daly, Patrick, Michael Feener and Anthony Reid (eds.). 2012. *From the Ground up: Perspectives on Post-Tsunami and Post-Conflict Aceh.* Singapore: ISEAS.

Feener, R. Michael. 2007. *Muslim Legal Thought in Modern Indonesia.* Cambridge, UK: Cambridge University Press.

———. 2013. *Shari'a and Social Engineering: the Implementation of Islamic Law in Contemporary Aceh.* Oxford: Oxford University Press.

Hefner, Robert. 1993. "Islam, State and Civil Society: ICMI and the Struggle for the Indonesian Middle Class." *Indonesia* 56:1–35.

———. 1997. "Islamization and Democratization in Indonesia." In *Islam in an Era of Nation-States: Politics and Religious Renewal in Muslim Southeast Asia*, edited by Robert W. Hefner and Patricia Horvatich, 75–128. Honolulu: University of Hawai'i Press.

Heryanto, Dadang. 2008. "Sekali Lagi, Cerita Khalwat di Negeri Syariat." *Modus Aceh.* May, No. 6, http://www.modusaceh-news.com (Accessed 24 June 2008).

Kloos, David. 2014. "In the Name of *Syariah*? Vigilante Violence, Territoriality, and Moral Authority in Aceh, Indonesia." *Indonesia* 98:59–90.

Mardira, Salman. 2010. "WH Melanggar, Hukumannya Harus Lebih Berat." *Aceh Kita*, 14 January http://www.acehkita.com/berita/wh-melanggar-hukumannya-harus-lebih-berat (Accessed 19 November 2013).

Miller, Michelle Ann. 2004. *Rebellion and Reform in Indonesia: Jakarta's Security and Autonomy Polices in Aceh.* London and New York: Routledge.

Mir-Hosseini, Ziba. 2006. "Muslim Women's Quest for Equality: Between Islamic Law and Feminism." *Critical Inquiry* 32:629–645.

Mukhtar, Sidratahta. 2006. *HMI dan Kekuasaaan.* Jakarta: Prestasi Pustaka Publisher.

Pasandaran, Camelia. 2013. "North Aceh Head Bans Women from Dancing in Public." *The Jakarta Globe*, 26 May.

Ricklefs, M.C. 2001. *A History of Modern Indonesia Since* c. *1200*. Third Edition. Stanford: Stanford University Press.

Saragih, BT and Hotli Simanjuntak. 2013. "Aceh City to Ban Women from Straddling Motorbikes." *The Jakarta Post*, 30 January.

Siapno, Jacqueline A. 2002. *Gender, Islam, Nationalism and the State in Aceh: The Paradox of Power, Co-optation and Resistance*. London: Routledge.

Siegel, James T. 2000. *The Rope of God*. Ann Arbor, MI: The University of Michigan Press.

Wadud, Amina. 1999. *Rereading the Sacred Text from a Woman's Perspective*. New York: Oxford University Press.

CHAPTER 6

Teungku Inong Dayah: Female Religious Leaders in Contemporary Aceh

*Eka Srimulyani**

This chapter focuses on female ulama in Aceh, known locally as *teungku inongs*.[1] I will concentrate in particular on *teungku inongs* of traditional Islamic educational institutions, known as *dayah*. In this chapter, I argue that, even though there are relatively few female ulama (as compared to their male counterparts), their roles as social agents and religious authorities are significant in the broader constellation of Islam in contemporary Aceh. Apart from being influential religious leaders within their local communities, some of these female ulama are also active in broader areas of social life. This chapter is based on several stories of *teungku inongs* from different areas in Aceh. The discussion of these figures will be organized around the major bases of their authority, either through their ties of kinship to a male religious figure or on the basis of their own personal and professional accomplishments. I will analyse these two ways of assuming authority in terms of 'ascribed power' and 'achieved power,' respectively.

In Java, most *nyais* (wives or daughters of the *pesantren* leader, *kiai*) in traditional *pesantrens* have historically come from the immediate families of a *kiai* (see Srimulyani 2009) and have therefore assumed authority through the 'ascribed power' of kinship. However, according to my observations, the *teungku inong dayahs* in Aceh have more diverse ways of assuming authority and asserting agency. While some of these female religious leaders come from established families of *dayah* teachers, others have established themselves through the initiative of founding and leading their own *dayah*.[2] The

* The data presented in this chapter were gathered during my postdoctoral research project that was funded by the Royal Academy of Arts and Sciences, The Netherlands (2010–2012). I would like to thank Sehat Ihsan Shadiqin for assisting me with the interviews and transcribing some interview data.

1 The word '*inong*' in Acehnese means woman, or wife.

2 Comparable to the institution of *pesantren* in Java, the *dayah* constitutes the main model of traditional Islamic education in Aceh. I will use the term *pesantren* when referring to the national or Javanese context, while for Aceh I will use the term *dayah*.

 | DOI: 10.1163/9789004304864_007

different ways in which these female ulama assume authority reveal significant aspects of the diverse processes informing the construction of female religious authority in the context of Acehnese Islam.

Although recent research has increasingly focused on the position of Muslim women in Indonesia, as yet little attention has been paid to the specific roles of female ulama. Traditional forms of Islamic historiography rarely deal with female religious leaders, and this general trend is also reflected in many works on Indonesian ulama (Azra 2002, xxi–xxxviii). In 2002, the Indonesian publisher Pustaka Gramedia Utama issued a book titled *Ulama Perempuan Indonesia* (Indonesian Female Ulama), which was edited by Jajat Burhanudin (Burhanudin 2002). The qualifications that the editor of this book used to select female ulama are, however, problematic and several female ulama, such as Nyai Khoiriyah, who should have been included, are not mentioned in the book (Srimulyani 2008, 126).[3] Since 2004, The State Institute for Islamic Studies (IAIN, presently UIN) Ar-Raniry has published two volumes of the *Ensiklopedi Pemikiran Ulama Aceh*, but together they also contain entries for only two women. One of them was Tgk. Fakinah,[4] who was a *dayah* leader herself and who is regarded as an Acehnese heroine, for her role in the armed struggle against the Dutch at the end of the nineteenth Aceh. However, the roles of other female ulama associated with *dayahs* in Aceh, such as Umi Rabi'ah from Dayah Darussalam Aceh Selatan, were left unrecognized in these volumes. Similarly, organizations of *dayah* ulama, such as Inshafuddin or HUDA (Himpunan Ulama Dayah Aceh), have very few female members, let alone women in leadership positions.

This chapter is based on field research I conducted in Aceh between 2010 and 2012. The *teungku inongs* discussed in this chapter come from different areas in Aceh and from different social backgrounds. Some of them are immediate family members of a *dayah* leader, whereas others are from non-*dayah* families. I conducted interviews with them in their hometowns, or when they visited

3 Nyai Khoiriyah is the daughter of Kiai Hasyim Asya'ary of Pesantren Tebu Ireng, Jombang (East Java). She lived for almost 20 years in Mecca from 1938–1957. In my interviews with some *pesantren* leaders (or *kiai*) in Jombang, including the late Kiai Yusuf Hasyim (Pak Ud) who was the leader of Pesantren Tebuireng, she was recognised as a learned ulama. She herself was a leader of Pesantren Seblak, and a member or Majelis Syuriah of the national organization Nahdlatul Ulama (PBNU).

4 Tengku Fakinah was both a heroine of anti-colonial resistance and an Islamic scholar. She had several female pupils, such as Teungku Fathimah Batee Linteung, Teungku Sa'idah Lamjame, Teungku Fathimah Ulee Tutue, and Teungku Hawa Lamdilip. See Mardhiah Aly (1980).

Banda Aceh. By exploring their life stories, I aim to draw attention to the ways in which they established their authority. In the next section, I will explore the sociological and historical contexts of women in *dayah* education. This is followed by stories of some female *dayah* leaders from the field, and discussions of their agency and authority. The last part of the chapter focuses on their perception of women's issues, particularly within the context of Aceh's contemporary state Shari'a project.

Female Ulama: Roles and Limits

In Aceh, as well as at the Indonesian national level, women make up only a small minority of the official Ulama Council. At all levels, they are thus under-represented both in terms of the organization's leadership structure and in terms of its membership. There are only a handful of female members on the Council, most of whom have a university rather than a *dayah* background and work as lecturers at the IAIN. In the district of Aceh Besar two female ulama were involved in, and invited to, the activities of the District Ulama Council. Nevertheless, only one of them remains relatively active. Walidah Marhamah, from the *dayah* in Tanoh Meurah, has become a member of the Ulama Council in the district of Bireuen. Umi Hanisah from the district of Aceh Barat is another female ulama who has taken on a public role through membership in a formal ulama *dayah* organization, namely HUDA (Himpunan Ulama Dayah Aceh).

Yet, the positions of Walidah Marhamah and Umi Hanisah are exceptional compared with the positions of other *teungku inongs* with a *dayah* background. The exact number of female ulama active in formal Islamic organizations in Aceh, such as the Ulama Council (Majelis Permusyawaratan Ulama/MPU), Inshafuddin, HUDA, or MUNA (Majelis Ulama Nanggroe Aceh),[5] is not clear. My personal estimation is that they make up less than 5 per cent of these organizations.

A number of *teungku inong*—both *dayah* leaders and those who run more simple schools known locally as *balee semeubeut*—prefer to stay outside these formal organizations and engage their respective communities more di-

5 The MPU is an official ulama organization. The rest are non-official; Inshafuddin is associated with traditionalist ulama, HUDA is the organization of ulama *dayah*, and MUNA was related to one particular local political party (Partai Aceh/PA) at the time of its establishment.

rectly.[6] There are only a few *teungku inongs* who are also leaders of *dayah*. Other *teungku inongs*, graduated from *dayah*, go on to establish *balee seumeubeut* where they teach the religious congregation, usually only women, on a regular basis. Some *balee seumeubeut* are also used by children who learn to recite the Qur'an or basic Islamic teachings. Some female students from Dayah Seulimeum in Aceh Besar whom I met and had a conversation with during my fieldwork, expressed their intention to establish a *balee seumeubeut* in their village upon their return from Dayah Seulimeum. Some of them had spent more than ten years in the *dayah*, and delivered sermons to some religious congregations around the *dayah* on a weekly basis. Furthermore, they also taught their juniors in the *dayah*.

The ulama have a long and rich history in Aceh, and their roles in relation to state power have been particularly complex since the twentieth century (Feener, this volume). In 1953, a group of modernist ulama began an armed insurgency against the political centre in Jakarta, which is generally referred to as the Darul Islam (DI) rebellion. The initial DI movement originated from West Java with the proclamation of an Indonesian Islamic State by DI's founding father, Kartosuwiryo. During the 1950s, other regional movements for the establishment of an Islamic state in Sulawesi, Kalimantan and Aceh were associated with the Darul Islam (Formichi 2012). The DI movement in Aceh was led by a former Governor of Aceh, who was also an ulama, Abu Daud Beureueh. He was the leader of the modernist organization PUSA (Persatuan Ulama Seluruh Aceh, All-Acehnese Association of Ulama). The DI movement in Aceh was one of the most serious armed conflicts in Indonesia in the post-independence years.

During Suharto's New Order regime (1965–1998), the ulama and their organizations were to some extent 'politicized' or involved in the state or the government's (political) development programs (see Feener, this volume). The official state ulama organization was established in 1965. It was originally known as MUDA (Majelis Ulama Daerah Aceh), which was later changed into MUI (Majelis Ulama Indonesia), and then MPU (Majelis Permusyawaratan Ulama). The provincial MPU organization has four women in its structure of 45 members. At the time of my research, all of those MPU women members had university backgrounds and tended toward more 'modernist' religious orientations, rather than coming out of Aceh's traditional *dayah*.

Outside these state and official organizations, most of the *dayah*-affiliated ulama in Aceh are members of *dayah*-based ulama organizations, such as

6 *Balee semeubeut* is a simple and humble place for learning. Usually it is a semi-permanent building made from wooden materials.

PERTI (Persatuan Tarbiyah Islamiyah) and Inshafuddin. Since the end of the New Order regime, new organizations have also emerged, including HUDA and MUNA. Some Acehnese ulama such as Teungku Faisal Ali, the leader of Dayah Mahyal Ulum, are also members or leaders of the national organization of ulama called NU (Nahdlatul Ulama). Junior *ulama dayahs* have a separate organization called Rabithah Thalibah Aceh (RTA). None of these organizations have many female members, and they rarely engage with programs or activities that deal with women's issues. Only the RTA, through its Muslimat division, has played a visibly active role in promoting gender equity or equality in *dayah* life and in arguing against gender-based violence. RTA took on this role especially in the post-tsunami and post-conflict years, when many donors and agencies looked for local organizations to function as partners. During those years, RTA worked with organizations such as The Asia Foundation, which supported their programs through trainings, workshops and other activities. The Asia Foundation engaged *dayahs* and *dayah* people in their programs, particularly addressing the younger generation that was familiar with foreign institutions and organizations as well as with the wider gender discourse.

The state implementation of Islamic law in twenty-first century Aceh has affected various dimensions of socio-religious life in Aceh. In the educational sector for instance, the provincial policy of '*pendidikan Islami*' (Islamic education) was introduced in 2008 through a local regulation (*qanun*) on education in Aceh. This means that more emphasis has been given to Islamic education, even in the 'general' or 'secular' school curricula. State Shari'a legislation has also placed more restrictions on the relationship between men and women through, for example, legislation on *khalwat* (illicit proximity of marriagable men and women) and through the implementation of formal regulations on Islamic dress. To some extent, female religious congregations even seem to have replaced other gatherings for women such as the Pembinaan Kesejahteraan Keluarga (PKK/Women's Welfare Movement).

After the 2004 tsunami and the 2005 peace agreement that put an end to decades of armed conflict between the central Indonesian government and the Free Aceh Movement (Gerakan Aceh Merdeka/GAM), Aceh experienced another set of remarkable socio-political changes. One of the most important developments is that the political role of the ulama has increased as their formal structure became one of the main pillars of Acehnese autonomy (as mentioned in Undang-Undang No. 11, 2006). It is against this background, then, that this chapter looks at the agency of female ulama in Aceh. It will examine the roots and modes of their agency and their authority as religious scholars.

Women and Traditional Islamic Learning in Acehnese Society

This section explains how women have become part of the history of *dayah* education in Aceh, drawing attention to the differences between ascribed and achieved modes of power. In this section, I present the cases of two *dayahs* in Aceh, namely Dayah Darussalam and Dayah Mudi Mesra, to provide examples of women whose authority is 'ascribed' to them by virtue of their kinship ties to male *dayah* leaders. Social status, as Rosaldo and Lamphere (1974) have explained, can be ascribed or achieved and both modes can be important in explaining the social position of women. When power or social status is ascribed, this often happens through kinship relations and hereditary factors. This means that people assume a particular social status, political position, or leadership position through their (kinship) connections with a particular figure or leader. When social status or power is achieved, it is not so much kinship, but rather people's own struggles and efforts and achievements that serve to define their authority and position.

Acehnese *dayahs* have much in common with *pesantrens* and traditional institutions of Islamic learning elsewhere in the Indonesian archipelago (Dhofier 1982; Mastuhu 1994). However, there are also important differences between the *dayahs* in Aceh and analogous schools elsewhere in the region. In Java, large family networks between *pesantrens* emerged as a result of endogamous marriages among the ranks of the *kiais* (*pesantren* leaders) (see Dhofier 1982). In Aceh, such intensive networks of endogamous marriages are rare. This does not mean that the world of the *dayahs* is not also characterized by a form of hereditary authority. Rather, Acehnese people tend to think about the cross-generational transfer of *dayah* leadership in a different way. During my research, I found some women *dayah* leaders who originated from non-*dayah* families. This situation contrasts sharply with that of the pesantren *nyais* whom I observed during my earlier fieldwork in Java, particularly in East Java. All of the *nyais* whom I met there, and who have roles in the *pesantren* leadership, were from the immediate families of (male) *pesantren kiais*.

Two different terms are commonly used to refer to female *dayah* leaders in Aceh: *teungku inong* (female ulama) and *inong teungku* (wife of an ulama). *Teungku inong* are women who acquired their positions—and the power and authority associated with these positions—on their own, rather than through marriage with an ulama. *Inong teungku*, in contrast, is a term that is somewhat similar to the *nyai* in the Javanese context. However, while the term *nyai* can designate either the wives or daughters of a *kiai* (Marcoes 1992, 203–227), the Acehnese *inong teungku* refers only to the wives of the *teungku*. In Javanese *pesantrens*, the *nyai* is usually the *kiai*'s representative for the women's section of the *pesantren*. When those *nyais* have higher knowledge of Islam, they will have even more authority and take over the leadership of (a part of) the *pesantren*.[7] Comparing these *nyais* in Java with the *inong teungkus* in Aceh, then, one may say that the expectations of a *nyai* are generally higher than of an *inong teungku*. This is because, in Aceh, the *inong teungku* figure can be more easily separated from her husband's role as *teungku*. Some of my observations and interviews suggest that some *teungku inongs* even quit their own public religious roles, including their roles as religious teachers, once they become *inong teungku* (by marrying a *teungku*).

Women have been involved in *dayah* education in Aceh since at least the nineteenth century, as demonstrated by the life of Teungku Fakinah. Teungku Fakinah was married to Teungku Ahmad who then founded a *dayah* in Lam Krak, Aceh Besar, with the support of Teungku Fakinah's father. In 1873, Teungku Fakinah's husband died in battle against the Dutch, after which she took over his role in the armed struggle. She was reported to have some female students (Mardhiah Aly 1980).

In general, however, socio-cultural practices in Aceh have traditionally privileged men to study. This was partly due to the male tradition of *meurantau* ('leaving one's home area'), or *jak u timo* ('going to the East'), which means leaving one's village to study or work in another place (Siegel 1969, 54). To become an ulama, in other words, involved studying in *dayahs* that were far from home. In Javanese *pesantrens* this practice is called *santri kelana* while in Aceh it is known as *meudagang*, a term which originally means "to study," but also implies "to be a stranger, to travel from place to place" (Snouck Hurgronje 1906, 26). In the 1960s, James Siegel wrote that "[t]he result of the *meudagang* is the transformation of ordinary villagers into *ulama* [...] the *pesantren* student came back a different person" (Siegel 1969, 57). The term *meudagang* is still used for *dayah* students who leave their home or village to live in a *dayah* for the purpose of learning.[8] Today, both boys and girls engage in *meudagang*. Some *dayahs* in Aceh now have a remarkably large number of female students. One example is Dayah Ulee Titi in Aceh Besar, where

7 One of the *kiai*'s daughters in Jombang said that she had to leave her comfortable life in Jakarta when she decided to return home to take over the responsibility of developing the *pesantren* that she inherited from her parents after they died. Her brother formally took over the *pesantren*, but the presence of a *nyai* is needed for religious activities both in the *pesantren* and in the surrounding community.

8 The term *meudagang* is commonly used among (and for) students of traditional *dayahs* and rarely for students of modern *dayahs* or *pesantrens* such as Gontor 10 or Umar Diyan.

the female students outnumber their male counterparts. The history of Dayah Mudi Mesra suggests that the *dayah* already had a few female students around 1927, when it was led by Teungku Haji Syihabuddin bin Idris, but today the number of female students comprises half of the total number of male students.

The emergence of modernist organizations and movements in other parts of the Indonesian archipelago, for example in Java and West Sumatra, went together with attempts to modernize the system of Islamic education. In the 1920s, modern Islamic schooling in the form of *madrasahs* was introduced in Aceh (Sulaiman 1988). This development caused contestation among the ulama, because traditionalist religious leaders resisted the idea of teaching secular or general subjects and the practice of teaching boys and girls simultaneously in the same space. A meeting which engaged community and religious leaders was held in Kuta Raja (Banda Aceh) on 2 October 1936. The consensus was that teaching general subjects and the co-education system are not forbidden from an Islamic point of view (Husein 1985), and both the inclusion of general subjects and the coeducational model of learning for girls and boys in the *madrasah* system continue until the present.

Today, most *dayahs* in Aceh have both male and female pupils, and separate dormitories for boys and girls. In some *dayahs*, boys and girls who are at the same educational level are taught simultaneously by their teacher in one pavilion (Ac. *balee*) (Baihaqi 1976).[9] Over the past century, the number of female pupils studying in *pesantrens* or *dayahs* has increased. However, the number of women leaders of *pesantrens* or *dayahs* is still low, at less than ten per cent, at least according to official records, such as documents produced at the district and provincial level offices of the Ministry of Religious Affairs, or the Office for Dayah Education and Development (Badan Pendidikan dan Pengembangan Dayah).

This does not mean, however, that women are fully absent from *dayah* leadership, as we will see in the examples below. In Aceh, the *teungku* (sometimes also referred to as *abon* or *waled*) usually lives with his family in the *dayah* compound. His daily routine consists of teaching higher-level Islamic religious texts (*kitab kuning*) to senior pupils, who at the same time are also the instructors of younger pupils. If his wife is also a *teungku*, she may also teach the female pupils of the *dayah*. However, it is not always the case that a *teungku's*

9 *Balee* in this context is a semi-permanent place made of a wooden floor and it was traditionally the place for *dayah* students to learn. The compound of a *dayah* might have several *balee*, depending on the number of students studying in the *dayah*.

wife has a *dayah* background. On the other hand, there are also some *teungku inong* who do not owe their position to kinship ties of being the wife or daughter of a *teungku*.

Examples of both types of female religious leadership in the world of Acehnese *dayah* will be explored here with references to examples from two well-known *dayahs*, namely Dayah Darussalam and Dayah Samalanga (which includes Mudi Mesra and Dayah Muslimat) in order to provide examples of female religious leaders whose authority is ascribed to them on account of their relations, by marriage or kinship, to male *dayah* teachers (Ac. *teungku*).

Dayah Darussalam, founded at Labuhan Haji (South Aceh) in 1936, was once an important center of (traditionalist) *dayah* education in Aceh. Its founder was Abuya Mudawaly, whose contribution to the *dayah* tradition in Aceh may be compared to that of Kyai H. Hasyim Asy'ary in Java, because the majority of other *dayah* leaders in the subsequent period were the students of Abuya Mudawaly, before they went on to found their own *dayahs* or become *dayah* leaders themselves (Waly 1993). One of Abuya Mudawaly's wives was Umi Rabiah, whose knowledge of Islam was well-respected and acknowledged by the community. I first came to know about Umi Rabiah from the stories of one of Abuya Mudawaly's grandchildren, who referred to her as an *ulama perempuan* (female religious scholar). Several sources from Abuya Mudawaly's family mentioned that she used to say she would only marry a man who could defeat her in a debate on Islamic religious knowledge. As the story goes, only Abuya Mudawaly was able to surpass her knowledge and defeat her in a debate. After her divorce from Abuya Mudawaly, she went on to establish her own school, a *dayah* for girls in the village of Lam Pisang, near Dayah Darussalam.

The centrality of Dayah Darussalam at Labuhan Haji diminished considerably after the death of Abuya Mudawaly. The absence of a figure as strong as Abuya Mudawaly, in terms of religious authority and even political influence, was one of the reasons for this decline. The reconfiguration of *dayah* networks after his death was further driven by evolving socio-political dynamics of that time as Abuya Mudawaly and the traditionalist ulama that he represented came under increasingly pronounced public critique by Islamic modernists associated with PUSA. Over the latter decades of the twentieth century, however, there has been a considerable rapprochement between traditionalist and modernist ulama in Aceh with the spectrum shifting in the direction of modernizing reform.

Today, the heart of *dayah* education in Aceh has 'shifted' from Labuhan Haji, on the west coast, to Samalanga, on the north coast. One of the leaders of Dayah Mudi Mesra at Samalanga was Teungku Abdul Aziz, a former student of Abuya Mudawaly. He was married to a daughter of Teungku Hanafiah Abbas, the leader of Dayah Mudi Mesra from 1935–1964. When Teungku Hanafiah Abbas passed away in 1964, Teungku Abdul Aziz took over the leadership of the *dayah*. At that time the majority of the students were boys, although this would later change. Since 1989, the majority of students there have been girls. Teungku Abdul Aziz's brother-in-law, Teungku Jalaluddin Hanafiah, managed the girls' part of the *dayah* compound, which is called Dayah Muslimat. In this, he was assisted by his wife, Umi Ainiyah. While there were separate compounds for boys and girls, the *dayah* under Teungku Abdul Aziz's leadership also had a few female students. When Teungku Abdul Aziz and his wife, Umi Fathimah, moved into the compound of the current Dayah Mudi Mesra, many female pupils followed the couple and stayed with them there.

Over time, the number of female pupils grew steadily, and villagers established dormitories for them. It was Teungku Abdul Aziz's wife, Umi Fathimah, who initially developed the complex of the *dayah* for girls. She used to be called *mi nek* (grandma) by her pupils. One of her students, who is now an instructor for female pupils in Dayah Mudi Mesra, told me that she was an active woman who "just couldn't sit quietly." In her time, there were no male *teungkus* who taught female pupils; all female pupils were taught by women, and she was strict about maintaining this principle. After managing the women's section of Dayah Mudi Mesra for some years after her husband's death, Umi Fathimah made the pilgrimage to Mecca. Before she left, she handed over the leadership of the girls' section to her son-in-law, Waled Hasanoel Bashry (aka Waled Hasanon).

Waled Hasanon was a student of Teungku Abdul Aziz, and he later married his teacher's daughter and became his successor. Under their leadership, the *dayah* grew and developed further, with thousands of male and female students from all over Aceh going there to study. Today, it is the largest *dayah* in Aceh, in terms of student numbers, facilities, teachers and alumni networks. This growth was also accompanied by other changes to the *dayah*. Whereas in Umi Fathimah's time the female pupils were taught only by female instructors, under Waled Hasanon's leadership male instructors also teach in the female students' pavilion (*balee*), with a curtain separating the teacher from his female pupils.

The part of Dayah Mudi Mesra that initially was a *dayah* only for girls was named Dayah Muslimat. Teungku Abdul Aziz's brother-in-law and his wife, Umi Ainiyah, inherited and managed this part of the *dayah*. One of Umi Ainiyah's students told me that she used to teach some classes and sometimes also taught the students how to weave mats. In one of my discussions with her, I found that she was able to quote from memory passages from the *kitab kuning*, that is, the texts of the Islamic religious sciences that she had taught at Dayah

Mudi Mesra. One of her daughters married Waled Nuruzahri (Waled Nu), who then founded another *dayah* close to Dayah Muslimat, called Ummul Aiman. Waled Nuruzahri's wife is called 'Bunda' (mother) by her *dayah* pupils. She is involved in managing the *dayah* and she also teaches this *dayah*'s pupils.

Apart from their responsibilities in regular *dayah* instruction, some *teungku inong* are also active in social and religious activities in the community outside their *dayahs*. Those *teungku inong* maintained a relationship with the local population, not only through a regular *majelis taklim* (study group) to study classical texts, but also through the practice of Sufi rituals, which bestow on them a particular form of religious authority. One of the former students of Dayah Mudi Mesra described Umi Ainiyah as being both a *inong teungku* and a *teungku inong*, and said: "Even in her eighties, she was strong enough to lead the rituals and recite the *dhikr* herself, sometimes almost without any sleep." Because of her great standing in the community, Umi Ainiyah was often invited to religious and cultural ceremonies. Sometimes her schedule could be quite full and, for example, after delivering a sermon in a *majelis taklim*, she might be invited immediately for another event. Even at her advanced age, she maintains a busy schedule of leading Sufi rituals during the month of Ramadan. The local community refers to her as a 'religious leader' in terms of her socio-religious activities and leadership in the *dayah* and within the local community.[10]

The examples discussed above explain how religious authority can be ascribed through ties of kinship. For women, this means that they assume authority mostly based on the positions of either their fathers or husbands, or both—as in the case of Umi Ainiyah's daughter, who also inherited religious authority from her mother. In other cases, however, women can assume religious authority even without the support of kinship ties to other Islamic teachers. Their authority is 'achieved' through their own accomplishments in the study of Islamic religious sciences and mastery of ritual practice. The claims to authority of the female ulama discussed below derive from their studies of classical Islamic texts, and thus their power could be thought of as achieved rather than ascribed. At the same time, however, their authority is also elaborated in terms of the broader social contexts in which they operate. As they assume diverse social roles in their community, however, their religious learning remains the primary defining feature of their status.

---

10 Once, for example, I observed a woman who came with her family to see Umi Ainiyah to ask her and her congregation to pray for her late mother. Since Umi Ainiyah was away, the woman asked her daughter, who was also a *teungku inong*, and the daughter agreed to do it.

Teungku Fatimah Cut

Teungku Fatimah Cut was born on 28 December 1929 into a family without direct connections to the world of the *dayah*. From 1936 to 1940, she attended a Dutch colonial primary school. When she was fifteen years old, she started to study under the guidance of the charismatic modernist ulama leader, Abu Daud Beureuh. From 1941 to 1945, she received *dayah* education at Pesantren Darul Huda Bambi in the region of Pidie. In 1945, she married Teungku Hasan Is. She later continued her education at one of the *dayahs* in Lampoh Saka, Pidie, from 1966 to 1967. Teungku Fatimah Cut established her *dayah* in 1978, with herself as Director and her husband as Secretary. This is remarkable as I did not find this kind of relationship in my research on *pesantren* leadership anywhere in Java, where a *nyai* never occupies a position of authority higher than that of her husband. The highest position a *nyai* can assume is that of joint leader of the *pesantren* together with her husband. Since the death of her husband, Teungku Fatimah Cut's daughter has assisted her in managing the *dayah*. Together they have developed vocational training programs, including the production of local *batik* (although, eventually, this activity ceased due to the armed conflict that prevented them from obtaining the cloth from Java).

Although at the time it was still rare for women to pursue university education, after her *dayah* education in the late 1960s, Teungku Fatimah Cut went on to attend both the IAIN Ar-Raniry and the Akademi Dakwah in Jakarta, obtaining the degree of Bachelor of Arts (*sarjana muda*). According to Teungku Fatimah Cut, when she established her own *dayah* in 1978, it was Daud Bereueuh himself who gave it the name of Fathimiyah, referring both to a Muslim dynasty of medieval Egypt, and to her own name: Fatimah. Before Teungku Fatimah Cut established the *dayah*, she was already a well-known orator and preacher, who used to accompany Daud Beureueh while he was preaching (*mendakwah*). Over the course of her career, she became engaged with the modernist ideas of the time, and with PUSA, the organization led by Daud Beureueh. She incorporated modernist ideas into the syllabus at the *dayah* by teaching not only religious subjects, but also general subjects and vocational skills—while distancing herself from Sufi ritual practice and *tarekat*. At the same time she actively engaged in *dakwah* (proselytization) on tours all across Aceh.

Apart from engaging in religious activities, Teungku Fatimah Cut was also active in the struggle for independence. During the resistance against the Dutch after the Second World War, she became skilled in the use of weapons. Later, in 1967, she joined the Batalyon 113 in Kuta Bakti and eventually obtained the rank of corporal in the Muslimat army, or Muslim women defence force.[11] It is unclear to me whether this was the first time that Teungku Fatimah Cut was involved in state-driven activities. Nevertheless, her ensuing career clearly shows her close attachment to political activities and to state agencies and government officials. In the 1970s she embarked on a political career, as she occupied a seat in the district parliament for two periods, from 1971–1977 and from 1977–1982, for Partai Persatuan Pembangunan (Unity Development Party, PPP).

Teungku Fatimah Cut also engaged in business activities. She was a contractor, who managed several infrastructure projects in Aceh, and she was a member of the association of contractor organizations. This work was also recognized by the Indonesian government, and she was nominated to receive the 'Satya Lencana Award,' honouring significant achievements in the field of development under the Suharto administration. Through her connections at the national level she attracted support for her *dayah* from several foundations, including the Suharto family's Yayasan Darmais. Her abilities to obtain such funds for Islamic education under the New Order testify to her extensive connections to national elites, built through her experience in politics.

As a female preacher who travels around Aceh, Teungku Fatimah Cut is still a well-respected, articulate orator speaking fluently in Arabic, Japanese, and English as well as in Acehnese and Indonesian. Most recently, she completed a translation of the Qur'an into the Acehnese language.

Teungku Zahrul Husna (Umi Husna)

Teungku Zahrul Husna was born in September 1966 in Jangka Buya, Ulhe Glee, in the district of Pidie. She began her formal education studying Islamic religious sciences in a *dayah* nearby in her village.[12] After completing her elementary education in 1981, she continued her studies at Dayah Mudi Mesra in Samalanga. Teungku Abdul Aziz (Abon Aziz) was still alive at that time and so she had the opportunity to study directly under him. Teungku Abdul Aziz always selected the best of his students to be taught exclusively in one special class comprised of male and female students. During these lessons, men and women were separated by a curtain.[13] This special class had two class managers

11 Women's groups received military training and, where necessary, were also involved in combat.

12 The Dayah Babul Ma'arif, led by Teungku Haji Munir.

13 The students of this remarkable class included: Teungku Hanan (one of Abu Seulimeum's sons); Teungku Bulqaini Tunjungan, the leader of Dayah al-Aziziyah in Lueng Bata; and Teungku Faisal Ali, the leader of Dayah Mahyal Ulum al-Aziziyah Sibreh, who was elected

(*ketua kelas*): Teungku Faisal Ali for male students and Umi Husna for female students. While Umi Husna went on to found her own *dayah*, other female students in that group took up other kinds of religious leadership roles by establishing *balee seumeubeut*, and have thus also come to be recognized as *teungku inongs* by their community.

In 1994, Umi Husna, as one of the advanced students in the *dayah*, was instructed by Waled Hasanon to further her studies of Sufism under Abu Wahab at Seulimum.[14] She went there with some other selected students and they were accompanied by the wife of Teungku Abdul Aziz. Thereafter, she participated in the activities of the Naqshbandiyya Sufi order (I. *tarekat*) and eventually received a certificate (*ijaza*) indicating her initiation into that order. She then became a Sufi master herself and served to lead particular Sufi practices (*suluk* and *kaleut*) of the Naqshbandiyya in her community.[15] Like Umi Husna, Tengku Abdul Azis's daughter in law, Umi Ainiyah, has also been known as someone who leads Sufi rituals, particularly during Ramadan.

Umi Husna was married to Teungku Kamal, a student of Abu Syam Marpali of Dayah Babul Huda. The marriage was arranged by the two *dayah* leaders of Dayah Babul Huda and Dayah Mudi Mesra. After they got married, the couple settled in Blang Pidie, where they rented a small shop selling copies of the Qur'an, *kitab kuning*, and Muslim clothing. While her husband was finishing his education with Abu Syam of Dayah Babul Huda, Umi Husna started to teach children from surrounding areas, particularly Qur'an recitation. In 2000, they established a *dayah* to which they moved their activities. They called the

---

as the leader of Nahdlatul Ulama for the province of Aceh. All of the alumni who established their own *dayah* have al-Aziziyah's name applied to their *dayah*. Therefore, the *dayah* of Umi Husna and her husband was named Dayah Darul Kamal al-Aziziyah, and the *dayah* of Teungku Faisal Ali in Sibreh, Aceh Besar, is called Dayah Mahyal Ulum al-Aziziyah. Being the largest traditional *dayah* in Aceh today, Dayah Mudi Mesra has an extensive network in, and even beyond, Aceh. The *haul* (annual) meetings to commemorate the late Abon Aziz are attended by thousands of participants, including local and national government officials.

14 Someone who has been initiated into a Sufi order (*tarekat*) receives an *ijaza* (certificate), and s/he will have a right to lead the *tarekat* rituals, or become a *tarekat* leader.

15 *Suluk* is a type of retreat for Sufi practitioners who congregate with their *shaykh* for an intensive ritual regime of devotions and religious instruction. *Kaleut* (from the Arabic for 'seclusion') is a form of ritual retreat emphasizing the 'remembrance' (Ar. *dhikr*/I. *zikir*) of God, in which participants cover their faces with cloth so that they cannot see anything and cannot be seen by others. They do not talk but rather practice *zikir*. Both *kaleut* and *suluk* participants wear white clothes and cover their faces with a white cloth or a white-coloured *mukena* for women.

dayah Darul Kamal al-Aziziyah. In the local community, the presence of this new *dayah* has been met with enthusiasm and many local children now study there. The *dayah* has about 500 male and female students; some of them reside in the *dayah* compound (*santri mukim*), while others (*santri kalong*) return to their homes after the classes because they live nearby.

This *dayah* also has a class for adults through its *majelis taklim* activities. The *majelis taklim* for men used to be held every Friday afternoon after prayer and was managed by Umi Husna's husband Teungku Kamal until his death in 2001. The women have two meetings each week; one on Thursday afternoon for studies of Islamic jurisprudence (*fiqh*), ritual practice (*ibadat*) and religious ethics (*akhlaq*), and one on Friday morning for the recitation of the 36th chapter of the Qur'an (*wirid Ya Sin*). Umi Husna manages and leads all of these activities herself. This *dayah* also has a special class for the most talented students of the *dayah*, similar to Dayah Mudi Mesra Samalanga. It was Umi Husna, and not her husband who was responsible for teaching this special class. After her husband's death, Umi Husna managed and directed the *dayah* on her own, being a leader for both female and male students.

Umi Husna then also took over the management of the *majelis taklim* for men, in addition to the *majelis taklim* for women. It is very uncommon for women to give *majelis taklim* for an exclusively male congregation. Almost everywhere in Aceh (and across the Muslim world, for that matter), women are usually instructors only for groups of other women (Frisk 2009). At first, Umi Husna tried to find other male *teungkus* to replace her, but after the participants complained she resumed the position of instructor for the men's *majelis taklim* herself. Although Umi Husna admits that it can sometimes be uncomfortable for her, as a woman, to talk with her male participants about such sensitive issues as reproduction, bodily hygiene, and sexual relationships, she maintains that she feels obligated to explain things clearly and directly. As she put it: "After I have explained something, I will ask them whether they have understood it and say 'if you want to laugh you can laugh later, but what is important now is that you have understood this'."[16]

As someone who has been formally initiated into the Naqshbandiyya Sufi order with a license (*ijaza*) to teach it to others, Umi Husna is also allowed to lead the *suluk* ritual in her *dayah*. The story of Umi Husna and other women like her demonstrates the extent to which some Acehnese women can attain considerable authority through their own studies of texts and ritual training. Dur-

16 *"Leuh lon syarah lon tanyong, peu ka muphom. Menyoe keunek khem ta khem enteuk, yang penteng muphom dile."* Interview on 3 September, 2011 at Aceh Barat Daya.

ing my earlier research in East Java, I also met with women in leading positions, such as Nyai Adlan, who inherited the leadership of a *tarekat* from her husband Kiai Adlan at the Pesantren Putri Cukir of Diwek Jombang (Srimulyani 2012, 53). However, Umi Husna's husband was not a Sufi leader, and her father was a military officer who had no ulama background. In contrast, then, to the women who have their leadership status ascribed to them, Umi Husna achieved her legitimacy and authority as a religious leader entirely on her own.

To preserve their autonomy, some (female) religious leaders prefer to have no official relations with the state, even if that means not receiving any state subsidies for their *dayah*. This is the case for Umi Husna, who was offered financial assistance by the government, but refused the offer in order to preserve the independence of her school. She also rejected offers to join formal ulama organizations or activities, arguing that she prefers to focus all her time and energy on her *dayah* and the *majelis taklim*. Unlike Umi Husna's *dayah*, Umi Fatimah Cut's *dayah* has received subsidies from both the local and national governments. As noted above, Umi Fatimah Cut's political work has provided her with access to far better connections with the state apparatus. Sometimes government officials visit her in her *dayah* in Lampoh Saka. Although she sometimes participates in activities sponsored by ulama organizations, she is not a formal member of the Acehnese Ulama Council (MPU) at either the district or the provincial level. Thus, neither Umi Husna nor Umi Fatimah Cut, as well as the other *teungku inong* discussed in this chapter, have been directly involved in any of the official institutions of Aceh's state Shariʿa system.

Nevertheless, a decade of formal state Shariʿa implementation has also had some significant effects on Aceh's female ulama. For example, the size of their community congregation and the topics discussed during their religious lessons appears to have increased over recent years. Although there are no precise numbers available on this, it is clear that there is a growing interest among the people to attend religious events like the *majelis taklim* organized by these *teungku inongs*. This growth has been fostered, at least in part, by the efforts of the state to raise a greater awareness of the importance of the Shariʿa through various official programs.[17] Some *majelis taklim* are even officially endorsed by the government, such as the religious congregation for the high ranking officials set up by the current governor as well as the vice governor. The *majelis taklim* organized by these female ulama also engage with prominent aspects of Shariʿa, as it is formally implemented in the province through discussions of high profile issues such as proper standards of Muslim dress, and the public

17 Interview with Tu Zainab, March 4, 2011 at Samalanga.

role of women, among others. In doing this, however, the *teungku inong* generally prefer to speak from a position of scholarly independence, and continue to work outside the formal institutional structures of state Shariʿa. Their distanced engagement with the official project for the state implementation of Islamic law further demonstrates the considerable agency that they can assert as religious authorities in their own right. As community religious leaders, they are consulted by the community on various matters, ranging from marital issues, family conflicts, inheritance, and even political affairs in the community, such as in the case of Islamic dress policies applied by the *bupati* (district head) of West Aceh district in 2010.[18]

In the post-tsunami/post-conflict period, some female religious leaders in Aceh have forged international connections, taking up the opportunities of a new cosmopolitanism through programs on gender and society conducted in the framework of the recovery of Aceh. Some *teungku inongs* have had the opportunity to join training and internship programs outside Aceh. This has included both Indonesian national programs, such as workshops on gender in the Islamic State University Syarif Hidayatullah in Jakarta, and an engagement with international initiatives and discourses that were introduced by international agencies and partner NGOs working in Aceh (see Afrianty 2015, and her contribution in this volume). Other *teungku inong*, however, have chosen not to engage with such networks. Many of them have other trans-local connections of their own, particularly in the form of Sufi orders, through which they engage with ideas and forms of ritual practice that expand their networks well beyond Aceh.

Views on Gender Issues

Aceh's long history of rule by female monarchs (Ar. *sultana*), as well as the prominence of female local chieftains and female heroines fighting against the Dutch all demonstrate that women in Aceh have for a long time assumed roles of public leadership (Reid 1988, 641). The Acehnese tradition of matrilocality may be one reason for the relatively high position of women (Siegel 1969). In Aceh, *teungku inongs* have played roles in the performance of Islamic religious

18 This policy, which was widely understood as prohibiting women from wearing trousers (I. *celana panjang*), invoked public debate both at the local level and at the provincial level through the local media. Among the religious figures consulted on this issue, both by the media and by the community through their religious congregations, were also *teungku inongs*, such as Umi Hanisah (see below).

duties such as bathing the corpses of Muslim women, as well as in cultural (*adat*) ceremonies, such as the *peusijeuk* that is commonly performed during marriage ceremonies, birth celebrations, and funeral rites.

However, while *teungku inongs* are still invited to *adat* ceremonies, their role in these rituals appears to be no longer as dominant as it once was. Since the 1980s, *majelis taklim* have become more popular and important at both national and local levels. As in West Java, women in Aceh usually form the majority of *majelis taklim* participants (Millie 2011). *Teungku inongs* who possessed particular religious knowledge or expertise in religious teaching took the opportunity of the growing interest in *majelis taklim* to become instructors. The majority of the *teungku inongs* who became involved in this kind of religious congregations are graduates of *dayahs*. This is particularly true for the rural areas, whereas in urban areas some of the *teungku inongs* have received modern Islamic education, such as in a *madrasah* or PGA (Pendidikan Guru Agama—religious teacher education), or even higher Islamic learning such as at the Islamic State Institute (IAIN presently UIN) Ar-Raniry.

Against the background of the life stories and the roles of the female *dayah* leaders I have presented above, I turn now to explore the ways in which these female ulama perceive the position of other women within their communities, and what they think of the roles of women and gender relations in the household. Although public discourse on gender issues in Aceh has intensified during the post-tsunami/post-conflict period, most female *dayah* leaders have not participated very actively in these discussions. By contrast, many of their male counterparts from Aceh's *dayah* community regularly engage in the discussions, mostly by countering the concept of gender as they see it as a Western concept that is irrelevant for the Acehnese community. In general, however, public discourse on gender in contemporary Aceh is dominated by activists and ulama or experts with non-*dayah* educational backgrounds. But this does not mean that the *teungku inongs* do not have opinions on these issues. Let us therefore now take a closer look at the views of Teungku Fatimah Cut and Umi Husna.

Teungku Fatimah Cut is vocal in her criticism of some contemporary discourses on the role of women in Acehnese society. She does not agree with the restrictions that are placed on women in the name of Shari'a:

> *Alah mak ooo*[19] ... according to Shari'a law, are women allowed to go to the market? And to the paddy field? [Are they allowed] to help their husbands

19 This is an Acehnese expression that means "how sad" or "how beautiful."

> in the paddy field? In the paddy field their *aurat* is uncovered. Do we want to be like women in Saudi Arabia? [...] here, we have to go to the paddy field, women carry sacks of rice on their heads, women mind the children, women trade in the market. Are those activities not [in line with] Shariʿa? [If someone tells you that women are not allowed to this and that], let me know and I will come to make it clear to her/him.

She also criticizes current patterns of gender relations in some sectors of Acehnese society:

> See ... the men, and this is sometimes quite embarrassing, hang out in the coffee shops. They talk about America, but none of them feeds his family at home. I can say this, and I can prove this. Then, after finishing his coffee, upon leaving the coffee shop, such a man tells the owner to write it down [on his bill], as he has no money to pay for it now. How then can he possibly afford to support his family? [If everything is available and these men fully support their families], then they can tell their wives that they should just make themselves beautiful at home, sit down near the window without shopping tasks and without the responsibility for the livestock. Only if someone carries the rice for us, we can have perfume ... What do you think, do we agree with this as women? Do you think my ideas are bad?

Teungku Fatimah Cut is convinced that women should be independent and productive, saying: "You, women, are heroines. Do not give up seeking the truth and you will not be defeated; remember Khadija, remember Fatima, remember Aisha [wives and daughter or the Prophet Muhammad]." Teungku Fatimah Cut herself has always been productive and active, doing what she believed are good works (*amal*) for the betterment of the Muslim community (*ummat*), and she clearly does not want to be discriminated against for doing so. In her view, a Muslim woman should be strong and active and she should be allowed to pursue many professions. For this reason, she was astonished to hear of the case of a female sub-district head (*camat*) in Plimbang, Bireuen who was replaced by another district parliament member in 2010, simply because she was a woman and was therefore deemed to be unfit for such a leadership role by a few people including the head of the Bireuen district parliament, who brought the case to the public and received wider media attention.

Umi Husna has a somewhat different view, placing more emphasis on issues of modesty when discussing the mobility and activity of women in public space. According to her, as long as women wear proper dress and maintain their chastity, they can assume public positions in the state bureaucracy or in the community without a problem, particularly if there is no one else who could take on the position. Umi Husna has also, however, maintained that in principle, women should always cover their face unless they have to see others and deal with others in their work. In her *dayah* in Samalanga, female students are recommended to wear the full face veil (*chador*).[20] This influences her view on proper Muslim dress for women, although she herself does not cover her face.

Teungku Hanisah

I will now compare the two *dayah* leaders discussed above with another female *dayah* leader, namely Teungku Hanisah from West Aceh, who is also called Umi Hanisah. Umi Hanisah was born on 3 July 1968 in Peunia, West Aceh (Aceh Barat). She spent nine years studying in Dayah Darussalam in South Aceh (Aceh Selatan), a well-known traditionalist *dayah* in Aceh. After completing her *dayah* education in South Aceh she decided to pursue higher education in Meulaboh (West Aceh) where she obtained a bachelor's degree in Islamic education. She married a *teungku*, but later divorced because her husband did not support her public activities outside the household.[21] Her *dayah* education has given her a wide range of knowledge on Islam and a good understanding of *kitab kuning*. She has established and is leading a *dayah* in Padang Mancang, Meulaboh, that currently has approximately two hundred students.

Apart from her educational and leadership roles, she is specifically concerned with assisting victims of domestic violence, most of whom are women. Sometimes her *dayah* functions as a shelter for these women. Once, the local

---

20 The majority of female *dayah* students in Aceh are not obliged to (and do not) wear a face veil. In this regard, Dayah Mudi Mesra Samalanga is quite exceptional. The practice started quite recently in the 1990s. Before that, the female students covered their head with traditional *batik* cloth (*kain batik panjang*). Now, the chador has become their uniform and forms the identity of the *dayah* female students, although upon the completion of their study, the majority of them do no wear the chador any longer. In the surrounding community, women also do not wear the veil, and were not persuaded to do so through the religious congregations teachings or sermons, even if the instructors were from Dayah Mudi Mesra.

21 Interview with Umi Hanisah on 11 February 2009 in Banda Aceh.

people misunderstood her activities and claimed that she protected an adulterer, after which she had to leave her *dayah* for a while to avoid angering the community further.[22] Umi Hanisah won the Aceh Women Award 2010 for her active role in campaigning and providing assistance for abused women and children. This is indeed a very different way of using agency as a religious leader. This kind of work would generally be seen as under the purview of social workers, and it is not necessarily related to the religious activities attached to the agency and authority of *teungku inongs*. The role of female religious leaders in such activities suggests that the *teungku inongs* can now use their positions for different activities than would have been possible for the *teungku inongs* of earlier generations.

Umi Hanisah is also an active advocate of women's rights and is sometimes openly critical of positions taken by the local government. She was a candidate for Partai Aceh in the general legislative elections in 2009. The Partai Aceh won the local elections and gained a majority of seats in the provincial parliament, and even in a number of districts across Aceh. During the run-up to the 2012 elections for governor and district heads, I asked Umi Hanisah about her thoughts on gender and politics. She replied: "I will only vote for a woman. If there are no female candidates, I will not vote for any candidates. I have had enough of them [the current leaders] and of what they have been doing so far. I would like to see a change." The background to this statement was formed by a district-level law passed in her home district of Aceh Barat in 2010. The law, prominently endorsed by the District Head, Ramli Mansur, banned women from wearing trousers. Umi Hanisah agreed that Islam sets particular rules related to Muslim women's dress in the concept of covering one's *aurat*, but she disagreed with the prohibition on women wearing (a modest type of) trousers. Commenting on this issue, she said:

> I wear trousers sometimes for practical reasons. [...] Acehnese women should not be separated from their trousers as it is also their traditional dress. [...] I cannot understand why they always focus on women's dress. [...] [I cannot understand] why they don't care about having a better plantation system to improve the economy, or about developing good cooperatives.[23]

22 Interview with Umi Hanisah on 10 February 2009 in Banda Aceh.

23 Interview with Umi Hanisah on 27 February 2011 in Meulaboh.

Tu Zainab

Another female ulama of the same generation, Tu Zainab, presents yet another profile of religious authority. As a daughter of Umi Ainiyah and a grandchild of Abu Aziz Samalanga, she studied in a *dayah* before her marriage and now she spends most of her time in the *dayah*.[24] She currently runs 14 *majelis taklims* with more than 800 participants in total. She holds at least two such sessions every day, in which she teaches from the *kitab kuning* on basic principles of worship (*ibadat*), mostly related to matters of *fiqh* (jurisprudence). Her husband has supported her in taking on this task.[25]

Tu Zainab says that the majority of problems about which the *majelis taklims'* participants (almost all of whom are women) consult her are family matters, such as family conflicts and divorce. She says: "I tell them: do not always think that your husband is wrong, but look at yourself first. Maybe you also have a problem … we [sometimes] do not understand our roles [as wives], we always blame our husband … [but] we are not always correct …"[26] Such comments are quite common in religious congregations or sermons, and can be made either by male or female *teungkus*. Moreover, this discourse on the role of women as wives has been embraced by the general public, not only in Aceh but also Indonesia, and it used to be strongly emphasized in the gender ideology of the state (Blackburn 2004; Robinson 2009; Suryakusuma 1996). However, when I discussed this issue further with Tu Zainab, she also expressed her concern about the ways in which some husbands restrict their wife's public activities, and she recognized that there was some injustice in the unequal relationships within the household.

The four examples above suggest a variety of opinions on the social position of women held by Aceh's female ulama. Teungku Fatimah Cut and Umi Hanisah hold some broadly similar views. Their background as women who are active outside the *dayah* seems to influence the way in which they think of the position and the mobility of women. Umi Husna and Tu Zainab, on the other

---

24 She is known as Tu Zainab and not as Teungku Zainab. She most likely has had this title since she was young and it is probably the title used for members of the family of the ulama *dayah*. During my research, I found several other men and women who had this title, for instance Tu Rukaiyah and Tu Bulqaini from Tunjungan, both of whom are also *dayah* leaders.

25 He himself is known as 'Abati' and apart from teaching in an Islamic secondary school, he also has the task of accompanying his wife to her *majelis taklims*.

26 Interview with Tu Zainab on 4 March 2011.

hand, concentrate and focus on the *dayah* or *majelis taklim*. Umi Husna, for instance, avoids any activity outside her *dayah*.

As Kloos (2010) has argued, the fact that a female *dayah* leader is in favour of Shari'a law does not automatically mean that she cannot also engage in attempts to advance the social position of women. Also, even though there has been some critique on the effectiveness of the religious congregation model of *majelis taklim* in terms of addressing women's interests or improving their position, Millie (2011, 152) argues that it does provide access to "possible modalities in which agency can be exercised." All of the female *dayah* leaders discussed above manage religious preaching activities (*dakwah*) or *majelis taklim*, with women forming the majority of their participants. This provides them not only with agency but also with considerable religious authority in the eyes of their participants. Some *teungku inongs* also exercise this agency and authority through their roles in Sufi rituals. None of these activities seem to be strongly affected by the current state Shari'a project, but they are strongly situated within the socio-religious patterns of community life in Aceh.

Conclusion

The discussion on *teungku inong dayahs* in Aceh presents examples of two ways in which women in Aceh can assume agency and authority as religious leaders. Firstly, a woman can be a leader through her kinship with a male leader, not only in the religious sphere as discussed above, but also in politics. This confirms a model of ascribed power that exists in many Muslim communities. Apart from this ascribed power, however, some women in Aceh are able to achieve a particular position of religious leadership through their own efforts. Authority based on achieved power can give these female religious leaders agency analogous to that based on ascribed or relational power. Importantly, some of these women are also able to exercise their authority beyond the religious context by addressing issues that are relevant to contemporary socio-political realities of life in Aceh. Some of the female religious leaders discussed here engage in politics or activism for human rights, against domestic violence, or other issues. This is a new and different way in which they deploy their authority, which had previously been generally understood as confined to discussions of religious issues. Nevertheless, some others choose not to get involved in politics or social activism. Still, they too have become influential in different ways through their networks of students and teachers affiliated with *tarekat* (Sufi orders) and their role in community rituals, as well as through their leadership in the *dayah*.

Although there are relatively few female *dayah* leaders compared to their male counterparts in Aceh, their role is highly significant because they have an important influence on the social life of the community, particularly through informal public religious spaces. Even though their *majelis taklim* are sometimes limited to female participants, they have used these networks to establish and extend their authority in a wider community outside their *dayahs*. Therefore, even though most of them are not involved in the formal ulama organizations and institutions of state Shariʿa, their work remains significant in the complex social dynamics of contemporary Aceh.

References

Afrianty, Dina. 2015. *Women and Sharia Law in Northern Indonesia: Local Women's NGOs and the Reform of Islamic Law in Aceh.* Abingdon and New York: Routledge.

Azra, Azyumardi. 2002. "Biografi Sosial-Intelektual *Ulama* Perempuan: Pemberdayaan Historiografi." In *Ulama Perempuan Indonesia,* edited by Jajat Burhannuddin, xxi–xxxviii. Jakarta: PT. Gramedia Pustaka Utama dan PPIM.

Baihaqi. 1976. *Ulama dan Madrasah di Aceh.* Jakarta: Lembaga Ilmu Pengetahuan Indonesia bekerja sama dengan Departemen Agama.

Blackburn, Susan. 2004. *Women and the State in Modern Indonesia.* Cambridge: Cambridge University Press.

Burhanudin, Jajat, ed. 2002. *Ulama Perempuan Indonesia.* Jakarta: Gramedia Pustaka Utama.

Dhofier, Zamakhsyari. 1982. *Tradisi Pesantren: Studi Tentang Pandangan Hidup Kiyai.* Jakarta: Lembaga Penelitian, Pendidikan dan Penerangan Ekonomi dan Sosial.

Formichi, Chiara, 2012. *Islam and The Making of the Nation: Kartosuwiryo and Political Islam in Twentieth-century Indonesia.* Leiden: KITLV.

Frisk, Sylva. 2009. *Submitting to God: Women and Islam in Urban Malaysia.* NIAS Press: Denmark.

Husein, Ibrahim. 1985. *Persepsi Kalangan Dayah terhadap Pendidikan Tinggi di Aceh.* Paper presented at a seminar at IAIN Ar-Raniry, 21–23 February 1985.

Kloos, David. 2010. "Supporting Syariah, Advancing Women." *Inside Indonesia,* Juli–Sept 2010. http://www.insideindonesia.org/weekly-articles-101-jul-sep-2010/supporting-syariah-advancing-women-31071904.

Marcoes, Lies. 1992. "The Female Preacher as a Mediator in Religion: A Case Study in Jakarta and West Java." In *Women and Mediation in Indonesia,* edited by S. van Bemmelen et al., 203–227. Leiden: KITLV Press.

Mardhiah Aly, Ainal. 1980. "Pergerakan Wanita di Aceh Masa Lampau Sampai Kini." In *Bunga Rampai tentang Aceh,* edited by Ismail Suny. Jakarta: Penerbit Bhratara Karya Aksara.

Mastuhu. 1994. *Dinamika Sistem Pendidikan Pesantren: Suatu Kajian tentang Unsur dan Nilai Sistem Pendidikan Pesantren*. Jakarta: INIS.

Millie, Julian. 2011. "Islamic Preaching and Women Spectatorship in West Java." *The Australian Journal of Anthropology* 22:151–169.

Reid, Anthony. 1988. "Female Roles in Pre-Colonial Southeast Asia." *Modern Asian Studies* 22(3), Special Issue: Asian Studies in Honour of Professor Charles Boxer:629–645.

Robinson, Kathryn. 2002. "Gender Orders in Some Societies of the Indonesian Archipelago." *Kultur (The Indonesian Journal for Muslim Culture)* 2(2):1–20.

Rosaldo, Michelle Z., and Louise Lamphere, eds. 1974. *Women, Culture, and Society*. Stanford: Stanford University Press.

Siegel, James T. 1969. *The Rope of God*. Berkeley and Los Angeles: University of California Press.

Snouck Hurgronje, C. 1906. *The Achehnese* (2 Vols.). Leiden: E.J. Brill.

Srimulyani, Eka. 2008. "Negotiating Public Space: Three Nyais Generations in a Jombang Pesantren." In *Indonesian Islam in New Era: How Women Negotiate Their Muslim Identities*, edited by Susan Blackburn, Bianca Smith, and Siti Syamsiyatun, 119–138. Clayton: Monash University Press.

———. 2009. "Women Leadership in Islamic Educational Institution in Java and Aceh." *Kultur (The Indonesian Journal for Muslim Culture)* 4(2):159–173.

———. 2012. *Women from Traditional Islamic Educational Institutions in Indonesia: Negotiating Public Spaces*. Amsterdam: Amsterdam University Press.

Sulaiman, M. Isa. 1988. "Madrasah dan pembentukan elite modernis di Aceh." In *Bunga rampai Temu Budaya Nusantara PKA-3*, edited by Ismuha, 488–509. Banda Aceh: Seksi Seminar.

Suryakusuma, Julia. 1996. "The State and Sexuality in New Order Indonesia." In *Fantasizing the Feminine in Indonesia*, edited by Laurie J. Sears, 92–119. Durham: Duke University Press.

Waly, Muhibbuddin. 1993. *Ayah Kami: Maulana Hají Muhammad Waly al-Khalidy*. Singapore: Jew Printers & Binders Pte. Ltd.

CHAPTER 7

Muslim Punks and State Shari'a

Reza Idria

I came to know Dema when he was hiding at Komunitas Tikar Pandan, an NGO for cultural programs in Banda Aceh.[1] It was on 10 December 2011, and Dema had arrived there shortly after midnight. I still remember that he rushed to enter our building when we had just finished our weekly 'movie night' screening program. At the moment, he just told us very briefly that the Wilayatul Hisbah (the 'Shari'a police,' WH) were hunting punks outside our office and he wanted to be away from them.[2] No one at Komunitas Tikar Pandan knew him before. But, as the news spread quickly about the punk raid which had just happened that evening, it was not difficult for us to identify Dema due to his physical appearance, with spiked hair and chain-filled clothes, as someone from the hunted group.

We had heard the news about the punk crackdown through social media just before Dema entered our office. The information spread quickly. 65 youths were detained by a combination of civil police and the WH after being accused of falsifying their music concert permit. Dema eventually told us more about the concert he and his friends had organized, how all seemed to be going well with the event until the Banda Aceh authorities came to arrest them. The concert was entitled "Aceh for the Punk: A Music Parade and Fundraiser for Orphanages." It took place at the Aceh Cultural Centre (Taman Budaya Aceh) and featured punk bands from various parts of Indonesia including Jakarta, Bekasi, Lampung, Jambi, Pekanbaru and Batam. After three bands had performed on stage, officers of the police force and the WH, accompanied by the Deputy Mayor of Banda Aceh, stopped the concert. The officers stormed the venue, rounding up those who were dressed in punk style, mohawk hair,

1 I offer my sincere thanks to Michael Feener, David Kloos and Annemarie Samuels for their careful readings and suggestions that have sharpened and enriched my present work. I also want to thank Moch Nur Ichwan for helpful conversations at the early stage of this research. Part of this research was made possible by financial support from the Islam Research Programme Jakarta, a collaboration of the Netherlands Ministry of Foreign Affairs and Leiden University.

2 On the WH, see Feener (2013a, 219–249), as well as the chapter by Jan Michiel and Benjamin Otto in this volume.

 | DOI: 10.1163/9789004304864_008

tattoos, and chains. They were arrested and brought to the local police station. Many of them were badly beaten. Dema was fortunate and managed to escape from the sweeping. He fled on his motorbike and sought a place to hide from the police. I asked him why he came to Komunitas Tikar Pandan, rather than some other place. He said it was just unintentional. But he did not deny that he was familiar with our cultural-based organization activities and knew already where it was located.

Tikar Pandan's headquarter is housed in a sprawling, decrepit mansion set in a semi-rural area with fences wrought of living trees. It has been popular as a cultural centre in Banda Aceh since 2003. Formed under the conditions of military emergency, Komunitas Tikar Pandan was founded by a group of local artists and student activists, including myself, in order to create a space for creative activities. Framed in terms of a cultural movement and cultural critique, Komunitas Tikar Pandan had chosen the safest way to launch protests against the political violence of Aceh during the conflict. Komunitas Tikar Pandan was also one of the main critics of the BRR (the Rehabilitation and Reconstruction Agency) during the post-tsunami rebuilding program.[3] In 2007, Tikar Pandan further evolved to become the Liga Kebudayaan or 'Cultural League' with several divisions working and managing independently but remaining under one "umbrella" called Liga Kebudayaan Komunitas Tikar Pandan or Komunitas Tikar Pandan Cultural League. Those divisions include Sekolah Menulis Dokarim (The Dokarim Writing School), the Dokarim bookstore, TV Eng Ong & Institute Tukang Cerita (Institute of Traditional Story Telling), Metamorfosa Institute, *Jurnal Kebudayaan Gelombang Baru* (*The New Wave Journal*) and Tikar Pandan Public Library. In 2011, the Liga Kebudayaan Komunitas Tikar Pandan also launched a new division called Museum HAM Aceh or the Aceh Human Rights Museum.[4] Its facilities include a multi-purpose space which has been used as a museum and as a library dedicated to the memory of the conflict. Komunitas Tikar Pandan also uses this space to run film series, book readings, lectures and discussions concerning violence and human rights issues.[5]

---

3 For further discussion of Komunitas Tikar Pandan, see Grayman (2012). Komunitas Tikar Pandan's engagement in advocating the rights of Punk and other minority groups in Aceh has briefly been sketched in my "Cultural Resistance against Shariatism in Aceh" (2013), and recently in Hendrie (2014). The Komunitas Tikar Pandan website is www.tikarpandan.org.

4 For more on the Aceh Human Rights Museum program, see http://www.museumhamaceh.org/.

5 This project has been organized by Komunitas Tikar Pandan in cooperation with several human rights-based organizations, such as LBH Banda Aceh (Legal Aid Agency of Banda Aceh), KontraS Aceh (Commission for "the Disappeared" and Victims of Violence) and Koalisi NGO-HAM Aceh (Coalition of Human Rights NGOs Aceh).

Following the 2011 punk concert incident, a number of local civil society organizations and NGOs offered assistance to those who suffered from the police crackdown. The lawyers from Banda Aceh's Legal Aid Institution (LBH) offered to provide free legal aid to release the arrested punks. When Dema arrived at the Tikar Pandan house, he asked for advice on the situation. The LBH staff recommended that we provide a little space for Dema and his fellow punks to stay. In the meantime, they would provide legal aid. Tikar Pandan agreed to allow Dema to stay in its office's garage. Some of his fellow punks joined him there later on, but none of them stayed as long as Dema.

During the course of Dema's stay at Tikar Pandan, I sought out opportunities to get to know him better. This was not always easy. For example, I found that there was almost no chance to talk to him before the sun went down. I was not sure whether he was afraid of something or someone, or whether it was just a habit. Dema's daily schedule was the reverse of ours. As far as I could tell, he always went to sleep in the morning and woke up in the evening. He started his 'day' with leftovers found in the kitchen. He ate very little. Sometimes he asked the Tikar Pandan members for coffee and cigarettes but he never complained if people were unresponsive to his begging. Nights were spent surfing the internet, modifying his punk outfit and writing songs for his band.[6] Whenever I spent time in the Tikar Pandan office at night, he asked me to look at some song lyrics he was writing during his stay in our office. Unsurprisingly, these were all about protest and his critique of 'the mainstream.' I thought this would be the first time in my life to deal with a person who embodied such calmness. At times, Dema would also open up, and he easily spent hours talking to people he could trust.

Dema was born and raised in Banda Aceh. He repeatedly told me—with a smile on his face—that his ancestors came from the Arab peninsula. In Indonesia, descendants of Arabs are often associated with the family of the Prophet Muhammad and his companions. I sometimes called him 'Sayyid' or 'Habib,' as many people with Arabic ancestors are called. He told me his family did not use that *laqab* (honorific). Sometimes I joked that the Prophet would not be happy if he knew that one of his descendants has become a punker. Dema laughed at this, but then argued that there had been a lot of punks *avant la lettre* since the early days of Islam, even during the Prophet's lifetime.

---

6 In our discussions about punk, Dema explained that, for him, 'punk' actually covers a wide range of musical forms, including hardcore, black metal, and punk-reggae. Dema preferred the latter style to deliver his punk message. In pursuit of this, Dema and some friends formed a band.

'What?' I said, 'Who?' His answer surprised me. They were the Sufis, he said. The Sufis dressed and lived unlike ordinary people. Like punks, they were not interested in materiality. Also, there have been many cases of persecution of Sufis in Islamic history. I asked: "Do you consider yourself to be a Sufi, Dema?" "No," he answered immediately, "I am a punker."

Dema's family background and his views on early Islamic history inform some of the ways in which he understands and articulates his engagement with punk, and vice versa. Thus, he offers a striking example of the complexities that characterize the diversity of Muslim experience in contemporary Aceh. This descendant of the Prophet has rejected 'mainstream' society for several years. In a small city like Banda Aceh, his appearance draws attention. For many people, Dema and his fellow punks look like aliens who come from a place they do not know. As Faisal Ali, a leading Acehnese ulama expressed it: "Tattoos? Piercings? Dyed hair? That's weird for Aceh. We're not ready for that." To this he added: "This is our community, and in this community you are not allowed to act like that."[7] The "West" is commonly blamed for the behaviour of Dema and his friends. Punkers have been accused of being westernized and of seeking to force Western culture on Acehnese society. Dema himself did not really care about this. Having made the decision to reject society, he was prepared for society to reject him in return.

Punks in Aceh

The history of punk in Aceh, and in Indonesia more broadly, remains to be written. The first punk community began to become publicly visible in Banda Aceh around 1998. According to Dema and his friend Dedi Besi, punks emerged in the context of rising political tensions between Acehnese separatists and the central government in Jakarta following the fall of the New Order regime. At that time, punk activists worked hand in hand with student activists to promote the possibility of a referendum about Aceh's independence from Indonesia.[8] Many of the graphics, posters, murals and pamphlets in support of the referendum movement were created by punkers. While many of these punks were local university students, they distinguished themselves from other campus

7 See Patrick Win, "Anarchy in Aceh: Criminalizing Punk Rock under Islamic Law," http://www.globalpost.com/dispatch/news/regions/asia-pacific/indonesia/120202/aceh-punk-rock-islamic-law-shariah (Accessed 12 June 2014).

8 Interview with Dema, Dedi Besi and Jal Kayu, 6 January 2012, Banda Aceh.

activists by their punk attire worn during a series of public demonstrations. They formed several rock bands, playing gigs at the Banda Aceh Cultural Park (Taman Budaya Banda Aceh) as a means of voicing their protest to the ongoing political violence in Aceh.[9]

Despite these efforts, attempts to find a peaceful solution for the political crisis in Aceh proved unsuccessful during the early years of the 21st century. The situation changed dramatically, however, as a result of the devastating tsunami of December 2004. Like nearly all segments of society, Banda Aceh's punk community suffered great human losses. It took years for the community to recover. One punker told me that the re-emergence of the punk community in Banda Aceh started on 9 September 2009. His choice for this date to anchor his narrative—evoking popular punk fascination with the emblematic numbers of 999 and its associated 666—was intentional.[10] It appears, however, that punks had started to become visible again in post-tsunami Aceh even before this symbolic date.[11]

Dema claims to have been a punker since 1998. Looking back, he stated that the punk community of Banda Aceh would never have grown to its present size were it not for the event of the tsunami and the Helsinki peace agreement. The economic boom in Banda Aceh after the disaster was a significant factor, with reconstruction jobs attracting punks from different parts of Indonesia. In early 2011, the local daily *Serambi Indonesia* listed several punk groups active in Aceh, including Rantai Hitam (Black Chain), Museum Street Punk, Rock in Love, Damai Boleh Ribut Boleh (Peace Ok Chaos Ok), Netral, Anak Brutal (Brutal Kids), Ello, Tanggoel Rebel (Rebel Dam), Jusuid Guero, Black Green, Breume + Horizontal, and Lem of Gun.[12] Today, there are hundreds of punks in Banda Aceh, who congregate in a number of well-known spots, including the Dutch colonial cemetery (Kerkhof Peutjoet), the Tsunami museum and the Blang Padang green at the heart of the city.

Dema identifies two different types of punks. The first refers to those who choose to live as homeless 'nomads.' The second group consists of those who have stable addresses, and often have regular jobs, but who don punk gear and

---

9 Punks' strong relationship with students and civil society activists was also clearly seen in the event called "Occupy Banda Aceh," a public demonstration in front of the Governor's office on 11 November 2011. For more on this, see "Occupy Banda Aceh," http://www.acehkita.com/berita/hari-ini-aksi-occupy-banda-aceh/ (Accessed 12 June 2014).

10 Interview with Lowbat Boeloek, 20 January 2012, Banda Aceh.

11 For example, on New Year's Eve of 2008, punkers rallied around the city of Banda Aceh even though the MPU had officially banned the celebration of this holiday.

12 *Serambi Indonesia*, 11 February 2011.

hang out with other punks from time to time. The first group often considers the second to be 'posers.' In their view, these 'occasional punks' are mostly teenagers imitating a punk-look 'just for fun,' without the motivation to become a 'real' punk, that is, to commit themselves to the ideals of a punk ethic. Although many of his friends were highly critical of the posers, Dema was rather moderate in his view. He believed that the original punk community in Aceh also started as posers, after which some of them went on to become 'true punkers.'

Another striking senior figure within Aceh's diverse punk community is Dedi Satria, or Dedi Besi. Dedi was first attracted to the punk lifestyle and ideology when he was a student at Gajah Mada University (UGM) in Yogyakarta (Central Java). His sobriquet, Dedi Besi ('Iron Dedi') comes from his well-known habit of using scrap metal, especially rusty nails he finds on the streets, as clothing accessories. Dedi, who is often seen carrying around a small guitar, has been involved in a number of traditional music projects with local artists. He is also an occasional lecturer in archaeology at the Faculty of Arts and Humanities (Fakultas Adab) at the State Islamic University at Banda Aceh (UIN Ar-Raniry), an institution that has been central to the design and implementation of Aceh's current Islamic legal system (Feener 2013, 88–90). While this might seem strange to some, as I will show, complex relations to Islamic ideals and institutions characterize the lives of a number of prominent figures in Aceh's punk scene.

Lowbat Boeloek is one of the leaders of an Acehnese punk group called Tanggoel Rebel (Rebel Dam). When I interviewed him, he was finishing his studies in the Economics Faculty of Syiah Kuala University. Lowbat formed a community of punks during the early days of post-tsunami reconstruction. It included 27 members, who, according to Lowbat, shared solidarity, a sense of family, and a spirit of community service. He claimed that the punkers in his group regularly performed the five daily prayers (*salat*), and that they helped to clean Banda Aceh's streets of rubbish. While conforming to basic religious and civic ideals, Lowbat was highly critical of Aceh's Islamic legal system. In his view, aesthetic taste in hair and clothing styles were a matter of individual choice, not something the state had the right to aggressively intervene in. He emphasized that their choices of dress and deportment were sincere expressions, to be contrasted to the hypocrisy of those who claimed to be 'religious.' Punkers, he argues, ought to resist such hypocrisy.

The public profile of Aceh's punks has evolved considerably over the past decade. As the community grew and became more visible, the state Shariʿa apparatus (in cooperation with Satpol PP) started to crack down on them. These anti-punk police actions have attracted considerable attention both domestically and abroad (Balowski 2012; Hendrie 2014; Idria 2013; Moore 2012). In Jakarta and Yogyakarta, punks expressed their solidarity with their fellow-punks in Aceh. One group, called Solidarity for Aceh Punk United, rallied in front of the national police headquarters in Jakarta, on 19 December 2011. In Yogyakarta, punks gathered on 22 December to condemn the crackdown. International expressions of support for Aceh's punks took place in Moscow, San Fransisco and London, under the slogan "Punk is not crime." A Seattle-based metal and punk label, Aborted Society, initiated the "Mixtape for Aceh" project on 14 December, a project calling on punk music fans to create cassette and CD compilations of punk music, which were subsequently shipped to punk fans in Aceh early January. "Support Indonesian Punks," a Facebook campaign based in Sweden, called on punks around the world to post pictures of themselves in full punk attire. By 16 December 2011, 4500 people had signed up.[13]

Reactions—mostly online—were also heard locally as human rights groups in Aceh condemned the arrests. Aceh Human Rights Coalition executive director Evi Narti Zain said that the police actions were violent and illegal. Other human rights groups, such as LBH and KontraS Aceh, made similar statements. A particularly forceful response came in the form of an article entitled "Aku Azhari, Aku Seorang Punker: Apa Ada Masalah Besar?" ("I am Azhari and I am a punker: What's the big deal?"), posted on Facebook on 13 February 2011.[14] Within a few hours, more than 170 comments were posted. The author of the article, the Acehnese Azhari Aiyub, is a well-known figure in the Indonesian literary scene. While he does not regularly wear punk clothes or live on the streets like many other punkers, in his published writing he has expressed strong solidarity with Aceh's punk community. In his article, he identifies as a 'punker' in support of those whose human dignity was injured by the arrests and detentions of those involved with the 'Aceh for the Punk' concert. The main argument of his article, which ranged across a broad spectrum of topics from punk ideology to nihilist philosophy and anarchy, was that the existence of punks signified a powerful reaction to the increasingly pervasive hypocrisy and corruption of contemporary society.[15]

---

13 James Balowski, "Punks become latest victim of Aceh's abusive Shariah laws," *Direct Action* 38 (February–April 2012), online at: http://directaction.org.au/issue38/punks_become_latest_victim_of_acehs_abusive_shariah_laws (Accessed 12 June 2014).

14 http://www.facebook.com/note.php?note_id=10150142263646015 (Accessed 15 July 2011). This article has also been published in *Distraction Zine* 4 (June 2011).

15 Azhari told me that he had previously sent the article to several local mass media but they all rejected his article despite the fact that none of his submissions had been rejected by those publishers before. Interview with Azhari Aiyub, 16 March 2011, Banda Aceh.

In sharp contrast to these expressions of solidarity stood the responses of Islamic organizations in Aceh, most of which expressed their support for state officials and their crackdown on the punks. Several Muslim student organizations, including KAMMI, HMI and PII, signed a joined press release declaring their full support for any action to ensure the implementation of Shariʿa. Teuku Zulkhairi, a leading member of the Rabitah Taliban Aceh and a former President of Banda Aceh's State Islamic University Graduate Students Association, is one of the main figures involved in mobilizing popular support for the government's actions against the punks.[16] In an article entitled "Menyorot Komunitas Punk Aceh" (Observing the Aceh Punk Communities), Zulkhairi attacked those who defend punkers as "playing around with issues of Human Rights" and called those supporting punk people "whose way of thinking should be questioned."[17] The argument that appeals to 'Human Rights' (*Hak Asasi Manusia*) are subversive and dangerous to public order have a long and tragic history in Aceh. During the conflict, appeals to human rights were made by many Acehnese activists, including members of the Rabitah Taliban, in response to abuses committed by the Indonesian military. In the post-disaster, post-conflict period, however, appeals to Human Rights have come to be increasingly discounted by many Muslim groups in Aceh as symptoms of westernization and even Christianization—and thus as a threat to the implementation of Shariʿa.

Teuku Zulkhairi's statements are in accordance with sentiments common among many ulama, who support the project of state Shariʿa in Aceh. At the same time, they resonate with a set of concerns that have a broader basis in contemporary Acehnese society. Religious authorities and ordinary Acehnese commonly refer to the 2004 tsunami in Islamic terms, perceiving it as a critical moment in the moral development of the Acehnese Muslim community (see for example Idria 2010; Samuels, this volume). As Kloos argues in his contribution to this volume, the changes wrought on post-disaster, post-conflict Aceh have been regarded with suspicion as much as they have been welcomed. It is a common view in Aceh that cultural influences from 'outside' are threatening the moral foundations of Acehnese society. From this perspective, it becomes clear why it is feasible, or even plainly logical, for conservative opinion makers to compare the revival of punk to issues like human rights and foreign intervention. In this framework, recent changes—particularly the 'opening up' of Aceh as a result of the tsunami and the peace process—have come to be presented,

16 The Rabitah Taliban Aceh or RTA is an organization of students and alumni of traditional Islamic boarding schools (*dayah*) in Aceh.

17 *Harian Aceh*, 24 January 2012.

by some, as signs of the detrimental intrusion of Acehnese society by non-local, non-Islamic values. In the following section, I will move beyond the discursive level to examine how 'dealing with punks' has become part of state practices connected to the implementation of Shariʿa.

Punks and the Socialization of Shariʿa

Over recent years, the government of Aceh has situated the 'problem' of punks squarely in the context of the implementation of Islamic law. Government officials in Banda Aceh have stressed that they are driven by a desire not to punish the punks, but rather to 're-educate' them. Banda Aceh's former Deputy Mayor, Illiza Saʿduddin Djamal, who led the raid on the 'Aceh for the Punk' concert, characterized punk as a "a new social disease" (*penyakit sosial baru*).[18] She told the media that her motivation to take action against the concert was to intervene against a group whose lifestyle contravened Islamic law and local social norms. As she expressed it, "they must be re-educated (*kembali dibina*) in order to bring them back to the right path of Islam and the Acehnese culture."[19] In her view, the social disease of the punks must be cured through processes of education and socialization (*pembinaan*). In addition, she stressed that she viewed it as her responsibility—both as a government representative and as a mother—to guide those youngsters who had gone astray.

Behind these emotionally and politically charged justifications, there are problems with the government's response to the incident at multiple levels. One set of problems is procedural in nature. Critics of the legal handling of the 'Aceh for the Punk' crackdown have pointed out that the Deputy Mayor was not following standard regulations when the youngsters were arrested, and she subsequently asked security officials to detain and 'educate' (*membina*) the punks at the police academy in the mountainside town of Saree, where the detainees were under the exclusive authority of the state police. There, as the world saw through the photographs and videos that moved across the global mediascape, the detained punks were beaten, shaved, and jailed without trial.

Another, more important, problem concerns the apparent continuation of New Order practices within the framework of state Shariʿa. In mid-December 2011, I visited the detained punks in the boot camps in Saree to see how the

18 http://www.globalpost.com/dispatch/news/regions/asia-pacific/indonesia/120202/aceh-punk-rock-islamic-law-shariah (Accessed 12 June 2014).

19 http://www.tempo.co/read/news/2011/12/15/058371825/Anak-anak-Punk-di-Aceh-Ditangkap (Accessed 12 June 2014).

pembinaan process was carried out. I observed that the detainees were forcibly bathed in what was called a 'holy lake' (*kolam suci*), actually just a stagnant pond on the police barrack grounds, to 'purify' their bodies. After this humiliating 'cleansing' ritual, they were forced to perform a series of militaristic exercises.[20] The police officer in charge told me that the punks were undergoing *pembinaan* so that they could learn to physically and morally discipline both their bodies and their souls. When I asked who decided on this program of 're-education,' the same officer responded that the government of Banda Aceh had both allocated a budget and dictated the content of the program of 'instructing' the punks according to the standard operational discipline of the police camp.[21]

The Indonesian term for this kind of 're-education' (*pembinaan*) is derived from an Arabic root with connotations of literal 'edification.' The Indonesian form, however, comprises a prominent element of the jargon popularized by the authoritarian New Order regime, to justify its acts of repression. During the Soeharto era, the term was used euphemistically for indicating diverse acts of violence carried out by the state apparatus against its own citizens.[22] In Aceh during the conflict, *pembinaan* was often understood to refer to torture at the hands of the military. Given these associations, it is not surprising that critics of the government's actions against the punks in 2011, raised spectres of past atrocities, thus sparking sharp condemnation.

On more formal grounds, critics highlight the fact that no articles exist in either the provincial laws of Aceh (*qanun*; including those pertaining to Shariʿa) or the national legislation (KUHP) that would justify the state's arrests of the punks, or their treatment while under detention.[23] The Chair of the National Commission for Child Protection, Arist Merdeka Sirait, sharply condemned the detention without charge, the head shaving, the ritual cleansing and the military-style treatment, arguing that they were a breach of human rights.[24] Points of procedure, however, are only one—and one might argue only a minor—aspect of the differences of opinion between provincial government

---

20 Public humiliation in the forms of such mock 'purification' rites has been common in village vigilante enforcement of Shariʿa norms in many parts of Aceh. See Feener (2013a, 244–246) and cf. Kloos (2014; this volume); Otto and Otto (this volume).

21 Interview with a police officer at the Satpol Compound in Saree, 21 January 2012.

22 I derive this analysis of language from a conversation with James Siegel in Banda Aceh, December 2012. For a more general discussion of the notion of force in language, and how it was used by the New Order regime, see Siegel 1986.

23 Personal communication with staff members of the LBH Banda Aceh, Hospi Novizal Sabri and Fauzan Febriansyah, 22 January 2012.

24 Balowski, 2012.

officials and the public supporters of punks in Aceh. For on a larger, conceptual level their respective positions reflect a fundamental disconnect between their views on the legitimacy of the coercive enforcement of normative morality. Moreover, they also reflect dramatically divergent understandings of how outward forms of dress and deportment are seen in relation to interior spiritual and psychological states.

For Aceh's punks, and many of those concerned with their plight, the issue at hand is that of individual liberty and freedom of expression—a position that might be seen as reflecting particularly 'romantic' conceptions of the relationship between a person's inner self and its outward forms of expression. The dynamic of external forms in relation to the interior state of one's soul are, however, viewed differently by many of the architects and agents of Aceh's state Shariʿa system. For them, visible markers of sartorial style are not only reflective of the state of one's soul. Rather the adoption (or even enforcement) of particular forms of dress and deportment are seen as important means for instilling desired moral values in individuals—as reflected in the conceptions of *syiar* and *sosialisasi* that dominate the work of Aceh's Shariʿa Agency (DSI; see Feener 2013a, 202–212). Acehnese officials, who view Islamic law as a potential tool for programs of social transformation, aim "to use the new Islamic legal system to bring about sweeping social change in both the regulation of society and the character of individual Muslims to conform to a particular set of modern ideals."[25]

In pursuit of this project, institutions of Aceh's Islamic legal system devoted much of their attention to programs for 'socializing' Shariʿa laws (*sosialisasi*). *Sosialisasi* thus became the rubric under which their work was conceptualized, as the term came to be used in connection with a wide range of activities, from mass-media campaigns and religious sermons to roadside checkpoints and WH patrols. Common in all these *sosialisasi* programs was an overriding concern for outward expressions of piety, including 'respect' for Islamic symbols (*syiar*) and the wearing of 'proper' Muslim dress (Feener 2013a, 197–205). These concerns were often regarded by critics as focused on 'merely' symbolic aspects of Islam, while neglecting what they viewed as more 'substantial' concerns. Such critiques, however, often miss one important aspect animating state Shariʿa projects of *sosialisasi*: the ways in which the designers of the system perceive the connections between outward signs and inward states. Following a model of moral pedagogy well established in Islamic traditions, but ultimately reach-

25 Feener (2012, 286). A broader discussion is developed in Michael Feener's recent monograph (Feener 2013a).

ing back to Aristotle, the architects of Aceh's contemporary Islamic legal system see the enforcement of good habits of deportment as facilitating the eventual inward transformation of individuals.[26]

This ideal formulation of the state Shariʿa system, however, was not immune to compromise and contestation, especially since it came to be implemented through the machinery of an inefficient and unprofessional state with a long legacy of corruption, manipulation, and authoritarianism.[27] The WH, an institution that was conceived to be a major motor of *sosialisasi*, came to be regarded in some circles as little more than thugs for their heavy-handed treatment of individuals, and as such, as violating public standards of morality (Otto and Otto, this volume). With the increasing openness of public discourse in post-disaster and post-conflict Aceh, critiques of the WH's 'arrogance' and 'hypocrisy' spread beyond coffee house conversations to take a prominent position in popular media discourse (Feener 2013b).

Tensions between the ideal formulations of 'socializing' the Shariʿa by using the state apparatus of the legal system to facilitate public moral education and the exigencies of day-to-day practice in a highly contested political arena increasingly impacted the way in which the Islamic legal system actually worked, and the ways in which its work was popularly perceived. One of the major milestones along this twisted path came in 2007, when the WH was removed from the supervision of the State Shariʿa Agency (DSI) and placed under the authority of the public order police (Satpol PP). This move heightened negative images of the WH in the minds of many Acehnese, as the Satpol had a long history of association with authoritarian action, and was popularly regarded, in Aceh and throughout Indonesia, as the state's 'destroying force' (*pasukangusur*). Satpol's uncompromising and threatening public image was one that evoked conceptions of control, rather than moral persuasion. The WH were thereafter clearly seen as a Shariʿa 'Police force'—with all the negative connotations that such a designation carried for many in post-conflict Aceh.

The move to merge the WH with the Satpol PP was authorized by then-Governor Irwandi Yusuf. During the conflict, Irwandi had been a representative of the Free Aceh Movement (Gerakan Aceh Merdeka/GAM) and shared the

26 R. Michael Feener, personal communication, 16 May 2014.

27 On the internet, videos of the WH's harsh treatment of suspected offenders are numerous. For edited clips of a WH patrol and interviews with detained punks with English commentary and subtitles, see this documentary by Farish Noor and his team: http://www.channelnewsasia.com/tv/tvshows/inside-indonesia/going-it-alone/1104300.html (Accessed 12 June 2014).

former rebel organization's cynicism regarding the implementation of Shariʿa. GAM's leadership was (especially before the tsunami and the Helsinki peace agreement), extremely critical of Shariʿa and saw it as a tactic on the part of the central government to manipulate the needs of the Acehnese for independence (see Missbach, this volume). During the first half of his term as Governor, Irwandi expressed his opposition to the expansion of the Islamic legal system by curtailing state funding for its institutions and refusing to sign or implement the controversial Islamic Criminal Code (*Qanun Jinayat*), passed by outgoing members of the provincial legislature in 2009 (Großmann, this volume).

Foreign observers praised Irwandi as a secular and moderate governor who valued pluralism and freedom of expression. It might have been expected, then, that he would have been critical of the persecution of punks and their rights to free public expression. It became clear, however, that he was either unwilling or unable to intervene in any way to mitigate the treatment of those arrested and detained at the 'Aceh for the Punk' concert. Rather, Irwandi increasingly seemed to avoid alienating parties supportive of Shariʿa, a trend which grew stronger during his (failed) campaign for a second term in 2011. These political reconfigurations significantly contributed to shape the ways in which state officials responded to the 'Aceh for the Punk' concert, and further complicated a complex social landscape characterized by "the emergence of new and contested expectations and activities in the pursuit of Islamic religious and social ideals" (Feener 2013b, 17).

Aceh's Punks: Enemies of the Shariʿa or Enemies of the State?

Punk, at the very basic level, is a subculture best understood as being part youth rebellion, part artistic statement (Sabin 1999). During its heyday, from 1976 to 1979, it was a highly visible element of youth society both in the UK and the US. It manifested itself primarily in music, expressing a range of attitudes, from an emphasis on negationism (rather than nihilism), a consciousness of class-based politics (with a stress on 'working class credibility'), as well as belief in spontaneity and 'doing it yourself.' Ian Moran described punk as a 'Do-It-Yourself Subculture' (2011). Punk's 'DIY ethic' has implied a range of tactics for subverting mainstream culture. In this sense, it has been compared to other subcultures expressing an 'alternative' aesthetics, including the hippy movement, leading some to see the emergence of punk as a new manifestation of the counterculture of the 1960s (Sabin 1999, 4).

There is, however, considerable diversity within the punk scene and, as Sabin suggests, punk should not be reduced to the 'ideologically sound' prism of the

1980s and 90s. Instead, the diverse manifestations of punk should be viewed and analysed within their own specific contexts. In Indonesia, punk communities appeared mostly in large cities, such as Jakarta, Bandung, Surabaya, urban Bali, and Yogyakarta. In these places, punks were recognized as a distinct social presence with a particular public image. In the rather different social contexts of smaller cities, however, other dynamics informed the popular perceptions of the punks, particularly in relation to 'deviant' behaviour. In Banda Aceh, people generally knew very little (if anything) about the nature and the history of the punk community. As a result of this, the general public often tended to lump punks together with motorbike clubs and young beggars. During the post-disaster/post-conflict period, these views influenced broader public reactions to the diverse groups that emerged and either identified themselves, or were popularly identified with, 'punk' in this provincial context.

In Aceh (as elsewhere), punks highlight what they see as a sharp distinction between social convention and the free expression of one's 'true self.' The way that punks dress and behave in public are obviously troubling for the authorities in Banda Aceh. Police regularly intervene to break up gatherings of punks in parks and other public places across Banda Aceh. Their sometimes heavy-handed ways of doing so, have significantly furthered tensions with the punks. At the same time, the punks' continued insistence on the public display of their counterculture is a source of deep irritation for many state Shariʿa officials. As one WH officer in Banda Aceh told me: "Punkers have to respect the culture of Aceh and Islamic Law. If they do not do that, they have to leave Aceh. There is no place in Aceh for those who do not follow Shariʿa."[28] For supporters of the state Shariʿa system, public norms of dress and deportment are critical to their project of transforming Acehnese society in line with their understanding of Shariʿa ideas.

To further complicate the issue, one has to recognize that—contrary to dominant media polemics in Aceh—in reality there is no line dividing 'punks' and 'Muslims.' Dema, Lowbat Boeloek, and other punks I spoke to all maintained that many punks "are still good Muslims."[29] While acknowledging that there are diverse types of punks in Banda Aceh—including those who commit offenses against Shariʿa law, such as gambling and drinking alcohol—they asserted that some of them were diligent in prayer and fasting. Addressing this range of personal religious observance among Aceh's punks, they asked—rhetorically—in what ways this was different from Acehnese society more broadly.

28 Interview with 'Sy' (a pseudonym), 14 April 2012, Banda Aceh.

29 Interview with Dema, 29 December 2011, and Lowbat, 22 January 2012, in Banda Aceh.

The perception of a double standard leads to frustration among those punks who continue to uphold what they see as 'Islamic' belief and practice, while at the same time being persecuted by state Shariʿa officials. In this respect, the plight of at least some of Aceh's punks might be viewed in relation to the broader phenomenon of state action against 'deviant' groups.[30] According to Dema, Punks must unite and fight against such unjust persecution.[31] The 'Aceh for the Punk' concert that ended with the arrest and detention of punks, and from which Dema had fled to the Komunitas Tikar Pandan, was itself a major attempt by the punks to push back against their persecution by state officials.

The idea of the 'Aceh for the Punk' concert was conceived and developed during a series of meetings in which Lowbat had brought together many of Aceh's leading punks in search of ways to create a more positive image. The music concert was to be organized as a charity event to raise money for orphans. However, the most important message of this event is shown by the phrase they chose for the concert title, 'Aceh for the Punk.' Lowbat insisted that through this event they wanted to claim Aceh as a safe place for all to live, and for punks in particular. Their argument for the possibility of punks living harmoniously in 'Islamic' Aceh was based on the view, held by Lowbat, Dema and a number of other punks in Aceh, that their way of life is compatible with what they understand to be the ideals of the Shariʿa. Islam, in their view, cannot be limited by the narrow understandings of certain state agencies.

Ironically, the 'Aceh for the Punk' concert was part of a broader campaign of public activities through which Aceh's punks sought to demonstrate to their neighbours just how "normal" they were. Other activities of this campaign included their involvement in a broader activist scene, most notably through demonstrations against corruption and political violence.[32] For example, they joined in a peaceful demonstration in front of the governor's office during the celebration of the Human Rights Day. In addition, Lowbat claimed, punks helped the Banda Aceh government to clean the city by collecting garbage from the city streets and public places, despite the government labelling the punks as "the refuse of the society."

It seems that these efforts were successful, at least to some extent, before the crackdown on the concert. For example, Aceh's leading daily newspaper

---

30 For more on the campaign against 'deviant' religious teachings by the institutions of state Shariʿa in Aceh, see Feener (2013a, 120–126).

31 Interview with Dema, 29 December 2011, Banda Aceh.

32 Acehnese anti-corruption organizations such as GeRAK and MATa have acknowledged the involvement of punks as their regular supporters in public demonstrations against corruption.

accepted an article by a young writer, Makmur Dimila, titled "Punks are also Human Beings."[33] Providing information about Muslim punks and their positive activities in many parts of the world, Dimila argued that people cannot judge the morality of punks only by looking at their dress and hair styles. Dimila's arguments echoed those made by Dema, Lowbat, Dedi, and other punks who have attempted to broaden the perspective of their Acehnese neighbours by calling attention to the ways in which punks have established themselves in other parts of Indonesia. Thus, they often pointed to the "Muslim punk" community in Yogyakarta, who are known to dress like punks while, at the same time, being practicing Muslims. In addition to singing on the streets as punks do elsewhere across the country, this group regularly gathers in religious study groups they call "PUNKajian"—playing on the common Indonesian term for religious education (*pengajian*).[34]

Criminalization of Punk

Some of the fault lines of tensions between punks and state officials in Aceh can be traced through local media discourses. It was the popular daily newspaper *Harian Aceh* that appears to have first publicly cast punks in their charged symbolic role of opposition to the Shariʿa by publishing an anonymous letter to the editor, entitled '*Punk Ancaman Bagi Syariat Islam*' ('Punk is a Threat to the Shariʿa').[35] The letter warned readers about the presence of an "un-Islamic culture" in Banda Aceh and the author urgently demanded the local government to take serious action to counter this deviance, in order to defend the implementation of Islamic law.[36] The media campaign against Aceh's punks was continued in the largest local newspaper, *Serambi Indonesia*. Its headline of 6 January 2011 highlighted the story of a mother who had lost control of her daughter, after the latter joined a punk community. In her attempts to get her daughter back, she appealed for help from the WH. The story was complemented with a dramatic photo of the mother crying in front of the State Shariʿa Agency office.[37]

Such analyses of punks as threats to the social order and the family became a rather common element of media coverage of the clashes between the punks

33 Makmur Dimila, "Punk Juga Manusia," *Serambi Indonesia*, 19 January 2011.

34 http://punkmuslim.multiply.com/ (Accessed 2 February 2012).

35 *Harian Aceh* is a popular daily newspaper and owned by Muhammad Nazar, the former lieutenant governor of Aceh (2006–2012).

36 *Harian Aceh*, 5 December 2010.

37 *Serambi Indonesia*, 6 January 2011.

and the police (including the WH) during their raids and sweepings. As the issue was propelled to public prominence and the situation escalated, a number of parties attempted to intervene, inviting both police and representatives of punk communities to attend dialogue sessions. A number of such discussions were held in Banda Aceh, and in March 2011, the Law Faculty of Syiah Kuala University organized a public seminar on the issue. There, WH officers, punks, and academics sat together in search of "common understanding." However, physical clashes between the police and punks continued. Just before the start of Ramadan, on 29 July 2011, the WH conducted raids against punks at several locations in Banda Aceh.[38] During one of these actions, a punker named Rully (aka 'Oyie') was arrested and beaten by the authorities. A journalist from *Harian Aceh* told me that the beating occurred within sight of the Deputy Mayor of Banda Aceh.[39]

Many critics see the former Deputy Mayor's support of aggressive police campaigns against Banda Aceh's punks as related to her interest in promoting the city's struggling tourism industry. In December 2010, the municipal government had launched the "Visit Banda Aceh 2011" campaign, promoting the city as a centre of "Islamic Tourism" (*Banda Aceh Bandar Wisata Islami*).[40] In her attempts to crack down on the punks, the Deputy Mayor was able to draw on a larger base of public support motivated by concerns going beyond the city's 'Islamic' public image, including all those who were sympathetic to the broader project of state Shariʿa as a means of social and moral reform.

As elsewhere, punks in Aceh present a striking visual profile in public, marked by symbols including leather jackets, accessories, piercings, tattoos, and colourful Mohawk hairdos that serve to distinguish them from the majority of people in society. However, the divide between punks and supporters of the state Shariʿa system runs far deeper than the specifics of sartorial style. The issue is not only that they look very different, or even unsightly on the urban landscape of this 'Abode of Islam.' Rather, the architects and supporters of the Islamic legal system maintain that the 'correction' of such deviant outward behaviour is a necessary step toward effecting the transformations of individuals according to their understanding of religious ideals. Such views on 'improving' people through coercive measures of conformity with expressed

---

38 http://harian-aceh.com/2011/07/28/satpol-pp-dan-wh-keroyok-anak-punk (Accessed 31 July 2011).

39 Interview with Junaidi Hanafiah, a *Harian Aceh* journalist, 2 August 2011 at Banda Aceh.

40 One Acehnese cultural analyst (who prefers to be anonymous) told me that he was absolutely convinced that there is a strong relation between the raid of punks and the Islamic tourism program launched by the government. Interview, 26 February 2012, Banda Aceh.

public ideals stands in sharp contrast with what might be described as the Punk Ethic of rebellion against established social norms and its sharp critiques against perceived hypocrisy.

The response of the state has been the criminalization of punk. This strategy has served to impose a model of absolute distinction between the categories of 'punk' and 'Islamic.' Despite arguments by punkers such as Dema, Lowbat, and Dedi and their supporters that those two categories are by no means mutually exclusive, public opinion has been dominated by both government rhetoric and mass media discourse on punks as a source of "moral disorder" or "social disease." The crackdown on punks can thus be seen in relation not only to broader debates about human rights and freedom of expression, but also as reflecting particular dynamics of state attempts at limiting the range of 'acceptable' ways of being Muslim in contemporary Aceh. Yet, in the face of these attempts, Aceh's punks have responded by keeping up their efforts of broadening the possibilities of being Muslim and punk at the same time. Despite continuous harassment by WH and Satpol PP officers, in the years after the raid on the 'Aceh for the Punk' concert, punkers have maintained their presence in Banda Aceh's public space. The case of punk youth in Aceh thus demonstrates that state attempts to limit ways of being have not gone uncontested. In the process, punks, as well as other social groups in Aceh, continue to negotiate the limits of the state.

References

Balowski, James. 2012. "Punks become latest victim of Aceh's abusive Shariah laws." *Direct Action* 38 (February–April). Available at: http://directaction.org.au/issue38/punks_become_latest_victim_of_acehs_abusive_shariah_laws.

Feener, R. Michael. 2012. "Social Engineering through Sharīʿa: Islamic Law and State Directed Da'wa in Contemporary Aceh." *Islamic Law and Society* 19:275–311.

———. 2013a. *Shariʿa and Social Engineering: The Implementation of Islamic Law in Contemporary Aceh, Indonesia.* Oxford: Oxford University Press.

———. 2013b. "Hand, Heart and Handphone: State Shariʿa in the Age of the SMS." *Contemporary Islam* 7(1):15–32.

Grayman, Jesse Hession. 2012. "Humanitarian Encounters in Post-Conflict Aceh, Indonesia." Ph.D diss., Harvard University.

Hendrie, Doug. 2014. *Amalga Nations: How Globalization is Good.* London: Hardie Grant Books.

Idria, Reza. 2010. "Muslim Theological Perspectives on Natural Disasters: The Case of Indonesian Earthquakes and Tsunami of 2004." MA Thesis, Leiden University.

———. 2013. "Cultural Resistance to Shariatism in Aceh." In *Regime Change, Democracy, and Islam: The Case of Indonesia*, edited by Kees van Dijk, 180–201. Leiden: Leiden University. available at: http://media.leidenuniv.nl/legacy/irpfinal2013(2).pdf

Kloos, David. 2014. "In the Name of *Syariah*? Vigilante Violence, Territoriality, and Moral Authority in Aceh, Indonesia." *Indonesia* 98:59–90.

Moore, Rebekah. 2012. "Unwitting Dissidents: The Aceh, Indonesia Punk Case." Paper presented at the AMS/SEM/SMT Conference, New Orleans.

Moran, Ian P. 2011. "Punk: the Do-It-Yourself Subculture." *Social Sciences Journal* 10(1): 58–65.

Sabin, Roger (Ed.). 1999. *Punk Rock So What? The Cultural Legacy of Punk*. London: Routledge.

Siegel, James. 1986. *Solo in the New Order: Language and Hierarchy in an Indonesian City*. Princeton: Princeton University Press.

CHAPTER 8

Shari'a Police in Banda Aceh: Enforcement of Islam-based Regulations and People's Perceptions

Benjamin Otto and Jan Michiel Otto

Researching the Wilayatul Hisbah (WH)

In 2009, two weeks after I was given permission to do my research with the 'Shari'a police' (Wilayatul Hisbah/WH) in Aceh, I received a phone call that two perpetrators were caught.[1] I was told that if I would like to interview them, I should come to the office immediately.

> There he sits, at a table in the office of the Shari'a police, his face hidden behind his arms. My first respondent. I sit down next to him and ask him whether he is willing to answer some questions. He lifts his head. His face shows sadness, humiliation and despair, but he agrees to talk to me. He talks about his girlfriend, whom he plans to marry, that they slept together, how he was caught by the neighbours. He tells me how the neighbours beat him up, threw him into a rice field, pulled him out by his hair and insulted him non-stop. After this he was arrested by the Shari'a police. His left eye is swollen, as well as his lips and cheekbone. I feel sympathy for this man. All he did was have sex with the woman he loves, but he has been punished severely; physically and socially. Although I know about the strict prohibition of premarital sex in Aceh, this punishment feels disproportionate and unjust. At the end of the day I drive my motorcycle back to my house in the outskirts of Banda Aceh, my head filled with new information, contradictory emotions and thoughts about how to process all of this in my thesis. I pass the *warung kopi* (coffee shop) in

1 Benjamin Otto is a criminologist who conducted field research on the Shari'a police in Aceh. He currently works for the Amsterdam police force and volunteers for Amnesty International (Amsterdam office) as country coordinator for Indonesia. When this chapter refers to 'I,' 'me' or 'my' it is Benjamin. Jan Michiel Otto is professor of law and governance in non-Western countries and director of the Van Vollenhoven Institute for Law, Governance, and Development at Leiden University. He has published about Shari'a and national law in Indonesia and other Muslim countries.

 | DOI: 10.1163/9789004304864_009

> my *kampung* (neighbourhood), where I recently made new friends. We usually have a drink there, two or three times a day. The atmosphere is relaxed. The *warung* is like a second living room for all the men of the *kampung*. Here they brag about their newest sexual conquests and discuss the football results from the day before. My friends are sitting there as they always do. My thoughts still with the poor man who was beaten up so severely and who is awaiting his punishment at the Shariʿa police office, I join them. Taking a sip of sweet tea, one of the guys says: "Too bad you went home early yesterday. There was a couple having premarital sex just around the corner. We got them really hard."

These are my field notes from April 2009, describing the first case I encountered during my research on the implementation of Shariʿa-based criminal law by the Shariʿa police in Aceh. The fact that Aceh province introduced a series of Shariʿa-based regulations at the dawn of the twenty-first century has prompted extensive critique both within Indonesia and around the world. International media have reported on several of Aceh's new provincial regulations, including the introduction of punishments such as caning, which critics have argued are cruel and unusual.[2]

The case refers in the first place to the way in which the 'Shariʿa police' in Banda Aceh, the provincial capital, implement provincial legislation on *khalwat*, the prohibition of unmarried and unrelated men and women spending time together in an enclosed space without supervision (Qanun No. 14 /2003). The official name of what is often referred to by outside observers as the 'Shariʿa Police' is Wilayatul Hisbah; often called by its acronym WH (pronounced 'way hah' in Indonesian).[3] The case shows some of the complexities of this topic. The WH turns out to be not only a repressive police force; it can also act, in the case of excessive violence by community members, as a protector of perpetrators. Also striking is the ambiguity of people who on the one hand can react explosively when neighbours are caught committing *khalwat*, and on the other hand

2 In 2009, Aceh's provincial legislature passed a bill mandating even harsher physical punishments, including the stoning of convicted adulterers. The governor, however, refused to sign the bill into law and it has thus never been implemented. For more on this, see Großmann (this volume).

3 The Wilayatul Hisbah is not actually defined as a 'police force' in Aceh's provincial Shariʿa legislation. In practice, however, the institution appears at times as a kind of police force because of its joint operations with the civilian police (Kesatuan Polisi Pamong Praja, or Satpol PP). However, in common parlance they are also known as the 'Shariʿa Police.'

can be proud of having had premarital sex themselves. The main question of my research was how the Shariʿa-based law on *khalwat* was implemented by the WH, what the consequences were for ordinary people in Banda Aceh, and how people perceived these consequences. Meanwhile, as an inhabitant of a small *kampung* on the outskirts of Banda Aceh, I could also observe how local community members had their own time-honoured ways of dealing with people transgressing local norms.

When I arrived in Banda Aceh in March 2009, the place was completely new to me. However, Indonesia as a country was familiar. In 1989–1990, at the age of four, I lived for a year in a *kampung* in North Bandung, where I went to pre-school and played with Indonesian friends. Ten years later, I went back for a holiday trip and was happy that some of my old *kampung* playmates had remained friends. In 2005, then a student of criminology at VU University in Amsterdam, I went to Yogyakarta to study Indonesian (*Bahasa Indonesia*). I also carried out volunteer work at the local Legal Aid Bureau. Living for six months in a small middle-class neighbourhood, talking with friends, neighbours, colleagues, and driving around town on my motorcycle, I came to learn some lessons about Islam, crime, laws, and the police in contemporary Indonesia.

I learned, for example, that for many Muslims in Yogyakarta it was considered important to be a good, pious Muslim and to follow the Shariʿa (in the sense of 'God's path') and that some people did their best to break with their own frivolous pasts by trying to behave piously (see also Kloos, this volume). I also learned that there were many laws in Indonesia, some of them quite repressive, others protective, but that in practice evading the law was a national pastime, or sometimes even a necessity. It was not only the common people who did this; some policemen, officials and judges also routinely violated legal rules, or applied them arbitrarily. When dozens of motorcyclists were ordered to stop to have their driving licenses checked, some were formally punished, while others could bribe their way out. Some others again, were able to just pass, as the police decided not to bother them—seemingly because of their appearance as possibly well-connected persons (for example if the driver was, like me, exceptionally tall and of a white complexion). At the Legal Aid Bureau, I noticed how the police arrested people and intimidated them, which is a violation of the law. I also learned about all kinds of social rules, commonly referred to as *adat* (tradition, or customs), to which people were supposed to comply. Nevertheless, in spite of state laws, Islamic rules and *adat* norms, both crime and violations of religious and *adat* norms (including gambling, drinking, and prostitution) were not uncommon in certain circles in Yogyakarta. In fact, it sometimes seemed to me that, at least in some contexts, extramarital and premarital sex were as common in Islamic Indonesia as in libertarian Amsterdam.

My observations of such patterns of lawlessness were perhaps not new. Many legal anthropology studies of Indonesia have discussed the ineffectiveness of the legal system. One major line of argument in such work has been that state law is a modern phenomenon, foreign to indigenous communities and naturally bound to meet much social resistance rooted in local traditions (Von Benda Beckmann 2002). However, in Aceh the issue seemed to be a different one. Here the state, through the initiatives of provincial and local governments, has tried to impose new religion-based legal rules on today's society. Would such appeals to religion and/or custom in state law have more legitimacy, and would it therefore be implemented more effectively here? After Bandung and Yogyakarta, I was curious about the limits of law in Aceh, and especially of criminal regulations derived from Shariʿa. How were these rules implemented? What was their effect? Moreover, how did the project of state Shariʿa implementation relate to informal community action, including the kind of vigilante violence referred to in the example above?

In order to find answers to such questions, I first went to the courts and to the prosecutor's office to find out how many cases had actually been prosecuted, forwarded to the courts, and how many cases had resulted in actual punishments. In this way, I also hoped to locate perpetrators, and to interview them about their punishments and their perceptions of the Shariʿa-based law and the WH. This was not a great success. To my surprise, I found that the last case in which someone had been formally prosecuted was in 2007, and that for more than two years after that not a single case had been forwarded to the court in Banda Aceh for prosecution. I did collect a few names and addresses of former perpetrators but I found that these people had moved away without leaving their new addresses. Once, I had a door slammed in my face. Clearly, this was not a subject people liked to be reminded of. It turned out that I could not start my research with the perpetrators directly, and I had to begin at the other end, with the law and its agents. Thus, I decided to focus on the work of the WH, and particularly on their patrols and their raids. Fortunately, the WH allowed me to observe their routines and practices. Over a period of five months, I spoke to dozens of people about the Shariʿa-based criminal law and its implementation. In this period, I came to know about nine cases of people being apprehended for committing *khalwat*. I spoke to all of the perpetrators involved in these cases.

It is important to note that my research was carried out in the city of Banda Aceh. The implementation of Aceh's Shariʿa-based regulations, which are formally named *qanun*, is not uniform everywhere across the province of

Aceh, and there are considerable fluctuations in the rate of cases brought to court. As mentioned above, there has not been any caning since February 2007 in Banda Aceh, whereas in Langsa (East Aceh), 53 people were caned in the year 2011 alone.[4] Most of the community members I interviewed were men. For women especially, it is very shameful in Aceh to talk about having had sex before marriage. For me as a male foreign researcher, it was almost impossible to discuss the subject with women. In several cases, however, I had the chance to talk to both the male and female perpetrators at the same time, so this gave me the opportunity to interview some women as well. As a consequence the results presented in this chapter are based mainly, but not exclusively, on male inhabitants of Banda Aceh.

The next section sketches the legal background of the *khalwat* regulation and how it was supposed to mark a new era in law-society relations in Indonesia. In the third section, we will discuss the work of the WH, by focusing on its three main tasks: patrols, raids, and investigation of suspected *khalwat* cases. Section four deals with the question of what happens to the people who get caught for committing *khalwat* and how this experience is perceived by them. In the fifth section, to illustrate in more detail the actual practice of implementing the *khalwat* regulation in Banda Aceh, we will present a more extensive description of one of the nine cases encountered during the fieldwork. In the sixth section, we discuss some of the ways in which ordinary people think and talk, on a day to day basis, about the WH and Aceh's Shariʿa-based penal law. Finally, in the concluding remarks we will try to interpret the impact of the Shariʿa-based penal law on daily life in Aceh.

The New Shariʿa-based Regulations in Aceh

Until 1999, Indonesian law was 'made in Jakarta' and aimed at 'development' (*pembangunan*). Development under the New Order (1966–1998) stood for stability, economic growth, and a certain degree of redistribution. Suharto and his generals viewed law as an instrument of power and development policy. Law would help the government's orders be carried out in orderly ways, and pre-

4 It is important to note that the years 2007–2010 were a pronounced low-point in terms of formal Shariʿa criminal cases brought to court. There was, however, a temporary resurgence in some districts (*kabupaten*) in 2011—particularly in the run-up to the elections. Whereas my fieldwork was carried out from March to August 2009, I conducted an Internet-based survey of local Acehnese newspapers in the summer and autumn of 2011, to learn about recent court decisions and punishments throughout Aceh province.

scribe how people would become 'developed' (Lev 2000). With regard to both *adat* and Islamic law, Suharto's government was ambiguous. *Adat* law was formally recognized but in the practice of land administration it was often denied or overruled by the government (Safitri 2010). Shari'a was controlled by the New Order government by incorporating acceptable versions of it into national law, for example in the 1974 Marriage Act, and in the 1989 Religious Courts Act. Such measures, however, generally dealt exclusively with the administration of Islamic family and inheritance law. In Aceh, however, there already were precedents for official promulgation of Shari'a criminal legislation over the past half century (Feener 2013).

Aceh had been granted special autonomy status in 1959 in the domains of culture, religion, and education, as result of the Darul Islam rebellion, which ended in 1962. During the Suharto era, provinces and districts still had some legislative autonomy on paper, however in practice this was extremely limited. Governors and district heads used to receive 'prefab' draft-regulations from Jakarta in the form of a directive (*pedoman*) ready to be enacted. In short, although the New Order government promoted the image of Indonesia as a '*Negara Hukum*' (state based on the rule of law), law-making was undemocratic, the bureaucracy including the police was authoritarian and quite corrupt, the judiciary had lost its independence and was also corrupted whereas the government regarded human rights as an instrument of subversion, and legal aid as suspect. From the perspective of common people in search of justice, the better option was generally to try and 'fix' or 'negotiate' things with the administration through brokers or mediators rather than rely on the court system.

After the fall of Suharto in 1998, new efforts were made to realize the national idea of a *Negara Hukum*. Constitutional amendments reduced the role of the military in government, and strengthened democratic mechanisms, the roles of parliament and of the courts *vis-à-vis* the executive. A bill of rights was introduced. In 1999, Law 25 on regional autonomy gave districts and towns a considerable degree of autonomy to regulate their own affairs. Fear of separatist tendencies in the provinces of Aceh and Papua led the central government to granting special authorities to both provinces, allowing local administrators to create their own regulations.[5] Law No. 18/2001 on Aceh enabled the province to base its regulations on Shari'a. This was in line with a long tradition of the Acehnese taking pride in their reputation for being among the country's

5 For a more extensive discussion of the relationship between Islamic and national law in contemporary Indonesia, see Otto (2010).

most committed Muslims—as reflected in the popular soubriquet for Aceh, 'the Veranda of Mecca' (*Serambi Mekkah*). The province of Aceh had already once successfully demanded special status in the 1950s. The effect of that earlier special status had remained limited, but the ambitions of the special autonomy provisions of the post-Suharto period were higher.

In these developments, Aceh's provincial branch of the Indonesian Ulama Council (MUI, later re-established as MPU) played an active Islamizing role by issuing several *fatwas*. In 2002 and 2003, Aceh's State Shariʿa Agency (Dinas Syariat Islam/DSI), then led by Alyasa Abubakar, professor of religious studies at the State Islamic Studies Institute (IAIN, presently UIN) Ar-Raniry in Banda Aceh, was (among others) involved in the preparation of draft provincial regulations, referred to locally as *qanun*. Soon thereafter, the provincial parliament enacted several *qanuns* based upon those drafts. The two most relevant to this chapter are Qanun No. 11/2002, notably its subsection concerning Islamic dress codes, and Qanun No. 14/2003 on *khalwat*, which prohibits unmarried couples to be together in a secluded place. The sanctions contained in Qanun 14 are threefold, namely fine, imprisonment, and caning. The legislator has framed the latter typically as a provision of criminal state law (*tazir*) bearing no reference to the Qur'anic punishment of the *hudud*-crime of adultery (*zina*). Here, it may be noted that in nearby Malaysia, which in many ways has functioned as an example for the formal implementation of Shariʿa law in Aceh, the Islamic judiciary has been increasingly modelled on the generally more prestigious civil judiciary (Peletz 2013). Caning, moreover, is quite common in Malaysia and Singapore, including in non-Islamic contexts, being a legacy of British colonial law rather than an outcome of Islamic regulations (Lindsey et al. 2007, 245–246).

Getting to Know the WH

The physical condition of their office in Banda Aceh is very telling of the situation of the WH. On 1 January 2009, the WH moved from the well-maintained DSI premises to a lesser office, on the compound of the Mayor's Office, close to the offices of the Local Government Police, the *Kesatuan Polisi Pamong Praja*, generally known as Satpol PP, of which the WH formally became a unit. Remarkably, on 12 May 2009, the WH changed location again, allegedly because its office was to be renovated. The new building was in an even worse condition. Parts of the ceiling looked as if they could fall down any second and there were big cracks in the wall. The building they had used previously had not been very impressive either, but compared to the current place it had looked much better. Before 2009, when the WH was still part of the DSI, they had been located in a brand new complex. The rapid deterioration of their housing conditions seemed to be a reflection of the political priorities of the provincial government.

The WH is the 'police unit' responsible for upholding the provincial Shari'a-based regulations. The first legal document describing the WH's role was the general elucidation of Qanun No. 11/2002, the introduction of which reads as follows:

> The Wilayatul Hisbah as a supervisory institution is granted the role of warning, guiding, and advising, so that the cases of contravention of this Qanun that are submitted to the investigators, to be followed up and forwarded on to the courts, are cases that have been through a process of warning and guidance toward the offender.

Two years later, this was specified further in the Governor's Decree 1/2004 on the Establishment and Functions of the WH. This Decree stipulates that the role of the WH includes: a) providing guidance and spiritual advocacy, including informing the public of *qanun* relating to Shari'a; b) monitoring compliance with Shari'a legislation; c) rebuking, warning and providing moral guidance to those suspected of violating the Shari'a; d) trying to stop activities/conduct suspected of violating the Shari'a; e) settling violations through a village customary meeting (*Rapat Adat*); and f) transferring violations of the Shari'a to the police who are legally responsible for conducting investigations of criminal offences (UNDP et al. 2006, 48–49). Interestingly, none of these tasks really make the WH seem like a 'police force' in any conventional sense, as there are no provisions for arrest, detention, and the like.

Although the WH was created on paper as early as 2000 (Qanun No. 5/2000), it only became active in the field after the December 2004 tsunami. At first, only the provincial capital Banda Aceh had a WH unit, but one year later district offices had been established all over the province. There were other important changes as well. Originally, the WH was placed directly under the State Shari'a Agency. However, in January 2009, the WH was formally integrated with the public order police, the Satpol PP. The WH itself does not have the legal power to enforce the Shari'a-based regulations. For this, they need the support of the Satpol PP. To arrest, detain or even enter a living space, the presence of a Satpol PP member is a requirement. Co-operation between the WH and the Satpol PP is therefore prerequisite to enforce Aceh's Shari'a-based criminal regulations. However, the different institutional and social backgrounds of the two forces and its officers has made this very difficult to achieve. During my research, I noted that members of both units often regarded each other in a negative way. The Satpol PP was regarded by members of the WH as a bunch of rude, non-believing and violent men, whereas Satpol PP officers considered the members of the WH as "weak, hypocritical people without any explicit authority."[6] As one WH official put it: "They are rude people. They are also not happy with us. As soon as the Director is not around, they enjoy annoying and insulting us."[7]

In order to get to know the modus operandi of the WH, I joined their daily patrols. Although not all the patrols were the same, the following description from my notes gives a good insight into the daily work of the WH officers.

> The next day I go back to the office. I have been told that patrols are held three times a day. For safety reasons I am not allowed to join the WH officers in the patrol car, but I can follow them on my motorbike to see how they work and how the citizens react. The patrol is not as exciting as I thought it would be. We drive around for one hour, only stopping once. There is a big empty building where young couples could hide to seek some privacy, which is of course forbidden according to the law on *khalwat*. We search the building, without finding anybody. On the way back nothing much happens. Occasionally a WH officer shouts from the back of the pick-up truck to a woman that she should wear a headscarf. The woman either shrugs or looks away a bit ashamed. In any case it doesn't matter too much, because the pick-up truck continues its way back to the office. Back in the office I find out that the work of the WH officers is pretty much limited to the three daily patrols. In between these patrols, the officers sit around, drink coffee, and talk. This gives me a perfect opportunity to get to know these officers and learn about their backgrounds.

The starting qualifications to get a regular, salaried job at the WH are twofold. One needs to be able to demonstrate a general proficiency in Qur'anic literacy, and one should have a bachelor degree from a university.[8] After a while, I found out from my daily conversations in the WH office that the employees are not all equally pious and motivated to do their work. Some really hoped to contribute to the Islamization of Aceh, while others were interested only in their monthly paycheck. These differences were also clear when I observed the

6 Personal communication with a member of the Satpol PP, June 2009, Banda Aceh.

7 Personal communication with a member of the WH, June 2009, Banda Aceh.

8 Interview with an administrative staff member of the WH, Banda Aceh, April 2009.

officers doing their job. Some WH officers explained the Shari'a regulations to young couples with a lot of conviction and sincere belief, while others preferred to stay in the back of the car as often as possible. A good example of an officer with a seemingly relaxed attitude toward the task of Islamizing society is presented in the next quote. This is what this officer said five minutes after the patrol started: "Wow, it's pretty hot. It looks like there will be no perpetrators today."[9]

During my research, I witnessed three main practices through which the unit tried to uphold Shari'a-based law: daily patrols, clothing raids, and investigations of people suspected of committing, or having committed, *khalwat*. I will now describe three cases, one for each practice, in order to show how the WH tried to fulfil its task.

The Patrol

Occasionally the WH officers were assigned a specific task for their patrol. Visiting 'beauty salons' (*salon*) is an example of such a task.

> "Hey hey, it's 9 o'clock, we are leaving," the shift leader shouts. The WH officers gather around and get into one of the two departing pick-up trucks. I ask the shift leader where we are going today. He tells me that we will go to Peunayong, a district in the city centre, to check upon some beauty salons. Usually we drive around the city without a specific destination, so I am excited that I will get to see something new today. We arrive at the first salon. I join the five officers who enter the salon to see what they will do. The other fifteen officers wait outside in the truck. An intimidating transvestite (*bencong*) sits inside and asks us provokingly whether we want a massage. One of the officers starts to interrogate her. He asks whether there is prostitution, whether she closes during Friday prayer, whether this is indeed a women-only salon and similar questions.[10] The others look around. I join one of them upstairs. There we find several small rooms with mattresses on the floor. In one of the

9 Interview with a senior WH officer, June 2009.

10 Because of the Shari'a regulations it is forbidden to run mixed gender beauty salons. Women should be treated by women and men by men. In practice, an exception is made for transvestites: they can work in both male and female salons. Most of the salons are female salons, but almost all have a second floor with small rooms and mattresses, which suggests that there is also a male clientele.

> rooms, four young, barely dressed girls are resting. As soon as they see me, they start shouting: "Mister mister, you like me? Mister mister, come back, come here." It seems pretty clear to me that I have just seen my first Acehnese brothel. I ask one of the officers why they don't act upon this discovery. He answers that the girls could also be family or employees. He can only close the shop when the prostitutes are caught in the act. We thank the owner for her time and go back outside. This ritual is repeated a few times. After visiting five or six salons we head back to the office. Time for coffee.

During my research, all the salon check-ups were carried out during the morning shift. Although the odds of catching the prostitutes red-handed would probably be higher on a night patrol, the WH never did this. Curious about the WH officers' view, I suggested that they conduct this salon check in the evening, but none of them considered this to be a good idea. I could only conclude, then, that the WH did not really want to stop the prostitution in Peunayong, but they did want to pretend that they tried to stop it. Although I asked several WH officers, I was not able to find out whether the WH was actually ordered or pressurized to tolerate prostitution and if so, by whom, or whether they had other reasons for not closing down these poorly disguised brothels.

The WH usually went out on patrol three times a day. A few officers would stay at the office to answer the phone while the rest joined the patrol. The description above is an example of what the officers did during a patrol. Also, they often looked for hidden stashes of alcohol or for young couples trying to find some privacy in romantic places such as the pier in the harbour district of Ulee Lhee. Another regularly chosen option was to just drive around for an hour, shout at some unveiled women to put on a headscarf, and return to the office. The average duration of a patrol was about one hour. If female officers joined the patrol, they always sat in a separate car.

Clothing Raids

Besides the daily duty of going on patrol, the WH occasionally organized a raid (*razia*). This meant that they set up a road block to check if passers-by were wearing proper Islamic clothing. The following two descriptions of one such raid are taken from my field notes of May 2009.

> "These pants are too tight. I can see the shape of your legs," an officer blurts. "You are not being a good Muslim." During the raid almost all

> the women and occasionally a man or two are pulled off the road to be lectured about the way they dress. About 80 per cent of the women passing are dressed improperly, according to the WH officers. Although almost all of them are covered from the ankle to the neck and most of them also wear a headscarf, they still don't pass the Shari'a dress code.

According to the Shari'a regulations, women should be dressed in accordance with Islam, which is generally interpreted as being completely covered except for their feet, hands and face.[11] In addition to this, the shape of the body should not be visible through the clothes. This automatically excludes jeans and many other 'western-style' clothes. For men, the dress code is less strict. Men should be covered up from knee to belly button. However, bare-chested men are a regular sight in Banda Aceh and that is not considered very shocking.

> When stopped on the road, the women have to hand over their identity card ("KTP"). Then they get a five-minute lecture from one of the WH officers about how decent Muslim women should dress. None of the women speak up. Some bow their heads in shame, while others look angry or annoyed. I try to interview some women. The ones that are ashamed prefer to leave as soon as possible. The others are willing to talk. They tell me that they don't agree with these raids. They feel discriminated against because only women are being lectured. They also feel violated in their right to dress the way they want. And most of all they feel the WH is being hypocritical. They have read in the newspaper about a WH officer caught for having sex with a high-school girl and other scandals. Now they are being lectured by officers from the same institution about the way they dress. They feel wrongly accused and that upsets them. After being lectured the women are allowed to pick up their KTP. They have to register before their card is returned and they are allowed to continue on their way. After two hours the WH calls it a day. Hundreds of forms are completed with names of improperly-dressed women and no arrests have been made.

---

11 Qanun No. 11/2002, article 13(1) states that "Every Muslim is required to dress in accordance with Islam (*Setiap orang Islam wajib berbusana Islami*)." The latter is defined as wearing "clothes that cover one's *aurat* (intimate parts of the human body), which are not transparent, and which do not show the shape of the body (*pakaian yang menutup aurat yang tidak tembuspandang, dan tidak memperlihatkan bentuk tubuh*)."

During the five months in which I observed and followed the WH in Banda Aceh, only two such 'clothing raids' were organized. What happened with the names of the women who were lectured was unclear. I never saw anyone process these forms in a computer programme or check the names of the first raid with the names of the second raid. Strangely, whereas Aceh's Islamic dress codes have been discussed all over the world, I found that the actual impact of these raids seemed rather marginal. Their infrequency, the lack of actual punishments, the fact that the WH looked upon virtually all women as perpetrators, and last but not least the outcome that in general women in Banda Aceh did not seem to change the way they dress; all these factors contributed to the marginality of such official state enforcement measures. Obviously, in this case the state-sponsored 'Shariʿa norms' went far beyond commonly accepted practices. At the same time, as we have seen already at the beginning of this chapter, (particular segments of) local communities had their own, sometimes violent, way of defining, and dealing with, moral transgressions.

Investigations

The third part of the WH job, which potentially had a much greater impact on the lives of those people targeted, was to respond to tips from Banda Aceh citizens about the whereabouts of couples arrested for (or suspected of) committing *khalwat*. The WH often received phone calls or text messages from worried or upset neighbours. Whenever the tip was considered serious, the WH set out for the given location to take the perpetrators into custody. On rare occasions, the WH themselves caught people in the act during a patrol, such as in the case of a 'rocking car' in the harbour district,[12] but in most cases they depended on tips from the residents of Banda Aceh.

The following field notes from July 2009 show that the WH depended not only on the tips of the local population to make an arrest, but also on their permission to do this.

> The last patrol of the day is already over and I sit with the WH officers who await the end of their shift. Every now and then a text message comes

12 "Mobil Goyang," *Serambi Indonesia* (1 June 2009). In this case, the WH spotted a wobbling car during their patrol. Officers approached the car to see what was going on. When they reached the vehicle, they found two people having sex in the car. These two people were immediately arrested.

> in with reports of people committing *khalwat*. No action follows. They believe them to be just prank messages. Then the phone rings, and this time it seems like there is an actual case. After a short discussion, the shift leader decides we have to pull out. When we arrive at the 'crime scene' a lot of people have already gathered around the two suspects. One of the WH officers questions the witnesses and the head of the *kampung*. I notice there is a vivid discussion, for some people disagree completely with the officer. After ten minutes the WH officers retreat. They tell me that the *kampung* security men have decided to solve this matter themselves.[13] They do not allow the WH to take the suspects into custody.

This case shows the limited power of the WH. Although Qanun No. 14/2003 aims to discourage premarital sex, the WH cannot do much without the permission of the villagers. In this particular case, the villagers preferred to solve the matter themselves. But in other cases, I was told by villagers that the WH had been called by angry community members and requested to arrest the suspect. There were also cases, as we have learned from the first case discussed in this chapter, in which the violence used by local people against the suspects was so brutal that concerned villagers asked the WH to arrest the suspects for their own safety.

Whether local community members want the WH to intervene or not depends on several factors. Usually a distinction is made between original inhabitants of the *kampung* and 'people from outside' (*orang luar*, or *pendatang*), that is, recent newcomers. When perpetrators originate from the *kampung* where they are caught, the matter is generally solved 'within the family' (*secara keluarga*) or 'according to custom' (*secara adat*) between the neighbourhood leader (*Geuchik* or *Kepala Lorong*),[14] the family and sometimes some

---

13 Many *kampungs* have their own security arrangements. Usually all the (young) men from the *kampung* (*pemuda kampung*; literally 'village youth') take turns patrolling at night. This may be once a week or every other week.

14 All over Indonesia local administration is divided into several levels. Towns (*kota*) like Banda Aceh and rural districts (*kabupaten*) are divided into sub-districts (*kecamatan*). Sub-districts have offices headed by the Head of the sub-district, the *Camat*. Physically, a sub-district hosts a number of *kampungs*, a kind of urban villages, which have a name, a history, a community and local leaders with which the *kampung* dwellers identify. Administratively, sub-districts are further divided into local units which, in rural areas, are called 'villages' (*desa*). The heads of these units, the Village Heads (*Geuchik/Kepala Desa*) are popularly elected, and have an office, a staff, and some consultative bodies of community members. Aceh's Regional Regulation No. 7/2000 on the Establishment of Adat Life employs the Acehnese adat term *Geuchik* to refer to the Village Head rather

respected members of the *kampung*.[15] Among the nine cases I observed there was not a single case in which the person arrested by the WH was an original inhabitant of a *kampung*. The arrested perpetrators were always 'outsiders.' This can be explained by the absence of a family to solve the problem in a family way, and by a lack of personal concern among community members for the fate of an 'outsider.' Other factors can influence the decision to call the WH as well. The availability of a WH unit nearby or the local tradition to solve problems within the community are factors that influence this decision. The type of violation can also be important. If the offense is not considered that severe, the choice is often made to solve the matter within the *kampung*. When the crime is considered pretty serious or the offender has already been caught several times, the chances of the WH being called in increase.

Patterns of WH Practices of Dealing with Perpetrators

In the previous sections, I introduced the WH, its main tasks, and the atmosphere in which its officers carried out their work. In this section, I will analyze in more detail the third task, which is the investigation of accused perpetrators of the *khalwat* prohibition. From my field research, I gradually found out that the WH had developed its own ways of dealing with perpetrators of the Shariʿa-based *khalwat* regulation. Although every case was slightly different, I was eventually able to recognize a clear pattern. Based on my nine case studies, as well as various conversations and observations, the WH's practice regarding *khalwat* investigations may be schematized in nine distinct 'steps' or 'phases.' These are: 1) discovery, 2) internal handling, 3) 'arrest,' 4) detention and inter-

---

than the Indonesian term *Kepala Desa* (UNDP 2006, 50). Below this level, a form of neighbourhood organization has been established throughout Indonesia. In cities, the subdistricts are not divided in *desa* but in so-called *kelurahan*, the head of which (*Lurah*) is not elected, but is an appointed official. Below the level of *desa/kelurahan*, at the grassroots level, a few dozens of houses are grouped together as a neighbourhood block called *lorong* (literally 'alley'). Their head, a community member, is elected and called Pak Lorong. Pak Lorong is the voluntary local leader who provides a regular connection between the officials of the *desa/kelurahan* office and the members of their community.

15 Solutions like these commonly involve a 'peace making' ritual (*perdamaian*), featuring a public apology, possibly in combination with the imposition of a fine. Village leaders might go further, however, for example by pressuring the accused couple and their families into getting married on the spot (that is, at the nearest mosque).

rogation, 5) calling the family, 6) calling the press, 7) lecture by WH director, 8) reporting to the WH, and 9) stigmatization.

1) *The discovery*: WH officers rarely discovered a *khalwat* case themselves.[16] Thus, they were almost completely dependent on worried, jealous, or upset people (often neighbours) to tell them where they could find wrongdoers. The case mentioned in the introduction shows how brutal violence could occur when unmarried couples were caught by their neighbours in moments of illicit intimacy. Later, I learned that one neighbour was so worried about the perpetrators being beaten up that she called the WH. She figured that the arrival of the WH would stop the violence and bring them to safety.

When I asked one of the attackers in this case why they had reacted so brutally, he answered:

> When people have premarital sex, the whole *kampung* will be contaminated with this sin (*kena dosa*). Later all the villagers will be punished [by God] for that sin (*dihukum untuk dosa ini*).

The same man had told me several times before that he had had sex with more than one woman in his life, although he was not married. I could not understand the difference between him having premarital sex and his bragging about it in the coffee shop on the one hand, and his angry and aggressive reaction when he caught someone else committing the same 'crime' on the other hand. When I confronted him with my lack of understanding, he answered, with a serious tone:

> Actually having sex before marriage is forbidden. It is indeed a sin. When you get caught you will be beaten for sure. But when nobody finds out, it's ok.

This is an interesting example of how some young Acehnese men dealt with strict Shari'a regulations. Not all men I came to know in Aceh shared this opinion, but it seemed that everyone had to find a way of coping with the incompatibility of the temptations of everyday life and the desire to be a self-respecting Muslim. I could also deduct from the way this man and his

---

16 Often, young couples were found sitting in a secluded place outdoors. Apparently, these violations often were not considered severe enough to arrest and detain the suspects. In the nine cases I investigated, all suspects were caught while being together in isolation inside a house or building.

friends talked about what happened that punishing perceived wrongdoers was something they enjoyed doing. Beating up a 'sinner' brought a lot of excitement to the village and they considered it a legitimate way to express some aggression or frustration.

2) *Internal handling*: The head of a *kampung* was always informed when people were caught committing *khalwat*. He decided how the case should be settled and whether the WH should be called. There were several ways, I was told by local *kampung* dwellers, to solve the problem 'according to custom (*adat*).' One was by paying money, to be used for the common good. Another settlement involved ritual 'bathing' (*dimandikan*). The perpetrator would be literally washed with water, which symbolized washing away the sin. Less friendly were the solutions in which the perpetrators were 'washed' with sewage water or subjected to different forms of humiliation and/or physical violence.[17]

3) *The 'arrest'*: After the perpetrators were handed over by the head of the *kampung*, they were taken into custody by the WH. In all the cases I witnessed, the perpetrators were apprehended without violence. Officially, the WH did not have the legal authority to arrest and detain people. However, in practice this was often ignored. Even with the consent of the Satpol PP, WH officers were not allowed to detain people suspected of committing *khalwat*, but many people are unaware of this. Practices like 'bathing' the perpetrators may be seen as *adat* punishments. However, involving the WH meant that the conflict was not to be solved internally, on the basis of *adat* law alone.

4) *Detention and interrogation*: At the WH office, couples suspected of committing *khalwat* were separated and questioned to determine what had happened exactly. Detention could last from a few hours to a few days. During the interrogation, dubious methods were often used to find out the 'truth.' Threats, lies and insinuations were not uncommon. Alternatively, WH officers would lecture the suspects about religion. How much pressure was put on the suspect depended on the officer. Again, the WH did not have the official authority to detain people. Therefore, they used an alternative method. They did not lock the perpetrators up, but forbade them to leave the office area. By taking away their identity card, threatening them with prosecution and not informing them about the absence of legal grounds for such detention, perpetrators were *de facto* detained. In one

17 See Kloos (2014) for an elaborate discussion of handling *khalwat* violations within the *kampung*.

of the cases, a young student accused of committing *khalwat* told me that he did not have the slightest clue whether he was to be detained for a day, a month or a year.

5) *Calling the family*: As in *adat* law settings, close family members were called in to discuss what should happen with the perpetrators. Should the latter be forced to marry, or forbidden to meet again? Should they be punished at home as well, or was the arrest itself sufficient punishment? Usually the suspects were asked to contact their family to report to the station. Preferably the parents were called, but in cases in which they were not available, an older brother, uncle or even a nephew would do as well. In one of the cases I studied, both suspects had no family left because of the tsunami. The WH did not know how to solve this matter without family, so they handed the suspects over to the regular police. There, the unhappy couple stayed incarcerated until they gathered enough money to bribe themselves out.

6) *Calling the press*: Local journalists told me that they always got phone calls from the WH when a new couple was arrested for committing *khalwat*. Usually they wrote about the nature of the crime and the circumstances in which it occurred. When I asked at the WH office why the newspaper always had to be notified, a WH officer answered that this would prevent other people from doing the same. For many perpetrators this form of publicity was the worst part of the punishment. People were very ashamed when they were accused publicly of committing *khalwat*. As one suspect told me, "I am already ashamed enough towards my family and *kampung*. Why should all the people in the city be informed? Besides, it could cost me my job if my boss finds out."[18]

7) *Lecture by the WH director*: In the seventh phase, typically a meeting was held, chaired by the director of the local WH office, to decide what should happen to the perpetrators. In those instances I witnessed, the WH director was talking 90 per cent of the time, using the occasion to lecture them once more about their immoral behaviour. Usually the perpetrators stayed silent and nodded quietly, responding only when they were asked something. When the families from both sides and the director had decided on the fate of the perpetrators, and they themselves had promised not to make the same mistake again, they were released.

18 Interview with a male *khalwat* perpetrator, 18 May 2009, Banda Aceh.

8) *Reporting to the WH*: The release was not unconditional. At the Banda Aceh WH office, the accused had to return to the WH office at regular intervals thereafter to report in. In most cases, three such visits were stipulated. During these visits, they were lectured again about their misbehaviour and about the purpose of Islam. The perpetrators were free to choose when to come back, but their KTP would only be returned after the third visit. One of the perpetrators from my case studies reported twice, but did not feel like reporting again. Instead he went to the civil registry and applied for a new KTP, which he received two weeks later.

9) *Stigmatization*: After the suspects were released, the real punishment was often yet to start. As a result of the publication in the local newspapers, many other people were aware of the events that happened. In one case, the perpetrator was forced to leave his *kampung*. In another case, a perpetrator was allowed to stay, but nobody wanted to talk to her anymore. She eventually decided to leave the *kampung* herself, since, as she described it, "My neighbours don't talk to me anymore. Even the one I used to be close with does not dare to be friends with me anymore."[19] One girl was also suspended by her local school. She was photographed by the local newspaper wearing her school uniform. The school claimed that she had given it a bad reputation, and expelled her. A man involved in another case, who was held for two days, lost his job. As he described it, "I could not come because I was caught, and many people would like to work where I work. When I did not come the second day either, my boss gave my job to someone else." Although many people did not comply with the Shariʿa-based penal regulations, the stigmatization of those who were caught was typically a cause for great worry, especially when it concerned *khalwat*, which was considered a very bad sin. Just as in the case of the man from my *kampung*, whom I quoted above, sometimes the difference between acceptable and immoral behaviour seemed to be a matter of being able to avoid being seen and caught.

This pattern shows how the WH developed its own particular practices in the absence of formal prosecution by the public prosecutor and adjudication by the Islamic courts. This practice is not based on any official policy to deal with *khalwat* perpetrators as such, but the WH developed it by applying the limited means they had at their disposal. Whereas the abovementioned sequence of nine phases was applied in almost all cases observed during my field research, there were also exceptions. For instance, there was one case in which a perpe-

19 Interview with a female *khalwat* perpetrator, 5 May 2009, Banda Aceh.

trator was a friend of a well-known politician. This powerful friend arranged that the press would not publish an article in the newspaper about the case.

Being Caught by the WH

In this section, we would like to provide some insight into the experiences of those who were apprehended by the WH. Of course, the cases I studied were all different. The facts of the cases varied considerably, the backgrounds of the people who got caught were diverse and their ages also varied. Yet, from the nine cases observed, a few generalizations can be made about the people who were caught by the WH and how they felt about this. In the first place, those arrested were almost never powerful people. Secondly, their knowledge of Islamic regulations was often very limited. Thirdly, they usually did not know what their rights were and what punishment awaited them. In the fourth place, in almost all the cases I studied, the perpetrators were very ashamed of the situation they found themselves in.

In order to give some insight into the feelings of a perpetrator, we will now discuss the case of 'Adi.'[20] It is a 'typical' case in the sense that it shares the four features mentioned above with many other cases. Yet, Adi's case also has some special features. Firstly, Adi was a very serious young Muslim who tried to live his life as well as possible in accordance with his religion. Secondly, in his perception, he had done nothing wrong. It was only because the WH imposed its official interpretation of Islam on him that he was forced to see himself as a 'bad Muslim.' Thirdly, he was lucky enough to be released before the reporters arrived, so no article was published in the newspaper. Finally, long after the arrest, he still suffered from the humiliation and the shame he felt when accused of committing what many people saw as one of the worst sins in their religion. What follows are some selected field notes on Adi's case.[21]

> After having joined another patrol, one of the officers tells me that there are new perpetrators I can interview for my research. I join a young man and try to talk with him. His name is Adi, and he is 25 years old. He barely answers my questions and does not look up a single time. He keeps silent and it is clear that he is very upset because of everything that has

---

20 For privacy reasons all names of respondents have been altered for this chapter.

21 Field notes, 4 May and 18 May 2009, Banda Aceh.

happened in the past hour. I realize that I cannot interview someone who is this upset, so I get up and tell him that I will be leaving. For the first time he looks me in the eye. Quietly he asks me to stay a little longer. I sit down again.

After an hour Adi starts to talk. He tells me about his life, his family and his girlfriend. How happy she makes him and that he wants to marry her. He seems to be a serious young man. He studies diligently and is a good football player. He has often been asked by different teams to play matches for them. This is how he makes his money. Adi has been dating a girl for three years now. He is still head over heels in love with her. Everything seemed to go well, when suddenly his life was turned upside down. When he was talking with his girlfriend in his room suddenly the WH appeared. They were both arrested and locked up in separate rooms.

Adi is scared, he does not know what will happen to them and he is worried about his girlfriend. Although he thinks he has done nothing wrong, he feels guilty about bringing this shame upon his girlfriend. He is afraid that she will (be forced to) leave him because of this. He has never slept with her. Adi wants to wait until they get married. We talk all night long and I try to comfort him by telling him that they probably will not be caned and will be released the next morning. Then Adi asks me whether I can send a message to his girlfriend in the other cell. He types a text in Acehnese in his telephone and hands it over to me. I walk to the guards and tell them I would like to interview the girl as well. In the cell I try to talk to the girl and show her the message from her boyfriend. But she is so upset, that she does not look at me nor listens to what I'm saying. After a few minutes she finally realizes that I have a message from her boyfriend. At the moment I want to give her the phone with his message a guard comes in. He tells me that I cannot be alone in the cell with this woman according to Shariʿa law. This situation "comes close to illicit sex" he says, "please continue interviewing the boy." I head back to Adi and tell him I did not succeed. Nothing seems to calm him down, until he finally falls asleep.

The next morning the families of both 'sinners' arrive. They are not happy with the arrest of their children, but they are smart enough to hide their displeasure. They behave in polite ways and give the socially acceptable answers so that they can leave as soon as possible. The director of the WH and the two families agree that the two kids should no longer be allowed to be in the same room without an elder to keep an eye on them.

> A few days later, I try to contact Adi, but he does not answer his phone. Two weeks later during a football tournament, I see that Adi is playing for the opponent team in my second match. I say hello, but he pretends not to see me. After the game I approach him again, but as soon as he sees me, he walks away. I do not understand this, because I thought he had become sort of a friend. I ask one of his friends, who is a shared acquaintance, why he is acting like this. My friend tells me that Adi is trying to continue his life and does not like to be reminded of the incident. Even more importantly, he does not want other people to find out what has happened. He is willing to talk to me, but only if I promise not to tell a single soul.

Certainly, shaming perpetrators, which is commonly regarded as an effective sanction in traditional *adat* communities, is also a considerable element of state Shariʿa reinforcement in contemporary Aceh.

The General Public's Perceptions of the WH

In the previous section, we have seen what people go through, step by step, after they have been caught by the WH and how they respond to the situation. I found that perpetrators did not know beforehand what was going to happen to them. From interviews with other people in Banda Aceh, who had never been caught, it turned out that they too had little idea about how the WH actually handled cases. They did know, however, what the WH was established for and almost everybody had an opinion about it. Although not everybody thought the same way about the WH, several opinions and thoughts seemed to be widely shared among the population. These were the things that, during my five months of field research, I heard over and over again.

Among the people of Banda Aceh, the dominant opinion about the WH was not positive. First of all, the WH is seen as a police unit. Due to the general malfunctioning and corruption in the Indonesian police, and bureaucracy in general, the WH was automatically assumed to be malfunctioning and corrupt as well. Secondly, people felt that the actions of the WH were severely biased. In particular, women and poor people felt discriminated against. As one of my interlocutors told me:

> It is not fair that it is always just the poor people who are caught and punished. The law of Shariʿa [that is, local Shariʿa regulations] is not fair, because rich people never get caught. People with money can just

> pay and the problem is over. Poor people without money go to jail straight away or get caned.[22]

In a rather similar fashion, a female interlocutor blamed the WH for being discriminatory, asking: "Why always harass women instead of catching real criminals?"[23]

Another point raised by many people in Banda Aceh was the alleged immoral behaviour of certain WH officers themselves. In the past few years, there have been several newspaper reports about WH officers caught for adultery or premarital sex. On 19 April 2007, a 33 year-old WH officer was caught cheating on his wife with a 17 year-old high-school girl in a public toilet in Ulee Kareng, Banda Aceh.[24] Although he was caught red-handed, he was never caned or sentenced. On the night of 10 January 2010, three officers in Langsa allegedly raped an arrested suspect.[25] Although only a few cases of misbehaving WH officers had been reported by a newspaper, it was clear that the reputation of the institution had been ruined.

Many of these criticisms were confirmed by my field observations. Indeed, I did not see wealthy people being questioned at the WH office, or being caught during clothing raids for 'un-Islamic' ways of dressing. At the same time, I wondered why people's irritations and criticisms were invariably aimed at the WH, and not at the law which the WH has been assigned to enforce. For example, Article 22 in Qanun No. 14/2003 about *khalwat* gives the judge the discretionary power to prescribe either caning or fining as a punishment. However, fines are so high that the majority of the people can never afford to pay them. As a result, they will inevitably be caned. In the rare occasion that rich people have been caught and prosecuted, this has never resulted in a public caning. The rich can often buy their way out without being shamed publicly. In 2006, however, a politician—a member of the DPRD (District Assembly) of North Aceh—was arrested and sentenced to be caned. He appealed as many times as possible, but was never able to change the verdict. Still, the sentence was never executed. This is legally possible, because the law implements no timeframe that regulates when the punishment should be

---

22 Personal communication, unskilled worker (approximately 40 years old), June 2009, Banda Aceh.

23 Personal communication, Acehnese woman (approximately 30 years old), who was stopped during a raid in May 2009. I heard many similar complaints during the raids from women who were halted as well as from bystanders, both female and male.

24 "Ketika Polisi Syariat Berbuat Mesum," *Detik News*, 20 April 2007.

25 "Sharia Police Arrested for Rape," *The Jakarta Post*, 12 January 2010.

executed. Therefore, officially this man still awaits his sentence, but nobody believes this punishment will ever be carried out.

To put it more generally, most people seemed to be largely unaware that it is the law itself which is discriminatory. Another obvious example is the dress code, which is much stricter for women than for men, and thus forces the WH to focus on women. Still, women do not complain so much about the law itself, but rather about the fact that they feel harassed. As for the oft-heard complaint that the WH does not arrest the rich perpetrators, it was my impression that people often did not realize that the WH simply lacks the authority and resources to enter private houses where the rich supposedly violate the Shariʿa-based regulations, as well as other means required to do their job properly.

Concluding Remarks

This chapter has discussed Aceh's Shariʿa-based regulations, especially the 2003 Qanun on *khalwat*, illicit behaviour between two members of the opposite sex. It shows how both local communities and the WH enforce Islamic moral norms as set forth in Aceh's state Shariʿa legislation. Finally, it presents evidence of the critical discourse ordinary Acehnese draw upon when they speak about the WH, and about the state Shariʿa system more generally.

Some scholars of Aceh's Islamic legislation have focused on how the laws fit in Indonesia's legal system, notably from a human rights perspective. Lindsey et al. (2007, 254) have concluded that, "Shariʿa in Aceh is thus an old theme but very new as a legal system [...] The question now is how will it develop?" Others asked similar questions such as "[h]ow far will implementation of 'comprehensive sharia' proceed in Aceh?" (Nur Ichwan 2007, 210). While some of the first reports in 2005–2006, including that of the International Crisis Group (2006), rang the alarm bell about the Shariʿa-based regulations, pointing at a range of serious human rights violations by the WH's predecessor, more recent observers suggest that "the implementation of this ideal has so far been less than complete" (Nur Ichwan 2007, 214). This chapter establishes some basic information about how 'it has developed' and 'how far the implementation has proceeded' in Banda Aceh. It must be noted that our findings definitely cannot be generalized across the whole province. However, they do provide concrete empirical data that can be of significant value in helping to understand the everyday workings and popular perceptions of this contemporary Islamic legal system.

So how do we assess the impact of the *khalwat* regulation and the way it has been enforced in Banda Aceh? To put things in perspective, we should make three observations. First, Aceh has a long tradition of taking pride in its culture, its way of being Islamic, and its claims to political autonomy, distancing itself from broader Indonesian national values. In many interviews, people made clear that they are firstly Acehnese, secondly Muslims, and thirdly Indonesian. Second, compared to the many years of bloody civil warfare between the Free Aceh Movement (GAM) and the Indonesian army, and to the humanitarian disaster of the 2004 tsunami, the newly introduced Shariʿa-based law simply has much less impact. Whilst some people showed me their discontent, their critiques were mostly moderate. Third, the use of physical violence against men and women who violate local norms concerning sexuality is not new in Aceh; rather, it is a long-established element of local culture.

When we look at the Shariʿa-based legislation as a whole, it is striking that political support for the Islamization of law is far from unanimous in Aceh. Aceh's legislature, the DPRA, which was elected in 2009 and dominated by former associates of the Free Aceh Movement (organized in Partai Aceh/PA), had not been very enthusiastic about such legislation. The former provincial Governor, Irwandi Yusuf (PA), even refused to sign the 2009 *qanun* enacted by the outgoing DPRA, which prescribes the punishment of stoning (*rajam*) for debauchery (*zina*) (see Großmann, this volume). Within the state apparatus, the WH does not rank very high. It is part of the regional public order police force, Satpol PP, which has less power and a lower status than the national police force. The WH lacks the basic legal authorities of a police unit, such as arrest and detention, and even within the Satpol PP, the WH does not stand in high regard.

Our study shows that the WH implemented and enforced the regulation on *khalwat* in three ways, namely through patrols, raids, and arrests after being informed by local communities. In Banda Aceh, as we saw in this chapter, the patrols and raids had very little effect. Field observations revealed an almost mysterious reticence on the side of the WH when it came to closing down brothels and the like (for which, obviously, they could have invoked the Satpol PP). The *khalwat* incidents, however, which were handled by the Banda Aceh WH about twice a month on average, did have considerable impact on the lives of the individual perpetrators. The WH's involvement of their families, and especially of the press, tended to stigmatize the perpetrators, affecting their social and economic position badly.

By intimidating the accused and keeping them uninformed about their situation, the WH in Banda Aceh has developed its own quasi-policing practice, without formally transferring cases to the police and the public prosecutor. During the process, it applies its own system of 'enforcement' consisting of the nine different stages described in this chapter. A close analysis of the actual relations between the WH and local communities and their leaders reveals the extent and limits of local authority. Local leaders, whether *Kepala Kampung*, *Geuchik*, or *Pak Lorong*, simply decide whether they transfer a case to the WH or not. And if the WH itself takes charge, they solve the matter in a much more informal way—working with local community leaders and the families of the accused, rather than by any kind of formal legal or Shari'a-based procedure. In fact, most literature on the introduction of Shari'a-based law in the 2001–2005 period seems to have overlooked the fact that, at the same time, other relevant regulations were enacted, such as Perda No. 7/2000 on the Establishment of *Adat*, Qanun No. 4/2003 on the Mukim governance structures, and Qanun No. 5/2003 on the Gampong governance structures. These by-laws serve to strengthen and formalize the role of traditional local community leaders in solving local conflicts, disputes, and other problems (UNDP 2006, 49–51), thus framing the work of the WH further. While the mandate of the WH has been constrained by weak legal powers *vis-à-vis* Satpol PP and other police units, the WH is also plagued by a lack of resources and a bad reputation among the population.

What, in conclusion, are the consequences of the state Islamic legal system for ordinary people living in the province's capital city, Banda Aceh? For most ordinary people, it seems, the consequences are quite limited. In many parts of the town patrols or raids by the WH never take place. In such areas, I saw women in their own neighbourhoods without headscarves, and in the outskirts of town I saw boys and girls sitting together without any apparent fear of reprisal. In the town centre and along the main roads, people do appear to pay some attention to the new rules. Yet, although patrols and raids intimidate and disturb people who are on their way, all the fuss usually results in just a verbal warning. Meanwhile, Acehnese are convinced that elsewhere, behind closed doors, drinking, gambling, and prostitution continue to occur, and that especially rich and influential people are never caught and punished by the WH. Therefore, if the goal of the state Shari'a project is to effectuate a drastic behavioural transformation to the extent that 'immodest' clothing, extramarital sex, drinking, gambling and prostitution would disappear, then the WH clearly has not been able to achieve its goal. So far, it has not been able to impose a set of strict socio-religious views and practices on a whole population. Instead, it seems that people mostly stick to their old ways, and that the impact has been rather modest.

At the same time, according to our findings, people who are caught committing *khalwat* can face serious consequences—even if the WH may treat them better than the local community. The end result of the WH's shaming policy is often sad for the 'perpetrators': a serious love affair must end, people feel the urgent need to move immediately to another area, or one loses his or her job or place in an educational institution. The case studies also show that the chances of being caught are much higher for 'outsiders,' who do not belong to the local community. In one exceptional case, the perpetrator seemed not to be affected at all by the WH, and did not really care about changing his behaviour. Finally, we asked how people perceive the WH, the Shariʿa-based law and the way it is implemented. Although some respondents enthusiastically expressed support for the WH's hard line on immorality, the interviews reveal considerable discontent, focusing on the way in which the law is enforced. In general, the image of the WH is negative. People's discontent concentrates on what they see as discrimination toward poor people and women, coupled with the view that the WH officers themselves do not practice what they preach. Due to some incidents reported in the press, and because members of the police are generally seen as corrupt, WH officers are often portrayed as hypocritical sinners with double standards.[26] Since the gap between prescribed norms and effective practice is rather common in Indonesia, the discontent is only moderate; particularly because people have been more concerned with other graver matters related to the resolution of armed conflict and the consequences of the tsunami.

When asked about the Shariʿa itself, people usually reacted in a positive way. Since Islam in their view is by definition something good, the same goes for the divine law. It is not up to humans to have critical opinions about it. In this sense, people cannot but praise Allah and extol the virtues of Islam, and this also seems to apply to the Shariʿa as well. However, the relation between religion, Shariʿa-based norms, and local cultural norms turns out to be very complex. In fact, people are more ambivalent than they appear to be when they just speak about Islam and Shariʿa. As was noted in the introduction, people condemn others on the basis of strict norms, which in practice they themselves do not comply with. It seems that they tolerate or even endorse non-compliant behaviour as long as it takes place in secret. Clearly, double standards prevail in communities too. For when I asked people in favour of a strict law on *khalwat*

26 "Mengaku petugas WH perkosa remaja putri" (Confession of WH official raping young girl), http://indonesiaindonesia.com/f/75320-mengaku-petugas-wh-perkosa-remaja-putri/ (Accessed 24 February 2013); "Kasus mesum anggota WH belum diproses hukum" (Sexual offence case of WH member not yet in legal process), http://www.antaranews.com/view/?i=1185878646&c=NAS&s= (Accessed 24 February 2013); "Berbuat mesum seorang polisi syariah NAD ditangkap warga" (Police official committing sexual offence in Aceh Province caught by community), http://www.antaranews.com/print/1176971136/berbuat-mesum-seorang-polisi-syariah-nad-ditangkap-warga (Accessed 24 February 2013).

whether—if they were to be caught—they would prefer to be dealt with by the WH or have the matter settled 'according to custom' (*secara adat*), they invariably said that they preferred to have the matter settled 'by custom.'

On the political aspects of the Shariʿa system, moreover, many people in Aceh are indifferent. As noted above, the introduction of all Shariʿa-based laws cannot be said to be '*the* expression of *the* aspiration of *the* Acehnese,' since their elected political representatives are seriously divided on the issue. In addition, people do not take the trouble to investigate the substantive content of the province's Islamic legislation. This also helps to explain why people hold the WH responsible for discriminatory behaviour, without realizing that this is at least in part caused by the law itself. Additionally, people do not often discuss the fact that Aceh's newly acquired legislative autonomy has not only led to the reinforcement of religion, but also strengthened *adat* as a basis for law and conflict resolution. In this context marked by ambiguities of all kinds—legal, political, administrative, religious or cultural—the WH in Banda Aceh has definitely not become a fanatical Saudi-styled 'morality police,' as some had feared. Its implementation of the Shariʿa-based *khalwat* regulation has manifested itself mostly in moral stigmatization rather than physical punishment. Moreover, the WH has mostly targeted lower classes. While the WH is accepted because of its religious foundation, its particular forms of implementation have provoked considerable criticism. When it comes to sanctioning misbehaviour, people value the continuing presence of local leaders and traditional *adat* rather than the bureaucratized WH. As a result, the WH effectively lacks the power to truly transform society.

References

Benda-Beckmann, F. von. 2002. "Who is Afraid of Legal Pluralism?" *Journal of Legal Pluralism and Unofficial Law* 47:37–82.

Feener, R. Michael. 2013. *Shariʿa and Social Engineering: The Implementation of Islamic Law in Contemporary Aceh, Indonesia*. Oxford: Oxford University Press.

International Crisis Group. 2006. *Islamic Law and Criminal Justice in Aceh*. Asia Report No. 117, Jakarta/Brussels.

Kloos, David. 2014. "In the Name of *Syariah*? Vigilante Violence, Territoriality, and Moral Authority in Aceh, Indonesia." *Indonesia* 98:59–90.

Lev, D.S. 2000. *Legal Evolution and Political Authority in Indonesia*. Den Haag: Kluwer Law International.

Lindsey, T. and M.B. Hooker, with Ross Clarke and Jeremy Kingsley. 2007. "Shariʿa Revival in Aceh." In *Islamic Law in Contemporary Indonesia: Ideas and Institutions*, edited by R.M. Feener and M.E. Cammack, 216–256. Cambridge: Harvard University Press.

Nur Ichwan, Moch. 2007. "The Politics of Shariatization: Central Governmental and Regional Discourses of Sharia Implementation in Aceh." In *Islamic Law in Contemporary Indonesia: Ideas and Institutions*, edited by R.M. Feener and M.E. Cammack, 193–215. Cambridge: Harvard University Press.

Otto, J.M. 2010. "Sharia and National Law in Indonesia." In *Sharia Incorporated: A Comparative Overview of the Legal Systems in Twelve Muslim Countries in Past and Present* (Law, Governance, and Development), edited by J.M. Otto, 433–490. Leiden: Leiden University Press.

Peletz, Michael G. 2013. "Malaysia's Syariah Judiciary as Global Assemblage: Islamization, Corporatization, and Other Transformations in Context." *Comparative Studies in Society and History* 55(3):603–633.

Safitri, M.A. 2010. "Forest Tenure in Indonesia: The Socio-Legal Challenges of Securing Communities' Rights." PhD diss., Leiden University.

UNDP. 2006. *Access to Justice in Aceh. Making the Transition to Sustainable Peace and Development in Aceh.* Report made in partnership with the Agency for Rehabilitation and Reconstruction, the National Planning and Development Agency, The Syiah Kuala University, IAIN Ar-Raniry, the International Development Law Organization, and the World Bank.

CHAPTER 9

"That is Jakarta's Project": Views from the Acehnese Diaspora on Shariʿa, Self-determination and Political Conspiracy

*Antje Missbach**

> The way I see Shariʿa is implemented in Aceh, it serves more the political interests of the central government, but this is not how Shariʿa actually ought to be.
>
> Online correspondence with an anonymous informant based in Sweden, September 2011[1]

∴

Most chapters in this volume analyse the perspectives on Shariʿa and its implementation by Acehnese who live in Aceh. There are, however, several thousand Acehnese living overseas for various lengths of time. While physically distant, many of these diaspora Acehnese have been actively engaged with political developments back in Aceh for years. Their views on religious and political developments should not be ignored, as they add an important dimension to broader discourses on Shariʿa and society in contemporary Aceh. State Shariʿa has changed not only aspects of life in Aceh, but also the views on the role of Islam as part of Acehnese identity across the Acehnese diaspora.

This chapter discusses the highly critical views with regard to the implementation of Shariʿa in Aceh, as held by some Acehnese residing outside their

* I would like to acknowledge the constructive criticism that I received on earlier versions of this chapter from Melissa Crouch, Michael Feener, Kristina Großmann, David Kloos, Annemarie Samuels and Anne Looker. Needless to say, all remaining inadequacies remain my sole responsibility.

1 Throughout this chapter I will not reveal the names of my interlocutors as I have promised them to protect their identities before obtaining information that can be considered rather sensitive. However, some details on how I recruited my informants, their general backgrounds as well as their current residencies are provided throughout the chapter.

 | DOI: 10.1163/9789004304864_010

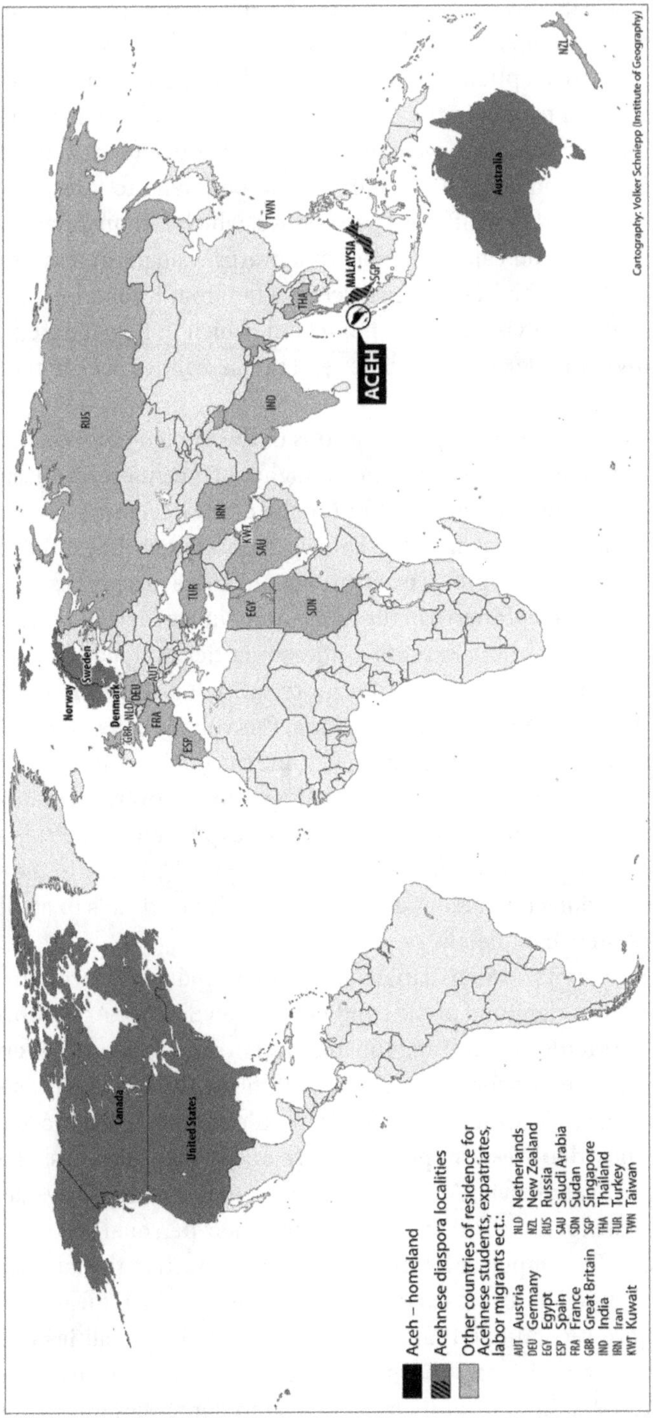

MAP 2 *The Acehnese diaspora in the world*

homeland, and asks why Acehnese diasporans have developed such different views from those prevalent in Aceh itself. As has been observed in various case studies, diasporic perceptions of homeland developments often differ dramatically from those of people in the homeland, in spite of all the instantaneous telecommunication methods available since the late twentieth century (Carruthers 2008; Winland 2002). People in the diaspora tend to interpret homeland developments from a different perspective, which is more often than not shaped by what I would call 'emotional time warps.' Caught in between longing for the homeland and yet being disconnected from it for a long time can result in rather biased views on the homeland, which in turn develop almost independently from the current debates and social realities back in the homeland.

When it comes to evaluating perceptions of the implementation of Shari'a in Aceh, it is striking to see how the thoughts of Acehnese in diaspora in Europe and Australia differ greatly from many of their fellow Acehnese back home. During my inquiries into the subject I discovered that rather hostile stances and outright disapproval exist among Acehnese diasporans in relation to the implementation of Shari'a in the homeland. Unlike their fellow Acehnese back home, many of whom express moderate criticism, followed by a wish for pragmatic improvements toward a more satisfying realization of Shari'a (Feener 2013b; Großmann, this volume; Idria, this volume), the opinions given by Acehnese diasporans ranged from describing the implementation of Shari'a in Aceh as "pure manipulation created by the national government in Jakarta to continue to control the politics in Aceh" (as expressed in the title of this chapter as "Jakarta's project") and as "besmirching Aceh's image in the eyes of the world as religious fundamentalists," to straightforward calls to abolish the state Shari'a system completely.

The diasporic views on Shari'a in Aceh cannot be understood without taking into account the background of the conflict between the Free Aceh Movement (Gerakan Aceh Merdeka/GAM) and the Indonesian state. Indeed, the very making of the Acehnese diaspora was the result of the conflict, which caused considerable numbers of GAM leaders to flee into exile abroad. Diasporic Acehnese have been exposed to Western (post-)modern and secular societies, especially when living in Scandinavia, Australia or the US, and therefore have accumulated manifold experiences that have affected their personal religious views and practices. More importantly, many of them left Aceh in the late 1990s and early 2000s, before Shari'a was actually implemented, which means that they often only have second-hand knowledge about the daily realities of Shari'a implementation back home. What seems to be even more crucial for their collective opinion-making, is that their diasporic fervour always was (and still is) more concerned with politics than with religion. This is because most diasporans see themselves as political refugees and victims of conflict rather than persecuted believers.

This is not to say that Acehnese in diaspora have not nurtured their religious heritage, especially in host societies that uphold cultural and religious values and norms that are different from theirs. It just means that religion was never the main trigger for their diasporization. In other words, religion was a means of developing strong group cohesion rather than a *raison d'être* for the diaspora. The reason for the Acehnese abroad to set up basic organizational structures was connected to their urge to support people back in Aceh from abroad during the conflict. While most of the diasporans lived in relative comfort and peace overseas, those remaining in Aceh suffered from the cruelties of the war, losing family members and property. As a number of scholars have pointed out in relation to other conflict-generated diasporas, the awareness of such diasporic privileges may trigger feelings of remorse (Lyons 2006; Radtke 2009; Skrbiš 1999). In order to deal with this notion of 'migration guilt,' many diasporans tend to provide remittances and other donations regularly.

Before delving more deeply into the question why the Acehnese overseas take a more critical position toward Shari'a than their fellow Acehnese in the homeland, it needs to be pointed out that, in their explanations, my informants tended to perceive Shari'a in political terms. Although they sometimes differentiated between, for example, Shari'a as a legal instrument for creating a 'perfect state' on the one hand, and 'man-made' written regulations and specific by-laws (*qanun*) determining everyday praxis on the other, they were often inclined to formulate their criticism against Shari'a implementation in blunt terms. Broadly, to them Shari'a implementation in Aceh meant a so-called bogus package deal, the terms and composition of which the Acehnese people had no say in. In their view, divine Islamic law, in this sense, was nothing more than a label for policies set by the central Indonesian state in Jakarta. None of the informants criticized in detail specific aspects of implemented laws and by-laws, or tried to be up-to-date in relation to debates about draft versions or additional regulations. As it turned out later in my research, especially during the second and third rounds of inquiry, most of them were not familiar with the contents of Aceh's contemporary Shari'a legislation. Instead, they rejected the very idea of implementing an Islamic legal system in Aceh. For them it was not about improving or adopting specific regulations, because in their eyes the concession of the Indonesian government to implement Shari'a was based on deceitful principles. Given their generally highly antagonistic stance against the national government developed during the time of conflict in Aceh, their anti-Shari'a positions were consistent, and not altogether surprising.

In order to place my findings within a wider context, I will first provide an overview of the development of the Acehnese diaspora. This will be followed by some observations about the religiosity of Acehnese in diaspora, which reflect their wish to preserve not only their cultural heritage but also their religious identity, especially in non-Muslim host countries. I will then introduce the main points of criticism that were put forward by my informants with regard to Shariʿa implementation in Aceh. Finally, I will analyse more thoroughly why the standpoints of the diasporans and the homelanders differ so widely from each other when it comes to the issue of Shariʿa in Aceh.

Acehnese in Diaspora

The largest contingent of Acehnese overseas lives in neighbouring Malaysia, which has been a home for many generations of Acehnese traders and businessmen (Reid 1969). The armed struggle for independence led by GAM founder Hasan Tiro, who himself had sought exile in Sweden, was for many the main cause for leaving Aceh. From the late 1970s onwards, there were several waves of emigration from Aceh across the Straits of Malacca, especially to Penang and Kuala Lumpur. Confronted with massive counter-strikes by the Indonesian military, GAM guerrillas left Aceh to escape retaliation, but also to continue their struggle for an independent state from abroad. Quite apart from those directly involved in the separatist conflict, ordinary Acehnese also had to cope for decades with the everyday realities of the ongoing conflict. Returning GAM guerrillas initiated several waves of aggression to resume the armed struggle, provoking renewed and intensified military reprisals. Civilians seeking refuge from the violence caused both by the guerrillas and the Indonesian security forces thus fled to Malaysia, adding to the Acehnese diaspora there. To an even greater extent, Acehnese were looking for economic opportunities in Malaysia due to the economic downturn and high unemployment in Aceh caused by the conflict.

At first, during the 1980s, Malaysia widely tolerated the Acehnese (and other labour migrants without proper work permits), because of its economic boom and the need for cheap labour. But during times of economic recession, and particularly following the Asian financial crisis of 1997, the Malaysian government sought to get rid of the foreign labour surplus (Battistella 2002; Pillai 1998; Rajaram, Kumar and Grundy-Warr 2004). Whereas many 'irregular' Indonesian labourers were deported back to Indonesia without much delay, however, Acehnese workers—with some exceptions—were mostly held in detention over a longer period of time (Missbach 2011a). Presumably, the Malaysian government did take the ongoing war in Aceh into consideration and tried to save the Acehnese from being sent back to a conflict area. Despite that, some hundred Acehnese were forcibly returned to Medan in 1998.

It was in these detention centres that many Acehnese became politicized by GAM-members, who were detained for involvement in the arms trade and for creating political unrest, as well as for basic immigration offenses. Apart from these involuntary meetings in prisons and detention centres, religious and social gatherings more generally served as regular venues for the Acehnese to discuss politics and exchange information. GAM members also tapped into a wide range of social networks in order to recruit young men, who would then be trained in Libya and later sent to Aceh to fight the Indonesian army (Aspinall 2009).

From the late 1990s onwards, Malaysia ceased to be a safe haven for the Acehnese. The Malaysian government took up a stronger stance toward unwanted refugees and irregular labour migrants, and even more so towards GAM leaders in hiding, leading to an increased number of arrests. As a result, more and more Acehnese applied to other countries for resettlement through the United Nations High Commissioner for Refugees (UNHCR). Although the number of Acehnese who were eventually resettled in Scandinavia, Canada and the US never exceeded 2,500 people in total (compared to at least 80,000 Acehnese in Malaysia at the peak of the Aceh conflict), this group turned out to be particularly influential with regard to developments in the homeland. People in Aceh directed their hopes to their countrymen in the West, expecting that they would be able to draw more international attention to the ongoing conflict and the human rights violations by the Indonesian military, and therefore to attract substantial international support for the Acehnese call for independence (Missbach 2011a). Not only did the Acehnese of the Western diaspora produce and circulate GAM propaganda and raise funds for GAM; they also served as contact points for Indonesian government officials and foreign diplomats, once the time for peace negotiations to end the almost thirty-year long conflict had arrived (Morfit 2007).

Current estimates of Acehnese living in Malaysia range between 20,000 and 30,000 people, as many have returned to Aceh since the end of the conflict.[2] Aside from Malaysia, there are significant Acehnese communities in Denmark, Sweden, Norway, Australia, Canada and the US. These communities have developed since the late 1990s and consist of numbers ranging between 200 and 500 people per country. Most of them came as refugees, while a few were self-

2 Providing exact figures on Acehnese in Malaysia is difficult, as some enter(ed) irregularly.

exiled GAM members. Some could also be primarily categorized as economic migrants. In addition, we find Acehnese expatriates, economic migrants and students in a number of other places, including New Zealand, Singapore, Egypt, the Netherlands, Germany, Taiwan, Thailand, Russia, Spain, France, Turkey, Iran, the United Kingdom, Austria, India, Kuwait, Sudan and Saudi Arabia. As the numbers of Acehnese in those countries remained either too small, or their temporary residence too short, one could not find any community building or diasporization as was the case for the Acehnese in Scandinavia, Australia and North America. At most, there are student organizations or business networks.

During the time of conflict, most Acehnese in diaspora tended to see their stay overseas as temporary, and insisted that they would return one day when Aceh was peaceful and, preferably, independent.[3] Resulting from this dominant homeland focus, social integration into the host country society did not appear to be particularly desirable for Acehnese in diaspora. Instead they tried to maintain their links to the homeland by preserving their cultural and linguistic characteristics while in diaspora. At least, this was the case in the first few years following their resettlement. After the end of the conflict, those Acehnese who did not return to Aceh often opted for a more active integration into the host society (Missbach 2010; 2011a). Over the years, some had taken well to life in diaspora and the advantages of the Western welfare state, affordable health insurance and education for their children, or even what could be called westernized lifestyles. Others kept insisting that they wished to return, yet at the same time were very suspicious toward the peace process, fearing that it might not hold. At the same time, despite welcoming the peace in Aceh, there were also widespread feelings of disappointment among the diasporans. People felt that their personal 'sacrifices'—leaving their homeland while supporting the struggle for Acehnese independence both financially and morally—were somehow left unrewarded. Although only a small number of diasporans publicly rejected the Helsinki peace deal and pledged to continue the struggle for Aceh's independence through non-violent means (Missbach 2011a; 2011b), many diasporans whom I got to know during my research still favoured the idea of Aceh's separation from the Indonesian state.

In this chapter, I concentrate mostly on the Acehnese communities in Europe and Australia and their views on, or engagement with, the implementa-

3 In the interviews I conducted most interlocutors would use the term (*me*)*rantau*. The concept of *merantau* means leaving home for a certain amount of time to gather experience, learn new skills and make one's fortune. In theory, there are no limits on how long one can be in the *perantauan* (i.e. foreign country).

tion of Shariʿa in Aceh.[4] In my previous fieldwork among the Acehnese diaspora, which was focused on the topic of long-distance politics, I did not deal primarily with issues related to religious developments, whether in Aceh or in the diaspora.[5] For the purpose of this chapter, however, I visited some of my interlocutors in Australia again to conduct additional interviews. In addition, I contacted some of my former key informants in the US, Denmark, Sweden, Malaysia and Germany, distributing a questionnaire about their opinion on the outcome of Shariʿa implementation in Aceh, and following up with conversations over email.

Given the massive socio-economic differences between, for example, Acehnese in Sweden (who tend to have more free time to spend on diasporic activities and online communication) and the Acehnese in Malaysia (who generally have to work harder due to a lack of state social welfare, and who often do not have the same quality access to internet compared to their fellow Acehnese in the West), in my analysis I need to take into account a certain response bias. Not all requested informants replied, yet those who did were very generous with their time in sharing their views with me, allowing for additional enquiries. As their answers often raised new questions, vivid long-distance dialogues took off. The decision to discuss all matters of concern only on a bilateral basis, and never in (online) group discussions, allowed me to dig deeper in what interested me the most, namely their personal views on the implementation of Islamic law. All quotations in this chapter are derived from interviews and email correspondence that took place between August and October 2011. Most interviews were conducted in Indonesian, except for one, which was held in German. Since most of my interlocutors preferred anonymity, I refrain from providing any detail that could be used to uncover their individual identities.

Nevertheless, some general background information about my informants' whereabouts and their current situations might be helpful to better grasp their responses in regard to the implementation of Shariʿa in Aceh. All my interviewees were men, and were in their mid-30s and mid-40s. Like the majority

4 It has to be acknowledged that the exclusion of Acehnese who live, work and study in Egypt, Saudi Arabia and the Sudan from this scholarly inquiry is very unfortunate, as they possibly hold very distinct opinions on Shariʿa implementation in their homeland when compared with their fellow countrymen based in the West.

5 Fieldwork for my PhD thesis, titled "Long-distance politics in transition: Aceh's diaspora during and after the homeland conflict (1976–2009)," was carried out between November 2006 and October 2007 in Malaysia, Aceh, Denmark, Sweden, Norway and the USA. I revisited Aceh and Malaysia in 2008 and again in 2009.

of Acehnese diasporans they would generally not be considered elites, hailing from the lower to middle socio-economic strata of society instead. Most of them had enjoyed basic religious education in a *dayah* (religious school) while receiving primary education and had also finished high school. Some had attended university for some time, but often had not graduated due to the worsening conflict back home. Before leaving for Europe or Australia, many had spent several years living in Malaysia. At the time of the interviews, most were working in blue-collar jobs, some were furthering their education and some were unemployed, in some cases already for more than two years. Especially since the economic recession hit Europe in 2008, they found it difficult to find new jobs. Unemployment was generally experienced as a burdensome circumstance, often accompanied with intensive homesickness and frustration. Having a lot of free time, however, also enabled some of them to become more active on behalf of their diasporic organisations, as demonstrated by their increasing involvement in cultural activities and traditional celebrations as well as their participation in political discussions in online forums.

With regard to their political alignments, none of my informants had fought for GAM in Aceh during the conflict, even though some had sympathised with or were even loosely aligned with GAM. In general, they became more attracted to GAM while they were already abroad and some even assisted GAM leaders as contact persons. Whereas their political commitments during the time of the conflict were rather clear, over the post-conflict years these informants developed more nuanced political standings. In particular, they became more critical of former GAM leaders, as well as GAM's political successor, the Aceh Party (Partai Aceh/PA). In general, while many of them expressed public support for the peace process, in private some continue to hold aspirations for an independent Aceh.

Religiosity in the Acehnese Diaspora

Although the study of global diasporas has grown exponentially over the last decades, so far only a few scholars have focused on the links between diaspora and religion (Baumann 2004; Sökefeld 2004; Vertovec 2004). If scholars of diasporas consider religion at all in their research, it is mostly in relation to various aspects of life in the host country, for example how Muslim immigrants loosen or revive their religious identities when confronted with non-Muslim majorities (e.g. Saint-Blancat 2002; Schiffauer 1999). By comparison, relatively few studies have paid attention to the impact diasporans have on religious developments in the homeland (Dean 2011). Unlike long-distance politics, nationalism, and diasporic impacts on homeland politics, which have all served as common topics for academic inquiry (Lyons 2006; Shain 2002; Skrbiš 1999), neither the diasporic impact on religion in the homeland nor the changing perception of homeland religion among diasporans has been researched thoroughly.

Undoubtedly, Islam is an inextricable constituent of 'Acehneseness' (Lindsey et al. 2007, 216). According to the Indonesian Ministry of Religious Affairs, 98.8% of the Acehnese population is Muslim.[6] Although Islam is not the one and only determinant, the construction of Acehnese identity encapsulates Islamic beliefs, practices, customs, and holidays (Siapno 2002). This said, Islam is also of crucial importance for the identity of Acehnese diasporans. In this, the Acehnese are by no means exceptional, as other ethnic diasporas also utilise religion to frame their identity. For example, Kristin Langellier (2010, 79) wrote about the Somalis overseas that their ethnic and "cultural authenticity is perceived to be largely coterminous with Islam." Many scholars have observed the Acehnese self-depiction as more pious compared to other Indonesian Muslims. Even non-Acehnese have adopted this self-image and tend to describe the Acehnese as "staunch Muslims" (Suryadinata 2002, 63). Proud to be one of the first entry points for Islam in the Indonesian archipelago, Acehnese even refer to their homeland as the 'Veranda of Mecca' (*Serambi Mekkah*) (Aspinall 2009; Reid 2006).

As described by Vertovec (2004, 282), "[u]pon settling in a new environment, immigrants often soon set about collectively organizing themselves for purposes of religious worship. The formation of associations is one prominent kind of socio-religious organization." This is also true for the Acehnese in diaspora: They not only transferred their ethno-religious heritage to the new countries of residence but also started to set up religious and other meeting points, thereby reconstituting "cultural patterns and social relations in new settings" (Vertovec 2004, 282). For Acehnese migrating to Malaysia, the shifts and adaptations in regard to language, custom, culture, dress and religion were relatively minor, as Acehnese and Malays share many cultural traits. Hence Acehnese have been able to blend into Malay(sian) society without much trouble. In the past, specific Acehnese mosques were erected; however, these are now generally open to Muslims of any ethnic background.[7] Today, many Acehnese also

---

6 Indonesian Ministry of Religious Affairs, "Population by Religion, 2009." http://www.kemenag.go.id/file/dokumen/PeddkAgama09h1.pdf (Accessed 6 December 2011).

7 Some older Malaysians of Acehnese descent from the area of Yan, also known as Kampung Aceh, claimed that building a *meunasah* (prayer hall, which also serves as a sleeping place for unmarried men) was one of the first things that needed to be organized after a group of Acehnese decided to settle down outside their original area. In fact, the Acehnese who came

attend mosques for the general Muslim population that are not marked in any specific way as being 'Acehnese' mosques.

For Acehnese diasporans in the West, however, bringing and nurturing their Acehneseness (*keAcehan*)—including their Islamic identity—was often a more conscious decision. Getting precise definitions from my informants of what actually constituted Acehneseness was difficult, since many thought of Acehneseness as self-evident. Nevertheless, whereas Acehnese in Aceh tend to understand their Acehneseness in Indonesia as, primarily, an incompatibility with what they consider 'mainstream Indonesianness,' it means something different in the diaspora. Perhaps, to offer a very basic definition, Acehneseness overseas could be understood as the feeling of belonging to an ethno-religious 'imagined community' based on shared symbols of language, culture, and religious traditions that are preserved and often re-imagined by diasporans living far away from the homeland. As Martin Baumann (2000, 327) has observed for diasporas generally: "[m]ore often than not it [i.e. the cultural-religious point of reference] involves an identificational difference of the diaspora group in contrast with the society's dominant cultural and religious norms and orientations."

Coming from a developing country and moving to a Western host country often created feelings of 'strangeness' and difficulties in adjusting to mainstream mundaneness and common lifestyles, which in turn could then trigger a stronger urge to reorient oneself towards one's ethno-cultural roots and one's traditional religious affiliation. In the words of a former informant, "since I am here [in Denmark], I am more Acehnese than back home, [back in Aceh] I used to speak more Indonesian, now my Acehnese is better and I also pray more regularly" (quoted in Missbach 2011a, 155). With regard to his increased observance of Islamic ritual practice, this Acehnese man was no exception, as other scholars have observed that "paradoxically, migration to the lands of unbelievers strengthens the religious commitment of the migrants" (van der Veer, quoted in Baumann 2004, 172).

In this particular case, it was obvious that increased religious commitment was also understood to be equivalent with a self-perception of being more Acehnese. Self-assurance about religious and ethnic identity *vis-à-vis* the host country majority is not only an internal matter within the Acehnese diaspora. From my observations, I gained the impression that Acehnese in Western countries often felt the necessity to prove to their friends and families back in

---

to Yan in the course of the Dutch-Acehnese War at the end of the nineteenth century built a *meunasah* that can still be visited today.

Aceh that they could still be good Muslims and, therefore, be proper Acehnese even when living among non-believers. In order to assure their fellow country people in Aceh and in other host countries of their continuing commitment to Islam as part of their bona fides of 'Acehneseness,' Acehnese diasporans often send reports about their religious celebrations to Acehnese journals and tabloids and also circulate photographs of religious gatherings in email lists and online forums. A rather typical report (taken from the '*Aceh Goet*' list-serv, dated November 25, 2011) reads as follows:

> ACEH GOET—Denmark: We celebrate Aidul Adha in a sports building Celebrating religious holidays is a religious habit that has to be followed by every Muslim, whether living in the country of birth or abroad. We are part of the Acehnese overseas who live far away from their homeland, but nonetheless we still celebrate the religious holidays with what we have.

Defending themselves against both silent and public reproaches from the homeland, one of the diasporans explained to me:

> It is not true that the Acehnese lost their identity when living in an infidel country (*negeri kafir*). Quite the opposite, the feeling of Acehneseness (*rasa keacehan*) grew stronger when living in places like Sweden. There is considerable evidence, for example, of Acehnese in Sweden writing fluently in Acehnese. Yes, it is true there are also those who have lost their Acehneseness here in Sweden, but they are not many.
>
> Quoted in MISSBACH 2011a, 154

While living in diaspora, Acehnese try to maintain their language and traditions, including Acehnese Islamic religious rituals for all kinds of rites of passage (circumcisions for young males, weddings, funerals) and Islamic holidays (*Idul Fitri, Idul Adha, Maulid*). Whereas, for example, Islamic holidays in Denmark are celebrated in rented communal halls, schools or private houses, the Acehnese in Sweden gather in their own prayer hall-cum-community centre (Ac. *meunasah*) in Fittja (on the outskirts of Stockholm).[8] This *meunasah* is

8 Referring again to the aforementioned residential arrangements, it is not coincidental that there is a *meunasah* in Stockholm because most Acehnese in Sweden live on the outskirts of Stockholm. Whereas in Denmark, which hosts roughly the same number of Acehnese, there is no *meunasah* (yet) because the Acehnese diasporans are more dispersed across rural areas of the country.

open to everyone and, besides functioning as a prayer house, it is used for all kinds of religious, social, political and cultural events. It is used by Acehnese women for cooking and sewing, but also for Swedish and Acehnese language instruction courses and Qur'an reading sessions (Ali 2008). In particular, the religious education of the second generation, i.e. children born in Sweden, is seen as a high priority in order to familiarize them with their cultural heritage and their religious identity. The reason for this—as has been observed for other diasporas—is that "without a serious effort at teaching the rudiments of their respective languages, the maintenance of ethnic identity is precarious" (Safran 2008, 185).

In summary, Acehnese in the diaspora try to uphold religious practices in their everyday life as much as possible, even though this is done with many adaptations (be it the wearing of the headscarf or adjusting the daily fasting hours in the European summer). Even in host countries, such as Finland or Germany, where there are few other Acehnese diasporans, they strive to uphold their religious practices by coming together with Muslim immigrants of other ethnicities (including Muslims from Somalia, Iraq or Turkey) to observe major religious holidays. This is especially the case during the fasting month, Ramadan. Indeed, many Acehnese in the diaspora see themselves as 'good Muslims.' Their main concerns are to uphold their religious and ethnic identities—which are closely aligned in most imaginations of 'Acehneseness.' They promote their beliefs and even more so their cultural traditions (dance performances, food exhibitions and trade fairs) in public, while at the same time operating within the political limits of life in their host countries.[9] Based on my observations, they show no interest in radical Islamic or pan-Islamic movements, either within the host countries or back home in Aceh. Since I started my research on the Acehnese diaspora five years ago, I have never come across any explicit demand for the implementation of Shariʿa as a concern of high priority, either in conversations I had or in the diasporic online forums or reports.

9 See for example "Saman Dan Boh Rom-Rom Aceh di Panggung Global Fair Denmark," Press Release, 5 May 2010, http://www.waa-aceh.org/2010/05/saman-dan-boh-rom-rom-aceh-di-panggung-global-fair-denmark/ (Accessed 8 December 2011) and "Tarian Aceh Gemparkan Penyambutan Kemerdekaan Norwegia ke 196 tahun," Press Release, 18 May 2010, http://www.waa-aceh.org/2010/05/tarian-aceh-gemparkan-penyambutan-kemerdekaan-norwegia-ke-196-tahun/ (Accessed 8 December 2011).

Why Diasporans Criticise Shariʿa Implementation in Aceh

In August 2011, I visited an Acehnese *ustadz* (religious teacher), who had been living in diaspora for more than ten years, to ask him about his views on Shariʿa implementation in Aceh. From previous encounters, I knew that he was enthusiastically involved in a local Qur'an school to teach children (from diverse ethnic backgrounds) to read the Arabic text of Islamic scripture. He is a strong proponent of practicing Shariʿa, and has even written a PhD thesis on the matter. Unlike all my other interlocutors, he was wearing a *kaftan* (a 'Middle Eastern looking,' rather than traditionally Acehnese kind of Muslim dress) when I visited him in his house. Within the Acehnese community, but also in the wider Indonesian immigrant communities and even beyond, he enjoys a high degree of respectability. Yet, his interpretation of the social and political impact of Shariʿa implementation in Aceh, particularly with regard to the future, left me rather astonished. Unlike the moderate criticism I expected, he expressed rigorous criticism of the implementation of Shariʿa, and outright rejection of the way in which this law is supposed to operate in Aceh. Although he was obviously strongly committed to Islam and Shariʿa as defining standards of personal piety, his basic argument resembled to a large extent the objections raised against the imposition of Shariʿa by the more secular-minded GAM leaders in the diaspora, which I had come across many times before, and which has been referred to by other scholars as well (Schulze 2004; Aspinall 2009).[10] Paraphrasing his key argument gives a good impression of his views on this:

> Shariʿa is exercised only because of Jakarta's permission. The Indonesian government gave it to the Acehnese people, but made sure to keep the reins in its hands. Just like the Law of Special Autonomy for Aceh is a camouflage, the general political system in Aceh has also not changed much. Jakarta keeps cheating Aceh. How would it otherwise be possible that the Acehnese people remain poor, whereas the corrupt state officials wander off unpunished?

This statement combines a number of crucial tenets in the arguments upheld by diasporan Acehnese against the implementation of Shariʿa in Aceh, of which

10 For direct statements by GAM 'Prime Minister' Malik Mahmud, see, for example, "Ex-rebel leader slams Islamic law in Aceh," Reuters, 14 August 2006; "Syariat Islam Bukan Keinginan Rakyat Aceh," 14 August 2006, http://www.tempointeraktif.com/hg/nasional/2006/08/14/brk,20060814-81900,id.html (Accessed 13 October 2010).

I will discuss the most significant ones: 1) an unwanted gift from Jakarta; 2) that God's law should not be subordinated to the control of a the state; 3) that the Shariʿa regulations are unfairly applied; 4) that the Shariʿa legislation prioritizes a limited set of devotional and moral issues over broader social concerns; and 5) the fragility of Aceh's post-conflict society.

The Unwanted Gift

Despite practicing Islam and being pious Muslims who might—in theory—favour the idea of Shariʿa, Acehnese diasporans generally disapproved of the state implementation of Islamic law in Aceh, denouncing it as an "unwanted gift" from Jakarta. My respondents unanimously asserted that former Indonesian President Abdurrahman Wahid offered Aceh the chance to implement Shariʿa law in Aceh only to divert attention away from the actual causes of the conflict. Whereas Hasan Tiro and his followers rebelled because of what they understood to be economic exploitation and political paternalism, many Acehnese joined GAM because of the military oppression that governed their daily lives in Aceh. After many years of conflict, people in Aceh yearned for peace. One way to end the conflict without further bloodshed would have been to arrange a referendum for independence similar to the one held in East Timor in August 1999. While Wahid temporarily entertained such a possibility (Aspinall 2009), eventually he arrived at the opinion that Indonesia could not afford to lose another province, especially not one that contributed significantly to the national state budget through its rich reserves in oil and gas.

Many in the Acehnese diaspora maintain that President Wahid made the offer of Shariʿa as a deliberately political manoeuvre, and that he was well aware of the deeper political implications it entailed. After all, the Acehnese, who are known for their Islamic piety, could not easily reject such an offer without compromising their reputation as particularly committed Muslims. It can also be assumed that Wahid purposely tried to weaken foreign-based GAM leaders, who had always been suspected by people back in Aceh of being less devout believers, by involving local Acehnese ulama in the political process (Aspinall 2009).[11] GAM leaders had long been able to avoid clear statements about their views on the role of Islam in the state structure of a future inde-

11 Demands for introducing Shariʿa had existed in Aceh long before GAM took up its struggle for independence. It was, in fact, one of the core demands forwarded by Daud Beureueh, the local *Darul Islam* leader in Aceh (Feener, this volume).

pendent Aceh. Because of Wahid's manoeuvring, however, they were forced to speak out against the implementation of Shariʿa (Aspinall 2009; ICG 2006). Afraid of losing their place of authority to local ulama by being labelled as 'bad' Muslims, some GAM-leaders tried to rebuff such defamation by stating that Islam was already fully integrated into the Acehnese identity, and that Jakarta's endorsement of Islamic law was not required for Acehnese to become better Muslims (Kingsbury 2007). Still, GAM's attitude towards Shariʿa implementation remained a difficult balancing act.

Given GAM's intention to find international (and especially Western) support for their cause, playing the 'Islam card' never appeared attractive. Having Aceh portrayed as 'Islamist' by foreign media would surely diminish any hope for international solidarity. On the other hand, any explicitly secularist approach carried the risk of alienating the Acehnese people back in the homeland. When the Wahid-led government tried to redefine the conflict and, most importantly, the causes of the conflict, by fostering the impression that the Acehnese people had been striving for religious goals rather than political self-determination, this effort was tantamount to hijacking GAM's discursive supremacy over the conflict. Hence, according to my respondents, Jakarta's push for the imposition of Shariʿa in Aceh was nothing more than a 'smear campaign' aimed at depicting the Acehnese as "terrorists" (*melebel orang Aceh sebagai teroris*), "discrediting Aceh in the eyes of the world" (*membangun image buruk aceh di mata internasional*) and "making [Aceh] look like a nursery for fundamentalists and Islamic militants."[12] By doing so, Aceh was put on par with "Mindanao, Pakistan, Afghanistan and other places of that kind," especially after 9/11, according to another interlocutor's retrospective analysis.

Although the armed conflict was formally brought to an end when GAM and the Indonesian government signed the Helsinki Memorandum of Understanding in August 2005 (in which GAM agreed to officially renounce its demand for independence), it seems that the idea of an independent Aceh is still attractive to many Acehnese in diaspora. This is clearly reflected in the statements of many diaspora Acehnese, such as that "even though demands for independence are not in accordance with world politics today, for Aceh it will remain the main issue."[13] In relation to the epigraph, about how Jakarta utilizes and

12 "*Sepertinya Acheh identik dengan fundamentalis, militan ataupun sejenisnya.*" Email correspondence with the author, 28 September 2011, 30 September 2011 and 10 October 2011.

13 "*Tuntutan kemerdekaan ini boleh saja tidak sesuai dengan percaturan politik dunia saat ini,*

therefore controls the politics in Aceh with the help of Shariʿa, another respondent from Sweden stated that "it would take a substantial amount of time for [the Acehnese] to study Shariʿa" so that it could be applied for the benefit of the Acehnese people. However, "such a venture would only be successful if Aceh was truly allowed to govern itself." Quintessentially, as long as "there are still collisions with Jakarta-made laws, an equitable Shariʿa remains to be utopian."[14]

God's Law

Tightly connected to the diasporans' contention about Jakarta's 'trick' in offering the Shariʿa to the Acehnese is another argument, namely that Shariʿa—understood as the law of God—should not be subordinated to a secular legislature. From the perspective that regional laws, including Aceh's Shariʿa law, ought to comply with national law and especially with Pancasila, Indonesia's official state philosophy, it appears, in the words of one of my informants, that Indonesia's "man-made laws, which are just an adoption of the former colonial legislature, are above god-made laws."[15] This point of criticism is related to the arguments described above, but differs in coming to the issue from a more religious perspective. The position of most diasporans on the implementation of Islamic law is complicated by their attitudes toward the Indonesian government. Many maintain a commitment to the ideal of independence, and this seems to be stronger among Acehnese in Australia and Europe than for many of those residing in Malaysia.

Exemptions

Most of my interlocutors saw the implementation of Shariʿa as an instrument of control in the hands of the national government that—although supported by some Acehnese ulama—had "nothing to do with real Islamic law as it ought to be according to God." One major bone of contention concerned the many

---

tapi hal ini akan tetap menjadi persoalan utama Acheh." Email correspondence with the author, 30 September 2011.

14 Email correspondence with the author, 4 October 2011.

15 "*Hal ini sangat paradok karena undang-undang buatan manusia (Pancasila +* KUHP *Indonesia adopsi dari bekas penjajah Belanda) diatas dari undang-undang buatan tuhan (syariat Islam)*." Email correspondence with the author, 4 October 2011.

loopholes in the current Shari'a regulation. Even though my interlocutors did not consent with the existence of the law and regulations in the first place, they went on to criticize its unequal application. Although the Shari'a is ideally applicable equally to all Muslims, my informants criticized what they saw as clear evidence that some Muslims seemed to be more equal than others under the current state system of Shari'a in Aceh (Feener 2013b). Three informants in particular pointed out the exceptions to the enforcement of Shari'a in reality, as enjoyed by members of the military, the police and other state officials.[16] One of them even went as far as to call it a "racist policy," because non-Acehnese people working and living in Aceh who do not hold an identity card listing a permanent address in Aceh are allegedly exempt from Shari'a. Moreover, my informants kept citing examples, in which violators of Shari'a law had managed to escape punishment due to their prominent position. For example, in April 2007, Puji Wijayanto, the head of the district court in Sabang was caught red-handed in a hotel with a woman who was not his wife.[17] Being suspected of having transgressed Law No. 14/2003 on *khalwat* ('illicit proximity,' see Feener, this volume), if found guilty, he would have been caned between three and nine strokes and/or been forced to pay a fine of between Rp. 2,500,000 and Rp. 10,000,000 (US$250 and US$1,000) (Paragraph 22). Although Puji resigned from his post voluntarily, and was then transferred to the High Court in Yogyakarta (though as a non-active judge), he was not punished in accordance with the Shari'a legislation. My informants not only noted the blatant case of exceptionalism, but also argued that this exemption had strengthened their suspicion that "Shari'a was after all an anti-Acehnese affront by Jakarta," demonstrating clearly who was in charge in Aceh.

16 The example provided by one informant (and not without a healthy portion of mockery) was an incident in which a young Javanese soldier who was departing from Aceh kissed his Acehnese girlfriend goodbye in front of the onlooking media. When the photograph of the kissing couple appeared in the local media, it provoked so much criticism in Aceh that the soldier's supervisor felt obliged to provide a public apology on behalf of his protégé. See: "Tentara, Asmara, dan Air Mata," Garsip, No. 46, September 26, 2005, http://arsip.gatra.com/2005-10-02/artikel.php?id=88737 (accessed 17 October 2011).

17 "Berbuat Mesum: Ketua Pengadilan Negeri Kota Sabang dicopot," *tempointeractif*, 23 May 23 2007, http://www.tempo.co.id/hg/nusa/sumatera/2007/05/23/brk,20070523-100464,id.html (Accessed 13 October 2011).

Limited Concerns

Closely connected to the argument about exemptions, is the more general criticism of the very limited concerns dealt with by current Shariʿa regulations (Großmann, this volume). In fact, this criticism reflected similar debates among Acehnese based in Aceh (see Feener 2013b; Idria, this volume). So far, the enacted *qanun* deals primarily with "moral wrong-doings." In the words of an informant: "I see the enforcement of Shariʿa in Aceh as misguided (*salah kaprah*) because it regulates only minor issues, such as gambling, adultery, and the consumption of alcohol, as well as the requirement for women to wear headscarves in public, even though Islamic law is far more wide-reaching."[18] People in the diaspora generally believe that such moralistic issues are less crucial for Aceh's current political and economic developments. Instead of improving the collective morals and strengthening religious modesty, they are more concerned with issues such as social justice and coming to terms with the violent past that was very much characterized by widespread and so far unpunished human rights violations.

In the eyes of my informants, ordinary people (*rakyat kecil*) gained little from the implementation of Shariʿa. According to them, the beneficiaries of the implementation of Shariʿa in Aceh were not only the government in Jakarta and the local ulama who were seeking a greater share in local power, but also the local enforcers of Shariʿa (the so-called 'Shariʿa Police,' Wilayatul Hisbah/WH). One Acehnese interlocutor even claimed that "arresting and whipping offenders had turned into a method of generating income for the Shariʿa police."[19] He had heard of stories in which WH officers stole the hand-phones of the people they arrested, so he simply referred to them as "thugs."[20]

With regard to callously chasing cases of rather minor moral offences, the WH has earned itself a very bad reputation (Otto and Otto, this volume). Especially before the budget cuts under Governor Irwandi Yusuf, the WH carried out raids that specifically targeted women on issues of Islamic dress. Additionally, there were widespread reports about nightly raids at hotels, where WH officers looked for unmarried couples. The local poor, who indulged in popular entertainment such as playing dominos, also fell prey to WH-raids, as their games fell under 'gambling activities.' Although, according to the law, the Shariʿa Police are not allowed to make arrests, there have been incidents in which

18 Online correspondence with the author, 28 September 2011.

19 Online correspondence with the author, 28 September 2011.

20 Online correspondence with the author, 10 October 2011.

they have taken matters into their own hands and overstepped their authority (Cf. Otto and Otto, this volume).[21] One interlocutor said that, "especially after the MoU, the WH, along with the judges [at the Shari'a courts], were getting crazy, as they would order people who have been caught gambling or drinking alcohol to be caned in front of other people."[22] The latter is understood to be extremely humiliating and disgraceful. Some public commentators from the Acehnese diaspora even went as far as to denounce public caning as a human rights violation (Muchtar 2009). However, there are also Acehnese in the homeland who express such criticism (see Großmann, this volume). In a letter to the editor entitled "Aceh doesn't need sharia law," a man who called himself Teuku Agam (probably a *nom de guerre*, as *agam* in Acehnese means not only 'man' but also stands for the armed wing of GAM) wrote:

> The public flogging of male and female sharia law offenders has greatly damaged the reputation and image of Aceh both nationally and internationally, and led to the sadistic and barbaric image of the Acehnese.
>
> *Jakarta Post*, 9 February 2009

When I was discussing with my informants the question of who benefits the most from Shari'a implementation and who does not benefit at all, one of my interlocutors complained that "it was the Acehnese people themselves who were most damaged by Jakarta's version of Shari'a, because for them daily life in Aceh has become tame and limited, as they have become restricted in their daily freedoms and always have to be wary of Shari'a raids."[23] Another interlocutor criticized the law by saying that "it is only women not wearing the headscarf who have become the subject of physical punishment, whereas the big corruptors walked free."[24] This perceived mismanagement of priorities—at times in

---

21 It has to be noted that 'vigilante justice' is a problem in Aceh, not only due to the transgressions of authority by the official WH, but also community retributions take place more frequently.

22 Online correspondence with the author, 28 September 2011.

23 "*Yang paling di rugikan adalah orang-orang Aceh sendiri, dengan di berlakukan syariat islam versi Jakarta, terasa sekali kehidupan ini jadi sangat di kekang dan sempit di Aceh, orang Aceh tidak bebas dan leluasa bergerak dan akan selalu was-was akan kena razia* WH." Online correspondence with the author, 10 October 2011.

24 "[…] *sebagai contoh, orang perempuan karena tidak menutup kepala kena hukuman, sementara koruptor bebas berkeliaran tanpa ada hukuman apapun. Apa ini namanya hukum (syariat)?*" Online correspondence with the author, 30 September 2011.

which Aceh faces a variety of economic and political challenges—brings us to the last point of my informants' criticism on which I want to elaborate.

The Fragility of Aceh's Post-conflict Society

Even though the armed conflict was brought to an end six years ago, Aceh is still in the middle of a post-conflict transition, the end of which is not (yet) in sight. Given the enormous socio-political, economic and cultural changes taking place in Aceh (see Feener, Daly and Reid 2011), my informants from the diaspora argued that the time is not yet ripe for Shari'a in Aceh:

> How is it possible to apply Islamic law in Aceh 'completely' (*secara sempurna*) if the war in Aceh has just finished and the society still suffers from economic instability and many other uncertainties? The central government in Jakarta has not yet fully clarified all uncertainties while Aceh remains to be cheated (*ditipu*) with regard to politics. So far, the division of power [between the central and the local government] has not been fully clarified [...] that is why Aceh remains highly susceptible to [renewed] conflict with Jakarta.[25]

According to the diagnosis of the Acehnese in diaspora, other issues, such as justice and reconciliation between the former conflict parties, as well as proper compensation for the conflict victims, were more important than the implementation of Shari'a. However, the diasporans often took a rather gloomy view when asked how likely they judged the chances for any of that to happen any time soon. The general pessimism towards their homeland and current political developments there becomes more comprehensible when taking into consideration the general bias of their news feed (see below).

In summary, having seen the wide range of dissatisfaction and complaints, it is not surprising that my informants would like to see the temporary suspension or even the abolition of state Shari'a in Aceh. Supposedly in order to avoid suspicions or allegations of not being good Muslims, one informant put it like this: "It is not that I am totally against Shari'a for Aceh, but there are so many issues that would have to be sorted out first."[26] Another respondent

---

25 Online correspondence with the author, 18 October 2011.

26 "*Saya tidak menolak* [*the implementation of Shari'a in Aceh*] ... *Maka harus disosialisasikan dulu objektif dan sasarannya.*" Online corresponence with the author, 26 October 2011.

recommended postponing the whole matter until the right time comes, without indicating when that time might be. The majority of my informants, however, rejected state Shariʿa completely: "I think Shariʿa should be abolished altogether, because the way I see it, it is doing more harm than good."[27] Another informant put it like this:

> It is time to think about Aceh's own interests. [We have to ask ourselves whether] the implementation of Shariʿa helps Aceh to prosper? If the answer is no, then this law needs to be revoked.[28]

Despite the bluntness of some of these statements, it is important to contextualize them further. The demand for the abolition of Shariʿa in Aceh is not necessarily tantamount to entirely secularized views on politics, as some of them pointed to Brunei and Malaysia as positive models worth replicating if Aceh could become an independent and developed state. It is probably safe to say that my informants did not wish to disengage religion from politics entirely, for—when asked more specifically—they still upheld the need for Islamic courts to regulate matters such as marriage, divorce, and inheritance, as is the case all over Indonesia.[29]

Of course, it needs to be emphasized that all these statements were made in private. The protected interview situation might have led some informants to express their views more bluntly. Although most of my interlocutors stated that Shariʿa was not as important to them as many other topics relating to current homeland politics, and therefore was discussed only rarely in public online forums, it still seems worthwhile to identify some reasons why the Acehnese diasporans took such positions in the first place. Taking into account their socio-political backgrounds, as well as their situatedness in diaspora helps to shed light on the formation of such collective stances.

---

27 "*Saya pikir sebaiknya di hapuskan saja, karena saya melihat syariat islam di Aceh lebih banyak kerugiannya dari pada mamfaatnya.*" Online correspondence with the author, 10 October 2011.

28 "*Jadi sudah saatnya acheh berfikir untuk kepentingannya juga. Dapatkah implementasi syariat islam memakmurkan acheh? Apabila jawabannya 'tidak,' maka hukum itu perlu dicabut.*" Online correspondence with the author, 30 September 2011.

29 "*Masalah kekeluargaan seperti perceraian, konflik perkawinan/pernikahan, saya kira pengadilan agama lebih cocok menanganinya.*" Online corresponence with author, 26 July 2013.

Interpreting Opposition to the Shariʿa

As mentioned earlier, the majority of diasporans had left Aceh before Shariʿa was formally implemented. The fact that they had not experienced the state Shariʿa system personally has important implications for understanding their opinion. My informants in Malaysia could rely on word-of-mouth accounts of the situation back home, as passed on by the large numbers of newcomers arriving from Aceh during the peak of the conflict—which happened to coincide with the introduction of the by-laws 12/2003, 13/2003 and 14/2003, and pre-dated the 2004 tsunami. In contrast, within the diaspora in the West, people relied firstly and foremostly on online media to gain information about the way Shariʿa was implemented in Aceh. Given the biased nature of both online media reporting and word-of-mouth communication, in general Acehnese diasporans only learned about the most contentious aspects of Shariʿa implementation, such as the raids of the WH to check women's clothing (*razia jilbab*), public canings and misconduct of WH members.

Looking for sensational news, online and print media often published reports about offenses against Shariʿa, such as gambling or inappropriate sexual conduct, on the front page and at prominent spots on their websites, so that it was generally hard to ignore them. Online newspapers hardly ever quoted, for example, the exact verdict of the Shariʿa court, so readers only learned about the penalty, and not the reasoning behind it. Although diasporans called and chatted with friends and family in Aceh more or less regularly, apparently this first-hand input could not help to adjust these biased impressions. Most likely, within such private conversations Shariʿa law does not play a big role in the first place. Therefore, it is not surprising that Acehnese in diaspora tended to view news about the implementation of Islamic law, and the apparent discrepancies between an abstract conception of Shariʿa and its formal application by the state implementation, more critically than people living in Aceh.

Although Acehnese in the diaspora still engaged intensively with the homeland, the interaction between them and the homeland had turned into one-way communication after the end of the conflict (Missbach 2011a). Generally, Acehnese in diaspora were not included in discussions about politics, let alone consulted by the relevant law-making bodies in the homeland dealing with such delicate questions as additional provisions or revisions to the Shariʿa. Hence, the influence of the Acehnese overseas on upcoming legal changes and adjustments of the Shariʿa by-laws in Aceh can be expected to remain minimal. For reasons that are not always entirely clear, the Acehnese in diaspora have not appealed to the responsible authorities in the homeland as being adequate dialogue partners.[30] It can be assumed that the local government's acceptance of the political arrangements of Aceh within the Indonesian state have further reinforced the gap between the community leaders in the diaspora and the political leadership in Aceh. Given these wider tensions and issues of trust between the local authorities in Aceh and the diaspora, the latter hardly qualify as desirable consultants.

Moreover, unlike with more purely political matters, be it rejecting the plans to split the province of Aceh or continuing to demand the formation of a truth and reconciliation commission, the Acehnese diasporans have kept rather silent with regard to religious affairs. In addition, I have noticed that, in online discussion groups and email lists used by diasporans, Shari'a is not a prominent subject matter. The primary trigger for the diasporization of the Acehnese overseas was the homeland conflict. Thus, their communal priorities were clear: homeland politics mattered more than religious issues. Unlike the great numbers of public statements (press statements, petitions, online newsletters and demonstrations) that focused on political issues in the homeland (for more specific examples, see Missbach 2011b), hardly any public statements on Shari'a were forwarded by the diasporans, except for very few radio interviews. How can this be explained?

Despite the assumption that Acehnese in the diaspora enjoy greater freedom of speech as compared to their fellow Acehnese in Aceh, who might face more immediate social control when making public statements, all of my informants indicated that I should anonymize them when quoting their opinion on Shari'a. Even far away from home, they were anxious of being denigrated or having their piety questioned. Anxiety was expressed as a fear of physical and psychological assault. For example, one informant stated that "[i]f I declared [in public] that Shari'a in Aceh is not important, in Aceh I would be completely destroyed (*diganyang*)."[31] For such reasons, all of my informants made clear at the beginning of our conversations that they were giving me their "personal opinion." In addition, during our conversations, they hardly generalised their views to be valid for other diasporans as well. However, once I had assured them I would protect their identities as well as I could, they appeared eager to speak their minds.

Nevertheless, it would be wrong to assume that my interviews offered a space for my interlocutors to articulate their frustration which they might not have

30 This even included an Acehnese diasporan who had written a PhD thesis on the just implementation of Shari'a. He was never consulted by the bodies responsible for drafting local by-laws.

31 Online correspondence with the author, 30 September 2011.

had been able to express elsewhere. Instead, it is more useful to reflect more on the context of the interviews, and especially on the so-called 'social desirability bias.' Rephrasing Kristin Langellier (2010, 67), I should ask: how actively were my informants trying to 'read' me (and my unspoken expectations) in just the same way as I was trying to 'read' them? I should also ask to what extent they might have adjusted their answers to the "regulating discourses of Islam and the West" (ibid.). Of course, it is extremely difficult to evaluate whether I—white, female, middle-class, presumably non-Muslim—might have unconsciously evoked the answers that I was given, or might have influenced their way of framing these, and the views I presented above must thus be read against this foil.

Conclusions

Although independence for Aceh currently seems to be entirely out of the question as a political alternative, and the peace agreement has been hailed as a great success by the Indonesian government, GAM, and the international community, a number of Acehnese in diaspora still hold on to the idea. This chapter has demonstrated that one way in which the diasporans foster their demand for self-determination is by (re)framing their protest against Aceh's membership of the Indonesian unitary state in terms of a rejection of state Shari'a. By arguing that Shari'a is not what the people in Aceh require to improve their welfare and general living conditions, they tend to see Shari'a solely as an "unwanted gift from Jakarta." The crux of this argument is that Shari'a has become the next political instrument in the hands of the national government used to 'interfere' in Aceh's internal affairs, namely by having the last say on what does and what does not fall within the range of Islamic law.

A common thread throughout many of my conversations with my informants was that "Islam is already strongly established as an integral part of the Acehnese society" (*Islam sudah melekat dengan orang Aceh, sudah sangat sebati dengan masyarakat*) and that therefore no additional Islamization from above is required (Muchtar 2009). My interlocutors' view of their own religiosity as superior, in comparison specifically with the Jakarta politicians and also with others (commonly condensed under the slightly negatively connoted term "*orang Java*," which basically refers to all non-Acehnese Indonesians), strengthened their resistance against what they saw as external political intervention in local affairs. For them, the implementation of Shari'a in Aceh was a mere political instrument used by the national government, which was, however, packaged in religious rhetoric. Unmasking the religiosity of the Shari'a discourse and instead reframing the issue in entirely political terms, allowed the diasporans to uphold their demands for political independence. Alternatively, as one diasporan put it: "the implementation of Shariʿa carries many political considerations that constitute a deception of the public."[32]

Having recapitulated the main stance represented in my interview material, it has become apparent that Acehnese in the diaspora often neglect actual developments of the implementation of Shariʿa and local discourses on it within Aceh, but nevertheless inherit strong opinions about it. It is clear, moreover, that by focusing solely on the Jakarta-Aceh relationship and thereby ignoring all the other provinces in Indonesia that also had Shariʿa-derived public morality by-laws (*perda*) implemented or demanded the implementation of Shariʿa, the diasporans seem to reflect a general unawareness or even ignorance of developments in other Indonesian regions. By ignoring or excluding trans-Indonesian trends, the diasporic Acehnese perpetuate the view of Aceh's religious uniqueness and political exceptionality (*Sebab amalan Islam di Acheh sangat berlainan dengan Islam di dunia lain*).[33] However, with Shariʿa-inspired by-laws now also on the books in a number of other parts of Indonesia, the significance of Aceh's 'specialness' might be seen as somewhat compromised.

What strikes me most in all the conversations I had is the deliberate avoidance of the fact that it was an Acehnese provincial government, which drafted and established the institutions tasked with the implementation of Islamic law in the province (see Feener 2013a). My informants scarcely seemed to take notice of the fact that the legal drafting bodies consisted of Acehnese intelligentsia, who thus helped to shape the laws as they currently are (see Großmann, this volume). When inquiring about such involvement, my informants generally discounted those ulama and academic scholars either as "fanatics" craving for more power in local politics or as Jakarta's "lackeys" (*kaki tangan*) depriving their own people of independence.[34] While dreaming the dream of an independent Acehnese state, the formation of which the diasporans have now re-imagined to take place in the distant future, the Acehnese in diaspora can envision a perfect state, in which the Acehnese people (maybe even in alliance with their fellow Acehnese from abroad) might or might not decide to implement Shariʿa. However, and so the often-repeated argument goes, as

32 *"Tapi ia melihat pelaksanaan syariat sekarang ini penuh nuansa politik yang merupakan pembohongan publik belaka."* (Muchtar 2009).

33 Online correspondence with the author, 26 October 2011.

34 Online correspondence with the author, 4 October 2011.

long as Jakarta has a say in Aceh, Shari'a will be seen as the extended arm of the Indonesian government and—even if reformed and amended—Shari'a à la Jakarta can never be quite right.

References

Aspinall, Edward. 2009. *Islam and Nation: Separatist Rebellion in Aceh, Indonesia*. Stanford: Stanford University Press.

Battistella, Graziano. 2002. "Unauthorized Migrants as Global Workers in the ASEAN Region." *Southeast Asian Studies* 40(3):350–370.

Baumann, Martin. 2000. "Diaspora: Genealogies of Semantics and Transcultural Comparison." *Numen* 47(3):313–335.

———. 2004. "A Diachronic View of Diaspora, the Significance of Religion and Hindu Trinidadians." In *Diaspora, Identity, and Religion: New Directions in Theory and Research*, edited by Waltraud Kokot, Khachig Tölölyan and Carolin Alfonso, 170–188. New York: Routledge.

Carruthers, Ashley. 2008. "Saigon From the Diaspora." *Singapore Journal of Tropical Geography* 29(1):69–86.

Dean, Kenneth. 2011: "Ritual Revolutions: Temple and Trust Networks Linking Putian and Southeast Asia." *Encounters* 4:1–25.

Feener, R. Michael. 2013a. *Shari'a and Social Engineering: The Implementation of Islamic Law in Contemporary Aceh, Indonesia*. Oxford: Oxford University Press.

———. 2013b. "Hand, Heart and Handphone: State Shari'a in the Age of the SMS." *Contemporary Islam* 7(1):15–32.

Feener, R. Michael, Patrick Daly and Anthony Reid (eds.). 2011. *Mapping the Acehnese Past*. Leiden: KITLV Press.

International Crisis Group. 2006. *Islamic Law and Criminal Justice in Aceh*. Crisis Group Asia Report 117, Jakarta, 31 July.

Kingsbury, Damien. 2007. "The Free Aceh Movement: Islam and Democratisation." *Journal of Contemporary Asia* 37(2):166–189.

Langellier, Kristin M. 2010. "Performing Somali Identity in the Diaspora." *Cultural Studies* 24(1):66–94.

Lindsey, Tim and M.B. Hooker, with Ross Clarke and Jeremy Kingsley. 2007. "Shari'a Revival in Aceh." In *Islamic Law in Contemporary Indonesia: Ideas and Institutions*, edited by Michael Feener and Mark Cammack, 216–254. Cambridge: Harvard University Press.

Lyons, Terrence. 2006. "Diasporas and Homeland Conflict." In *Territoriality and Conflict in an Era of Globalization*, edited by Miles Kahler and Barbara Walter, 111–131. Cambridge/New York: Cambridge University Press.

Missbach, Antje. 2010. "The Merits of Not Returning: The Search by Acehnese in the Diaspora for Political Participation in Post-conflict Times." *Review of Indonesian and Malaysian Affairs* 4(1):111–142.

———. 2011a. "The Acehnese Diaspora after the Helsinki Memorandum of Understanding: Return Challenges and Diasporic Post-conflict Transformations." *Asian Ethnicity* 12(2):179–201.

———. 2011b. *Separatist Conflict in Indonesia: The Long-distance Politics of the Acehnese Diaspora.* New York: Routledge.

Morfit, Michael. 2007. "The Road to Helsinki: The Aceh Agreement and Indonesia's Democratic Development." *International Negotiation* 12(1):111–143.

Muchtar, Bari. 2009. "Aceh Gegabah Memberlakukan Syariat Islam," interview with Tarmizi Age, September 9, *Radio Nederland*, http://www.rnw.nl/bahasa-indonesia/article/aceh-gegabah-memberlakukan-syariat-islam (Accessed 13 October 2011).

Pillai, Patrick. 1998. "The Impact of the Economic Crisis on Migrant Labour in Malaysia: Policy Implications." *Asian and Pacific Migration Journal* 7(2/3):255–288.

Radtke, Katrin. 2009. *Mobilisierung der Diaspora: Die Moralische Ökonomie der Bürgerkriege in Sri Lanka und Eritrea.* Frankfurt am Main: Campus.

Rajaram, Prem Kumar, and Carl Grundy-Warr. 2004. "The Irregular Migrant as Homo Sacer: Migration and Detention in Australia, Malaysia, and Thailand." *International Migration* 42(1):34–65.

Reid, Anthony, ed. 2006. *Verandah of Violence: The Background to the Aceh Problem.* Singapore: Singapore University Press.

Reid, Anthony. 1969. *The Contest for North Sumatra: Atjeh, the Netherlands and Britain 1858–1898.* Kuala Lumpur/Singapore: Oxford University Press.

Saint-Blancat, Chantal. 2002. "Islam in Diaspora: Between Reterritorialization and Extraterritoriality." *International Journal of Urban and Regional Research* 26(1):138–151.

Safran, William. 2008. "Language, Ethnicity and Religion: A Complex and Persistent Linkage." *Nations and Nationalism* 14(1):171–190.

Schiffauer, Werner. 1999. *Islamism in the Diaspora: The Fascination of Political Islam among Second Generation German Turks.* Oxford: Transnational Communities Working Paper WPTC-99-06, http://www.transcomm.ox.ac.uk/working%20papers/Schiffauer_Islamism.PDF (Accessed 19 October 2011).

Schulze, Kirsten E. 2004. *The Free Aceh Movement (GAM): Anatomy of a Separatist Organization.* Washington: East-West Center.

Shain, Yossi. 2002. "The Role of Diasporas in Conflict Perpetuation or Resolution." *SAIS Review* 22(2):115–144.

Siapno, Jacqueline Aquino. 2002. *Gender, Islam, Nationalism and the State in Aceh: The Paradox of Power, Co-optation and Resistance.* Richmond: Curzon.

Skrbiš, Zlatko. 1999. *Long-Distance Nationalism: Diasporas, Homelands and Identities.* Brookfield: Ashgate.

Sökefeld, Martin. 2004. "Religion or Culture? Concepts of Identity in the Alevi Diaspora." In *Diaspora, Identity and Religion, New Directions in Theory and Research*, edited by Waltraud Kokot, Khachig Tölölyan and Carolin Alfonso, 133–155. New York: Routledge.

Suryadinata, Leo. 2002. *Elections and Politics in Indonesia*. Singapore: ISEAS.

Vertovec, Steven. 2004. "Religion and Diaspora." In *New Approaches to the Study of Religion*, edited by Peter Antes, Armin W. Geertz and Randi Warne, 275–304. Berlin/New York: Verlag de Gruyter.

Winland, Daphne. 2002. "The Politics of Desire and Disdain: Croatian Identity between 'Home' and 'Homeland'." *American Ethnologist* 29(3):693–718.

Index

www.ingramcontent.com/pod-product-compliance
Lightning Source LLC
Chambersburg PA
CBHW071433230926
51846CB00001B/217
* 9 7 8 9 0 0 4 3 0 4 8 5 7 *